Monstrous adaptations

MANCHESTER
1824
Manchester University Press

Monstrous adaptations

Generic and thematic mutations in horror film

Edited by

Richard J. Hand and Jay McRoy

Manchester University Press

Published by Manchester University Press
Altrincham Street, Manchester M1 7JA, UK
www.manchesteruniversitypress.co.uk

British Library Cataloguing-in-Publication Data is available

Library of Congress Cataloging-in-Publication Data is available

ISBN 978 1 7849 9248 4 *paperback*

First published by Manchester University Press in hardback 2007

This edition first published 2015

Printed by Lightning Source

Contents

Acknowledgements

Richard J. Hand would like to thank the Arts and Humanities Research Council for a grant to support the research and completion of this book.

Dedicated to Sadiyah, Shahrazad and Danyazad (RJH)

Dedicated to Amy, and in loving memory to Peter Cohen and Willie McRoy (JM)

Contributors

Linnie Blake teaches film at Manchester Metropolitan University in the UK. She works predominantly on American genre cinema, particularly horror and crime. In her spare time, she raises strange children.

Guy Crucianelli is a recent graduate of the University of Wisconsin – Parkside. His recent research interests include the cinema of Tod Browning, Robert Bresson and John Ford.

Brigid Cherry is a lecturer in Media Arts at St Mary's College, University of Surrey. She has researched the female horror film audience and has subsequently published chapters in *British Horror Cinema* (Routledge, 2001) and *Identifying Hollywood Audiences* (BFI, 1999). She has also written on vampire cinema and is currently researching British fans of the television science fiction series *Stargate SG-1*. Her working environment is altogether Gothic, St Mary's College campus being based around Horace Walpole's 'little Gothic castle' at Strawberry Hill in Twickenham.

Ruth Goldberg is a member of the faculty at SUNY/Empire State College, where she teaches cinema studies, screenwriting and cultural studies. She also teaches regularly at New York University School of Continuing and Professional Studies and at the Escuela Internacional de Cine y Televisión, San Antonio de los Baños, Cuba.

Richard J. Hand is Professor of Theatre and Media Drama at the University of Glamorgan in Wales, United Kingdom. He is the author of *Terror on the Air: Horror Radio in America, 1931–52* (McFarland, 2006), *The Theatre of Joseph Conrad: Reconstructed Fictions* (Palgrave, 2005) and the co-author (with Michael Wilson) of *Grand-Guignol: the French Theatre of Horror* (University of Exeter Press, 2002). He has published journal articles and book chapters on diverse aspects of horror culture (such as theatre, radio, film, graphic narratives, and digital gaming) as well as adaptation studies.

Steffen Hantke has published essays and reviews on contemporary literature, film, and culture in *Paradoxa*, *College Literature*, *The Journal of Popular Culture*, *Post Script*, *Kinema*, *Scope*, *Science Fiction Studies*, and other journals, as well as in anthologies in Germany and the US. He is author of *Conspiracy and Paranoia in Contemporary Literature* (Peter Lang, 1994) and editor of *Horror*, a special topics issue of *Paradoxa* (2002), as well as *Horror: Creating and Marketing Fear* (University Press of Mississippi, 2004). He currently serves on the editorial board of *Paradoxa* and has served as advisor to the book review board of *College Literature*. He is chair for the 'Horror' area at the Southwest/Texas Popular Culture and American Culture Association. He currently teaches at Sogang University in Seoul, South Korea, as Associate Professor for British and American Culture.

Reynold Humphries is Professor of Film Studies at the University of Lille, France. He is the author of *Fritz Lang: Genre and Representation in his American Films* (Johns Hopkins University Press, 1988) and *The American Horror Film: An Introduction* (Edinburgh University Press, 2002), as well as articles on *Dracula's Daughter*, David Cronenberg and Michael Powell.

I. Q. Hunter is Principal Lecturer and Subject Leader in Film Studies at De Montfort University, Leicester. He edited *British Science Fiction Cinema* (Routledge, 1999) and co-edited *Pulping Fictions* (Pluto, 1996), *Trash Aesthetics* (Pluto, 1997), *Sisterhoods* (Pluto, 1998), *Alien Identities* (Pluto, 1999), *Classics* (Pluto, 2000), *Retrovisions* (Pluto, 2001) and *Brit-Invaders!* (Lindau, 2005). He has published widely on exploitation, horror and cult films and is currently writing a British Film Guide to *A Clockwork Orange* for IB Tauris.

Mikel J. Koven is Lecturer in Film and Television Studies at the University of Wales, Aberystwyth. He has published extensively in the area of folklore and film in such journals as *Ethnologies*, *Culture & Tradition*, *Contemporary Legend*, *Journal of American Folklore*, *Literature/Film Quarterly*, and *Scope*. He is co-editor of a special issue of *Western Folklore* on Folklore and Film, and co-editor of *Filmic Folklore* (Utah State University Press, forthcoming). Koven is also a contributor in Steffen Hanke's collection *Caligari's Grandchildren* (Scarecrow Press, 2007) and author of *La Dolce Morte: Vernacular Cinema and the Italian* Giallo *Film* (Scarecrow Press, 2006).

Jay McRoy is an Associate Professor of English and Cinema Studies at the University of Wisconsin – Parkside. He has written extensively on horror film, including the forthcoming monograph, *Nightmare Japan: Contemporary Japanese Horror Cinema* (Rodopi University Press). He is also the editor of the recent critical anthology, *Japanese Horror Cinema* (Edinburgh University Press, 2005).

Brad O'Brien is a graduate student at Francis Marion University in South Carolina.

Julian Petley is Professor of Film and Television and Director of Research for Screen Media at Brunel University. He has published widely on horror cinema, British cinema and television, and the press. His publications include *British Horror Cinema* (co-edited with Steve Chibnall) (Routledge, 2002), *A Young Citizen's Guide to the Media in Politics* (Hodder Wayland, 2002), and *Ill Effects: the Media Violence Debate* (second edition, Routledge, 2001).

Murray Pomerance is Professor in the Department of Sociology at Ryerson University. He is the author of *Johnny Depp Starts Here* (Rutgers University Press, 2005), *Savage Time* (Oberon Press, 2005), *An Eye for Hitchcock* (Rutgers University Press, 2004), and *Magia d'Amore* (Sun & Moon Books, 1999), as well as editor or co-editor of numerous volumes including *Cinema and Modernity* (Rutgers University Press, 2006), *From Hobbits to Hollywood: Essays on Peter Jackson's Lord of the Rings* (Rodopi, 2005), *American Cinema of the 1950s: Themes and Variations*

(Berg, 2005), and *Enfant Terrible! Jerry Lewis in American Film* (New York University Press, 2002). With Lester D. Friedman he co-edits the 'Screen Decades' series, and with Adrienne McLean the 'Star Decades' series, at Rutgers University Press; and he is the editor of the 'Horizons of Cinema' series at State University of New York Press.

Marianne Shaneen is a fiction writer, filmmaker, conjurer of the archaic yet-to-be, and 'sentimental insurrectionary' who lives in Brooklyn.

Andy W. Smith is Subject Leader for Performance in the Newport School of Art, Media and Design at the University of Wales. For the *Dictionary of Literary Biography* (Thomson-Gale, 2005) he has written critical profiles on Welsh dramatists Ian Rowlands and Ed Thomas. Andy has contributed to *Theatre of Catastrophe: New Essays on Howard Barker* (Oberon Books, 2006) and researches contemporary performance culture with a special interest in horror and genre.

Monstrous adaptations: an introduction

Richard J. Hand and Jay McRoy

The history of horror film is full of adaptations that draw upon fiction or folklore, or have assumed the shape of remakes of pre-existing films. From its earliest days, horror film has turned to examples of the horror genre in fiction (such as the Victorian Gothic) or legend (as diverse as classical mythology, biblical stories or the 'The Golem' from Yiddish folklore) for source material. In addition, the horror film abounds with more examples of sequels, prequels and remakes than any other popular film genre in the history of cinema. Whether it is a cliff-hanger ending that permits the return of a monstrous protagonist or, failing that, the emergence of sons, daughters or brides of various monsters, in many examples narrative finality seems unlikely as long as there remains a popular demand that makes such texts not only economically viable, but highly lucrative. Moreover, the same source material may be reinterpreted for different national cultures and contexts, or for different generations of filmgoers.

That the plots of these horror films frequently abound with adaptation on a thematic level is both striking and curious. From occultists and scientists abusing their knowledge to explore the radical potentialities of metamorphosis or transformation, to ancient curses or alien invasions that variably distort or transmute the human body (as well as the body politic), horror film thrives on the notion of transformation. Indeed, adaptation for the purposes of survival proves the impetus for many horror movie monsters. Of course, the ultimate and only certain adaptive journey in lived existence is that which takes us from being into non-being, or from life into death. In the phenomenologist Martin Heidegger's terms, we are each a *Sein-zum-Tode* (a being towards death); consequently, the subsequent and inevitable *Todesangst* has long been the predominant preoccupation of horror culture. Time and again in horror narratives, death and the fear of death is explored, demonstrated, threatened, confronted and even mocked and overcome. The adaptation that is the journey into death may be entropic or explosive, terrifying or titillating, terminal or merely a conduit for rebirth; whatever the presentation and effect, no film genre is more obsessed with the multiple possibilities of life into death adaptation than horror.

To account for why horror film narratives remain a consistently successful source for adaptations, be they generic or thematic, in horror cinema, one need consider horror's relation to the broad concept of *myth*. In his seminal study *In Frankenstein's Shadow: Myth, Monstrosity, and Nineteenth-Century Writing*, Chris Baldick makes use of the concept of 'myth' *à la* Claude Lévi-Strauss in order to investigate the enduring legacy and adaptive appeal of Mary Shelley's novel. Baldick argues that in spite of the plurality of interpretation, a literary text is a fixed entity, whilst a myth, in a Lévi-Straussian sense, 'is open to all kinds of adaptation and elaboration, but it will preserve at the same time a basic stability of meaning' (Baldick, 1987: 2). The word 'mythos' – as used by Aristotle – means 'the basic action'; hence, myth, or the 'mythic' connotations of a specific work, occupies a critical ontological space, one freed from the tyranny of a specific plot or character arc. The myth of a work exists at its simplest, most memorable and irreducible pattern. Myths are more organic than concretised text: they resist reducibility. A myth lives, and the 'truth' of it is not to be found in the earliest version but, as Lévi-Strauss claims, in all its versions. Applying the implications of this to *Frankenstein*, Baldick succeeds in distilling the core myth of Mary Shelley's novel in two sentences:

(a) Frankenstein makes a living creature out of bits of corpses.
(b) The creature turns against him and runs amok. (Baldick: 3)

In these two simple sentences, not only does Baldick claim that a multiplicity of potential interpretations is possible, but that a plethora of potential interpretations has been, and continues to be, demonstrated across a wide range of media, including stage dramatisations, comic book interpretations, sequels in the form of fictional prose, parodies in television sitcoms, or academic studies in the form of the kind of film criticism that comprises this collection. Each reiteration of the Frankenstein story contributes to the myth-making process, perpetuating and reinventing the myth that is *Frankenstein*:

> The vitality of myths lies precisely in their capacity for change, their adaptability and openness to new combinations of meaning. That series of adaptations, allusions, accretions, analogues, parodies, and plain misreadings which follows ... is not just a supplementary component of the myth; it is the myth. (Baldick: 4)

As a genre, horror abounds with mythic resonance.

The essays that follow engage generic and thematic adaptations in horror cinema from a wide range of aesthetic, cultural, political and theoretical perspectives. These diverse approaches further evidence the horror genre's obsession with corporeal transformation and narratological rearticulation. Additionally, they illustrate the extent to which the horror genre impacts its audience, confronting us with nightmarish scenarios and unsettling images that demand us to respond – to *adapt*. In their consideration of films that originate in works of nineteenth- and twentieth-century horror literature, Richard J. Hand, Guy Crucianelli, Julian Petley and Brigid Cherry interrogate the myriad alterations and re-envisionings filmmakers must negotiate as they transport tales of terror between very different modes of artistic expression. In the process, these essays shed welcome light upon some of the more neglected horror films of cinema's first century, including Thomas Edison's *Frankenstein* (1910), John S. Robertson's *Dr Jekyll and Mr Hyde* (1920), Jean Epstein's *La Chute de la maison Usher* (1928), and Bernard Rose's *Candyman* (1992). The four chapters that constitute the book's second section further extend the volume's examination of adaptation as both an aesthetic process and a thematic preoccupation. Steffen Hantke, for instance, reveals the practice of self-reflexivity in David Cronenberg's *Videodrome* (1983) and *eXistenZ* (1999), whilst Andy W. Smith dissects *The Faculty*'s (Robert Rodriguez, 1998) postmodern amalgamation of motifs from teen comedies and alien invasion narratives. Addressing the remake as adaptation, Jay McRoy reads Abel Ferrara's 1993 *Body Snatchers* as an historically- and politically-coded re-working of a text that, in keeping with its previous incarnations, variably melds terror with social criticism.

The chapters by Marianne Shaneen, I. Q. Hunter and Murray

Pomerance probe the fertile intersections of the horrific and the experimental in cinema, further enhancing this volume's focus on adaptation as a generic practice and thematic concern. Whereas the visual anarchy of avant-garde works by Ken Jacobs form the core of Shaneen's study, I. Q. Hunter deploys psychoanalytic film theory to interpret Terence Fisher's *The Gorgon* (1964) as a meditation upon how science and technology impact societal secularisation. Similarly, by exploring the experimental extremes of adaptation in horror film, Murray Pomerance's 'Marion Crane Dies Twice' reflects critically upon visionary director Gus Van Sant's daring and controversial remake of Alfred Hitchcock's *Psycho* (1960). Finally, the five chapters that bring this book to its conclusion understand adaptation in horror cinema as a useful point of departure for articulating numerous socio-cultural trends. Mikel J. Koven's topological essay on the filmic representations of urban legends proves a valuable companion piece to Brad O'Brien's reading of the strategic mobilisation of the Frankenstein and Dracula myths in Guillermo del Toro's *Cronos* (1993); similarly, Reynold Humphries analyses four films written and directed by Mario Bava between 1960 and 1966 – *La Maschera del Demonio* (aka *Black Sunday*, 1960), *La Frusta e il Corpo* (aka *Night is the Phantom* and *The Whip and the Body*, 1963), *Operazione Paura* (aka *Curse of the Dead* and *Kill, Baby . . . Kill!*, 1966) and *Sei donne per l'assassino* (aka *Blood and Black Lace*, 1964) – revealing how each work revisits the image of the 'martyrised' female body in Italian horror cinema. In her chapter, '"In the Church of the Poison Mind": Adapting the Metaphor of Psychopathology to Look Back at the Mad, Monstrous 80s', Ruth Goldberg explains how Mary Harron's *American Psycho* (2000) and Richard Kelly's *Donnie Darko* (2001) function as contemporary films designed to instigate a critical re-evaluation of a specific moment in US history that continues to haunt the popular imagination. Lastly, Linnie Blake brings the volume to a close with her interrogation of recent Western appropriations of Asian horror motifs. Buttressed by an analysis of Gore Verbinski's 2002 Hollywood remake of Nakata Hideo's *Ringu* (1998), Blake's chapter offers an insightful and timely investigation of adaptation in horror film as an increasingly trans-cultural activity.

We conclude our introduction with a perhaps surprising point of reference. Frank Zappa's song 'The Torture Never Stops' (*Zoot Allures*, 1976) is not only an example of trans-generic adaptation – it was apparently inspired by Roger Corman's Edgar Allan Poe movies – but it has a title which carries great resonance in the study of the integral link between horror and adaptation. Horror continues to re-work, re-envision and re-invent its manufactured myths through returning to the dungeon of its inspirations or impetuses. In so doing, horror film continues to take us on a journey that explores that most primal of adaptations: the agonising transformation from life into death, being into non-being. And even if the journey results in catharsis, or if the forces of death are occasionally surmounted, the next horror film we see may take us back to square one on our voyage.

In truth, when it comes to the monstrous adaptations of horror cinema, the torture never stops …

Part I

From page to scream: literary adaptation and horror cinema

Paradigms of metamorphosis and transmutation: Thomas Edison's *Frankenstein* and John Barrymore's *Dr Jekyll and Mr Hyde*

Richard J. Hand

Two great works of fiction at opposite ends of the nineteenth century continue to be paradigms of horror with the concept of 'adaptation' at their heart: Mary Shelley's *Frankenstein, or the Modern Prometheus* (1818) and Robert Louis Stevenson's *The Strange Case of Dr Jekyll and Mr Hyde* (1886). Both present mad scientists who experiment with adaptation in the sense of metamorphosis (reassembling dead body parts and bringing them to life) and transmutation (an elixir that releases and extrapolates an inner being). But the works are not merely concerned with adaptation on a thematic level. Although original and perennially defining moments in horror literature, both were, broadly speaking, examples of intertextual adaptation: *Frankenstein* draws extensively on classical legend and poetry, and the recent scientific experiments of Luigi Galvani and Erasmus Darwin; *Dr Jekyll and Mr Hyde* in its turn is unthinkable without James Hogg's *The Private Memoirs and Confessions of a Justified Sinner* (1824) and the true story of the double life of the Edinburgh criminal Deacon Brodie. Both works would find themselves the inspiration for many examples of adaptation into a range of media, such as caricature, comic journalism and, above all, theatre. Although Shelley and Stevenson wrote their influential 'horror' novels at opposite ends of a remarkably transformative century, the overarching condition and culture of the nineteenth century meant that both works were adapted to the popular stage many times in sensationalist melodramatic versions which exploited the potential for heightened horror and spectacle inherent to both works, a potential which continues to define the novels' appeal for cinematic adaptation. Early twentieth-century cinema adaptations of *Frankenstein* and *Dr Jekyll and Mr Hyde* drew their style and technique from European and American melodramatic adaptations more than from Shelley and Stevenson's original novels. In this chapter I will look at the Thomas Edison Company's *Frankenstein* (1910) and John S. Robertson's *Dr Jekyll and Mr Hyde* (1920), two intrinsically 'melodramatic' adaptations that nonetheless resonate profoundly over the subsequent legacy of popular horror culture. Indeed, I argue that as increasingly distant as these two films are, they can be seen as establishing paradigms of horror movie form.

The Edison *Frankenstein* was released in 1910 but, according to Wheeler Winston Dixon, 'most film histories were still treating the film as lost' as late as 1987 (Dixon, 2000: 116). It is a work that is often described as the first American horror movie, although William Selig's 1908 *Dr Jekyll and Mr Hyde* may have pre-empted it. Selig's movie, however, was very much a filmed play – 'complete with the curtain' (Mank, 1994: 3) – whereas the Edison company's *Frankenstein* is unquestionably cinematic (and, furthermore, *dramatic* more than *theatrical*) and uses technologies only possible with film editing and special effects. The first stage adaptation of *Frankenstein* on record was a short piece performed in 1821 (Willingham, 1994: 14) – three years after the book was published – and the first full-length production was Richard Brinsley Peake's *Presumption* (1823), which provided a 'curious mixture of thrills and arias' (Willingham, 1994: 14) and ends with an onstage avalanche. From the same era, H. M. Milner's *Frankenstein or The Man and the Monster!* (1826) is another suitably spectacular, melodramatic adaptation. In contrast to Shelley's novel and yet precursive to many film interpretations, including the Edison and James Whale versions, the monster is mute. Moreover, the frontispiece engraving in the published edition of the play script (Wischhusen, 1975: 107) shows the monster (O. Smith) as a somewhat 'noble savage' figure with the long hair that we will associate with the Edison creature. Milner's adaptation distils the original narrative into a succinct account of ethical dilemma, creation (the actual moment of which is, as in the novel, in ellipsis) and conflict, concluding in a terrific set-piece in which the monster 'leaps into the Crater (of Mount Etna), now vomiting burning lava' (Wischhusen, 1975: 120) leaving his creator lifeless on the summit on the volcano. Milner's concise adaptation is a thrill-ride of moral dilemma and melodramatic horror remarkably close, despite an intervening century, to the Edison *Frankenstein*, although the latter opts for an alternative ending to Frankenstein's 'just desserts' demise and supplies a polar opposite, yet equally melodramatic, happy ending with the creator vanquishing his unnatural monster.

Undoubtedly the potential for heightened fantasy and spectacle that the stage melodramas exploited were the same qualities that drew the Edison Company to *Frankenstein* in 1910. They were, however, not the only reason. Eileen Bowser has revealed that, after 1907, cinema was no longer such a novelty and there was thus an increasing demand for more sophisticated narrative: literary adaptations provided one solution (Bowser, 1990: 42–3). In 1908 there was a flurry of Shakespeare adaptations across the film industry after which the Edison Company produced one-reel versions of Goethe's *Faust* in 1909 and Dickens' *A Christmas Carol*, along with *Frankenstein*, in 1910. Not only were these and other adaptations dictated by the audience's demand for more sophisticated stories, but there was also a degree of moral panic in this. In July 1907 Edison himself had acknowledged that the success of the whole motion picture enterprise depended upon 'good moral tone' (quoted in Bowser, 1990: 37). The cinema was an irresistible target for those seeking a root cause for the social calamities they saw infecting the newly-arrived twentieth century. Cinema attempted to redeem itself by using 'the prestige of the classics' (Bowser, 1990: 43) through adaptation. Indeed, some film exhibitors at the time would meet with local schools to encourage teachers to use literary texts, which would soon be appearing in screen adaptations, on their curricula.

Edison's *Frankenstein* may have attempted to attain the prestige of the 'good morality' implicit in the adaptation of a literary classic, but it would not be unproblematic. This was a horror movie before the horror film genre really existed. As Dixon reveals: 'Many exhibitors found the film too horrid to show' (Dixon, 2000: 117). This controversy can be explained if we consider the decisions that are taken in the adaptation of the novel. Approximately one quarter of this one-reel film is devoted to the creation scene: it is not only the most dominant sequence but the focus of the narrative and the set-piece of the film. Yet, of course, in the original novel (and also in the Milner stage adaptation) it is what Mary Shelley chooses to leave in ellipsis, not dissimilar to classical Greek tragedy wherein acts of violence or murder occur strictly offstage. The Edison film decides to fill in the gaps of the novel and add a creation sequence: it wants us to *see* the monster come into being, a decision which either fulfils, fuels (or even nurtures) in the spectator a *desire* to see, or possibly leaves a viewer mortified. Regardless of reception, in explicitly showing us the birth of the monster, a huge step forward is made for what will become the horror genre. Arguably, the creation sequence in the Edison *Frankenstein* creates the horror genre.

The creation scene – a reverse motion sequence in which the monster comes into being, *ex nihilo*, into the black void above a cauldron – presents us with *Frankenstein* as *Faust*. Certainly, as Dixon writes, this is an 'alchemist's lair' and the 'supernatural overtones are more apparent here than in any later version' (Dixon, 2000: 117). Despite Frederick C. Wiebel Jr's arguments (Wiebel, 2003: 55–7), the resulting creature (played by Charles Ogle) is *not* a precursor to Boris Karloff and his iconic embodiment of the role for Universal in 1931. The Edison monster is more reminiscent of O. Smith's interpretation of the monster or numerous stage Calibans from nineteenth-century stage versions of Shakespeare's *The Tempest*: an image of unkempt 'savagery' who in physique, deportment and movement is antithetical to the graceful and heroic posturings of the Victorian melodramatic hero (clearly alive and well in Augustus Phillips' portrayal of Dr Frankenstein). Both Ogle and Karloff will share enormous feet, but Ogle's talon-tipped fingers seem to be precursive to *Nosferatu* (Murnau: 1922) while his unwieldy hands and wild hair combined seem to anticipate *Edward Scissorhands* (Burton: 1990). But overall his rough, hairy organicism – rather than the manufactured texture of all later Frankenstein monsters – makes him a primitive, missing link figure which would probably be very troubling to any anti-Darwinist spectators of the time. The special effects may be simple and obvious to us a century later, but nonetheless there is something horrific and effective in the reverse motion sequence: an empty void slowly filling with flesh. In this reverse decomposition, we see the face and gesticulating arms of the modern zombie, fetid and impossibly reanimated, all concluding in probably the least obviously human of all screen Frankensteins.

What the Edison *Frankenstein* establishes is how *seen horror* and special effects will become a central plank in the horror film genre. Ogle's makeup as the creature is most extreme, the most 'made up', in order to dehumanise the actor into monstrosity. Interestingly, according to David J. Skal, in 1928 First National Studios proposed *Frankenstein* as a project for the special effects technician Willis J. O'Brien to make a stop-motion animated monster (Skal, 1993: 128). The project fell through and O'Brien would go on to make *King Kong* (Schoedsack and Cooper: 1933) instead, the giant ape becoming an enduring landmark in horror animation. Film adaptations of *Frankenstein* would never venture into stop-motion animation but would remain as the Edison studios pioneered: a monstrous adaptation reliant upon special effects for an explicit creation sequence with an actor beneath extreme make-up at its conclusion.

If the Edison *Frankenstein* establishes special effects as a central plank in horror, John S. Robertson's feature film *Dr Jekyll and Mr Hyde* (1920) reveals another paradigm: the primacy of the actor in horror. John Barrymore was already a legendary stage actor by the time he appeared in *Dr Jekyll and Mr Hyde*. His classical good looks earned him the nickname of 'The Great Profile'. He was devoted to theatre and yet had appeared in several films before *Dr Jekyll and Mr Hyde*, principally as a light comedian and/or love interest. It seems that Barrymore despised the 'lover' roles his good looks cursed him with; in this respect, *Dr Jekyll and Mr Hyde* must have been a dream come true. Moreover, Barrymore had a taste for the macabre and the Gothic: his first career was as an artist whose chief desire was to 'illustrate definitively the works of Poe' (Mank, 1994: 4).

By 1919, John Barrymore had been hailed as 'the successor to Richard Mansfield' (Garton, 1980: 79). Mansfield was one of the great US stage actors of the late nineteenth century and friend to the Barrymore family when John was a child. Mansfield's most celebrated stage role was as Dr Jekyll and Mr Hyde in an adaptation written specifically for him by Thomas Russell Sullivan in 1887, barely a year after the novel had appeared. The *New York*

Times described Mansfield's premiere in *Dr Jekyll and Mr Hyde* thus:

> The change from one to the other is made in full view of the spectators without resorting to any artificial device whatever [and in so doing gives] form and substance to a character entirely new to the drama. (10 May 1887)

Mansfield's monstrous transmutation was so terrifying that, when performing in London in 1888, the actor was, as Andrew Smith informs us, 'marked out as a suspect for the [Jack the Ripper] murders' (Smith, 2004: 77) and was obliged to curtail the production's run. Not only was Mansfield so convincing in his embodiment of schizophrenic transmutation, he also emphasised Hyde as a 'sexual sadist' (Smith, 2004: 77): a decision not implicit in Stevenson's story but one which will cast a long shadow of influence over the adaptations of *Dr Jekyll and Mr Hyde*, not least Barrymore's interpretation of Hyde as an evidently syphilitic menace.

Just as Sullivan's dramatisation would compete with other stage adaptations of the novel, cinema would find *Dr Jekyll and Mr Hyde* to be an immensely popular source text for screen adaptation. There were numerous versions after Selig's 1908 production, including four in 1920 alone. If the Edison *Frankenstein* established the creation scene as a horror film paradigm, then in the case of *Dr Jekyll and Mr Hyde* it is the transformation sequence. Early screen adaptations of the novel make extensive use of dissolves and rapid edits. The nature of film technology, even in its earliest days, facilitated this. Indeed, in the case of the Thanhouser *Dr Jekyll and Mr Hyde* (1911), S. A. Nollen reveals that editing was used so that two actors (James Cruze and Harry Benham) took the respective roles of Jekyll and Hyde (Nollen, 1994: 168). With John Barrymore's realisation of the initial transformation, however, we witness a return to the principles of virtuoso theatrical performance inaugurated by Richard Mansfield.

Although in the full transformation episode some extremely effective editing is used to facilitate Jekyll's complete transmutation, the first section is entirely dependent on the actor. After painful deliberation, Jekyll swallows his potion and is thrown into melodramatic paroxysm before he leers up as Hyde. As a performer, Barrymore crams numerous components of physical adaptation into a concise period of time. We see the classically postured matinée idol transform into the monster, a transformation that uses his dishevelled hair, jutting chin, bulging eyes, rippling eyebrows, wrinkled forehead and a radical shift in posture and pace and rhythm. An edit is used to allow a classic, eventually clichéd, hand transformation before we return to Hyde with the detailed makeup which will become more extreme – and pointedly degenerate – as the film proceeds.

Barrymore may be paying homage to, if not competing with, Richard Mansfield's theatrical precedent, but what he establishes in his performance is the role of the virtuoso actor in horror film. The centrality of Barrymore's transmutative performance in the film is confirmed by contemporary reviews which clearly see *Dr Jekyll and Mr Hyde* as a vehicle for Barrymore's talents. Moreover, the verity of both Jekyll and Hyde are seen as being in perfect balance. *Variety* stated that the story is 'ridiculous, judged by modern standards' (2 April 1920), but this did not diminish Barrymore's astonishing performance; while the *New York Times* (29 March 1920) suggested that 'everything that distinguishes [the film] ... is centered on Mr. Barrymore's flawless performance' which is 'on as high a level as has ever been attained by anyone'. In our own time, Ramsey Campbell claims that 'John Barrymore [remains] the screen's most frightening Mr Hyde' (Campbell, 1986: 129). The challenge – and dramatic 'legitimacy' – of Barrymore's performance in the dual roles will draw Fredrick March and Spencer Tracy to it in 1931 and 1941 respectively, with March winning an Oscar for his interpretation. More widely we may wish to consider the theatrical actors who step from the classical stage (or 'serious' cinema) into the horror movie: Michael Redgrave in *Dead of Night* (Cavalcanti et al.: 1945) is one example, but more familiarly we may consider Vincent Price, Peter Cushing and Christopher Lee; right up to Anthony Hopkins' Oscar-winning performance as Hannibal Lecter in *The Silence of the Lambs* (Jonathan Demme: 1990), it feels like Barrymore's towering performance not only makes inhabiting such roles possible for the 'serious' actor, it throws down the gauntlet. Similarly, while *Spider-Man* (Sam Raimi: 2002) may abound with CGI splendours, its greatest sequence is probably when Mr Osborn meets the Green Goblin: Willem Dafoe in a Barrymore-style dressing gown in a room with a mirror. It is a scene not dependent on special effects but the skills of a virtuoso performer.

The other pioneering horror film achievement in *Dr Jekyll and Mr Hyde* is Jekyll's waking-nightmare towards the end of the film, a scene in which, we are informed by the intertitles, 'outraged Nature took her hideous revenge', sending the 'creeping terror' of his other self out of the 'black abyss'. The creeping terror takes the form of a gigantic spider which crawls across Jekyll's bedroom floor before mounting the bed and then *mounting* – the violent sexual connotation is unmistakable – Jekyll. On close observation it can be seen that the giant spider is not a superimposed tarantula, but a superimposed sequence of Barrymore in a spider costume with the head of Mr Hyde. This short episode consolidates another paradigmatic moment of horror film: a dream sequence wherein the broad fantasy of the overall narrative is extrapolated into an intensely disturbing moment of the grotesquely irrational. In conventionally narrative-driven horror movies such moments of the grotesquely irrational can only inhabit nightmares and are imbued with symbolic verity. Other more recent yet classic examples of hideous dreams with acute symbolism include the dreams of the guilty in the shocking finales to *Deliverance* (John Boorman: 1972) and *Carrie* (Brian De Palma: 1976), the sexual anxiety of the maggot-birth dream in *The Fly* (David Cronenberg: 1986) and the paranoid nightmare sequence within *An American Werewolf in London* (John Landis: 1981). In *Dr Jekyll and Mr Hyde*, the spider-Hyde is not the symbol of guilt, anxiety or paranoia, but the symbol of Jekyll's terminal descent into degeneracy and doom; after all, he does not awake in the cold light of a slightly more rational world, but as Mr Hyde.

The figure in Jekyll's nightmare is not a Peter Parker Spider-Man but a hideous monster caught mid-adaptation. These half-human, half-animal figures have a pan-cultural resonance, appearing in such diverse places as the legend of mermaids; the paintings of Hieronymus Bosch or Joe Coleman; or as the half-woman, half-spider 'mad Arachne' in Dante's *Purgatory* or the Spider-Anancy trickster man in Caribbean folklore. In Carl Jung's psychoanalytical theory, such figures are physical embodiments of *dissociation* or 'a splitting in the psyche' which is, 'in reality ... an inner psychic state' (Jung, 1964: 24). It is not surprising that such ghastly hybridity has a special place in horror culture, including films as diverse as *The Fly* (Kurt Neumann: 1958) and *The Thing* (John Carpenter: 1982). Just as the Hyde-spider mounts and probably violates Jekyll, such monsters have a sexual resonance as evidenced in the half-girl, half-spider in the classic *Quiet, Please* radio play 'The Thing on the Fourble Board' (Wyllis Cooper: 1948) or in the *Masters of Horror* television drama 'Deer Woman' (John Landis: 2005): in these examples, the alluring females reveal a bestial lower body that erupts as the ultimate *vagina dentata*.

Regardless of its broad cultural resonance, the half-spider is an important metaphor in looking at the Barrymore legend. During the making of *Dr Jekyll and Mr Hyde*, Barrymore filmed in the morning; in the afternoon he rehearsed *Richard III* for theatre; and in the evening he performed in a play called *The Jest*. Meanwhile, he was also planning his production of *Hamlet* and had begun his fiery relationship with the female writer Michael Strange. The run of *Richard III* in New York was cut short when Barrymore suffered a nervous breakdown and was admitted into a sanatorium. While recuperating, Barrymore drew a self portrait in which he caricatured himself as the 'Great Profile', combining the image of a spider with his own head: the Jekyll nightmare, in short. Indeed, it is a recurrent image in Barrymore's artworks – quite startlingly, he uses it as the frontispiece to his 1926 autobiography – and in terms of his craft as an actor, it takes us back to the genesis of *Richard III*. In *Confessions of an Actor*, Barrymore recalls a trip to the zoo:

> I was at the Bronx Zoo one day . . . looking at a red tarantula which had a grey bald spot on its back. This had been caused by trying to get out of its cage. It was peculiarly sinister and evil looking; the personification of a crawling power. I said . . . 'It looks just like Richard III'. (Barrymore, 1926: 99)

This makes us realise that *Dr Jekyll and Mr Hyde* is not just a major example of early horror cinema; it is also a valuable *theatrical* document for the history of Shakespeare production as well as a reflection and adaptation of Barrymore's concept and rehearsal practice for his concurrent performance as Shakespeare's *Richard III*. Although Barrymore would always be thoroughly dismissive of this film role (see Mank, 1994: 6), the mid-adaptive figure of spider-Hyde is a bridging juxtaposition between Jekyll and Hyde, but it is also a bridge between *Dr Jekyll and Mr Hyde* and Shakespeare, theatre and film, and popular and 'high' culture.

Dr Jekyll and Mr Hyde has become an inseparable part of the John Barrymore legend: a great performance surrounded by myth and metaphor. On the day of its premiere (Rivoli movie theatre, March 1920), the hysterical crowd smashed windows and broke down the door in their desperation to see the film. There are other anecdotes of audiences terrified by the film once they finally saw it. Other aspects add to the legendary status of the film, such as the sad fate of the female lead Martha Mansfield who died, aged 24, in 1923 when her dress caught fire on a film set. The role of Jekyll and Hyde stands as an emblem of the notorious duality of Barrymore's life: the talent and grandeur of the greatest American stage Hamlet juxtaposed with the scurrilous womaniser, bankrupt and alcoholic. One of the most famous anecdotes surrounding the film is connected with the young Tallulah Bankhead. Barrymore invited Bankhead to his dressing room. 'Were the Barrymore intentions professional or carnal?' (Bankhead, 1952: 75) she asked herself. When Barrymore invited her to play the lead female role in *Dr Jekyll and Mr Hyde*, she declined.

> Jack took it in his stride. [But then] he started to make little animal noises ... He rose and took my hands in his and started to lead me to a convenient couch. With such dignity as I could simulate under the fiery circumstances, I declined. With difficulty I withstood his pleading, [and] shortly found myself in West Forty-fifth Street, shaken and seared. What a crowded hour! Two propositions had been made to me. (Bankhead, 1952: 75)

A proposition each, as it were, from Jekyll and from Hyde. Thus Bankhead paints the picture of Barrymore as the real-life embodiment of Jekyll and Hyde, with the animal noises signifying the moment of metamorphosis. But what her autobiographical account reveals – probably unconsciously – is her own transmutation: when she first meets Barrymore she describes how 'my insides did nip-ups. My temples throbbed. My brow grew clammy'; she even confesses how Barrymore caused her to 'wax oozy' (Bankhead, 1952: 74–5).

As a final anecdote: Elaine Barrie Barrymore (his fourth wife) recalls how towards the end of his life (and before their divorce), she promised her alcoholic husband a drink if he would do the Jekyll and Hyde transformation:

> My blood ran cold. There wasn't a feature that was recognizable. His face was contorted by the presence of sheer evil. No! It wasn't even evil. This was no cliché of cruelty or bestiality ... This was utter amorality. The smile made you crawl with obscenity. The secrets of hell were unlocked [...] I almost fell into a faint [...] What an actor this man was! (Quoted in Mank, 1994: 7)

We see here utter transformation: not simply a two-faced or schizophrenic figure, but an example of total inhabitation and complete immersion producing two figures as different as a spider and a man. It is this remarkable transmutation that makes the role remain a milestone and a yardstick of horror performance.

Ian Conrich has persuasively argued about the hegemony of sound cinema in the study of horror film, as if horror cinema only began in the US with Universal's *Frankenstein* in 1931 (Conrich, 2004: 41). Examples of horror movies from the silent era in the US are perhaps as interesting as the contemporary and subsequent achievements in Germany. In the case of the Edison *Frankenstein* and John S. Robertson's *Dr Jekyll and Mr Hyde*, we are presented with two masterpieces of generic and thematic adaptation which, when analysed, are monumental moments in horror film history. Like their respective ur-texts, both films establish certain paradigms and can be seen as having an extraordinary resonance when considered in the light of subsequent horror film culture, including the realm of special effects, narrative and the centrality of the horror performer.

Painting the life out of her: aesthetic integration and disintegration in Jean Epstein's *La Chute de la maison Usher*

Guy Crucianelli

Introduction

Adapted from Edgar Allan Poe's story, 'The Fall of the House of Usher', Jean Epstein's 1928 film *La Chute de la maison Usher* incorporates nearly all the major avant-garde trends of the previous one hundred years and interprets them through an early twentieth-century modernist sensibility. In its treatment of the artist in self-imposed isolation – a figure whose heightened aesthetic experience infects his psyche and, consequently, his environment – Epstein's film links with nineteenth-century Romanticism, Decadence and Symbolism, as well as Edgar Allan Poe himself. Epstein exteriorises a disintegrating consciousness through a variety of cinematic techniques, from slow and reverse motion photography to the superimposition of multiple images. Epstein also employs rhythmically complex editing patterns that not only articulate the theories of the cinematic Impressionists, but can be related to Russian montage, as well as the more painterly films of other French avant-garde filmmakers of the 1920s, such as Fernand Léger's *Ballet mécanique* (1924). While the latter film is concerned more with the non-linear, abstract possibilities of cinema, the use of 'musical' and often dissonant juxtapositions are reflected in Epstein's film. *La Chute de la maison Usher* also touches on Surrealist theories, especially the emphasis on the transformative powers of the imagination. Ultimately the film is a sort of cryptic and anachronistic palimpsest whose modernist tendencies exist specifically in this blending and integration of a variety of aesthetic attitudes at the service of purely formalist concerns.

'General impressions'

Jean Mitry refers to Jean Epstein as the 'first real theoretician of the cinema' (quoted in Abel, 1984: 249). Beginning his career as a writer, Epstein's early book *Bonjour Cinema* (1921) was 'a witty parody of a film program [in which he] was already playing with the idea of "editing" together the diverse strands of modern life into something analogous to a film' (249). Epstein's theories, with their conflation of 'poetic and scientific language' (249), would greatly influence French avant-garde cinema and Impressionist cinematic theory in particular.

Among the many influences on Impressionist film theory, David Bordwell specifically mentions Jean Epstein's 'aesthetic of "approximation" and "the indefinite" (Bordwell, 1980 [1974]: 96), notions with obvious antecedents in nineteenth-century literary symbolism. Like Symbolist writers such as Stephane Mallarme, Charles Baudelaire and Edgar Allan Poe, Epstein envisioned an art 'based on suggestiveness and implication' (96) achieved through the 'investigation of cinematic specificity' (L'Herbier, quoted in Abel, 1984: 290), or *photogénie*, a relatively obscure 'free-floating signifier' (292) which alternately relates the ambiguous, hypnotic power of the cinematic image, as well as the 'unique visual and kinetic aspects' (290) allowed by the manipulation of materials *specific to* cinema – for example optical devices, montage and *mise-en-scène*. Epstein approached the concept of *photogénie* as something both scientific and metaphysical: 'The decomposition of an event into its *photogénic* elements is the first law of film, its grammar, its algebra' (292). While such theories appear more closely related to the conditions of abstract or 'pure' cinema, Epstein sought the same evocative 'musicality' within an open narrative framework.

Given its array of influences, *La Chute de la maison Usher* may be seen as the ultimate synthesis of Jean Epstein's theories on cinematic expression and a culmination of the director's tendency to weave diverse strands of source material into a puzzle-like whole. The film's scenario is itself composed of diverse strands; just as Poe himself often thematically referenced his own stories and poems through recurring images and motifs, Epstein's adaptation draws from several of Poe's works, allowing the director a wider assortment of narrative ideas upon which to perform his experiments. While the film adheres to the title story's basic framework, it borrows generously from Poe's 'The Oval Portrait', incorporating the latter story's emphasis on the almost-supernatural powers of portraiture. The film also includes other sly references to Poe's work. One portrait in the Usher house is labeled 'Lady Ligeia', and there are numerous shots of a clock's swinging pendulum, recalling Poe's 'The Pit and the Pendulum', along with overtly pendulous camerawork intended to destabilise viewers through the creation of a 'swaying' *mise-en-scène*.

In addition to employing this cross-section of Poe's material, Epstein alters crucial details of the title story in significant ways. While retaining the narrator of the story as a character, Epstein substitutes the first-person singular narration with a 'strangely fluctuating omniscienc[e]' (Abel, 1984: 463). Such an alteration allows for a more diffuse, indeterminate point of view that challenges and, at times, denies traditional image continuity and, thus, spectatorial expectations as well. Characters, for instance, enter or exit the frame from oblique angles; at other moments, they look off in directions that subsequent shots fail to answer according to conventional spatial logics. While this unhinged narration may also be seen as Epstein's way of transposing the gloomy, unsettling quality of Poe's prose, it is perhaps more closely linked to the director's desire for a specifically cinematic world capable of describing 'the perfect circle of an impossible simultaneity' (quoted in Abel, 1984: 293).

The 'approximate' POV

Edgar Allan Poe's 'The Fall of the House of Usher' opens with a detailed description of the narrator approaching the house itself. Epstein begins his adaptation with visual transpositions of Poe's imagery. A series of shots display a dark figure stumbling over a marshy landscape of weeds and bare black branches. Is this Poe's narrator-figure? If so, the shots in the opening sequence seem purposefully to hide or obscure his identity. The figure is shown in long shots that make it impossible to see his face, medium shots from the neck down, and as close-ups of legs stepping through black marshes. When we do get a close-up of the face, the eyes are cropped out of frame. Epstein emphasises this delayed narrative disclosure through his use of spatial ambiguity. In a scene owing much to *Nosferatu* (1922), the narrator enters a rural inn to inquire as to the whereabouts of the house of Usher. In *Nosferatu*, the inquiring character, Hutter, is easily distinguishable, his identity having been established in previous scenes and his position in the inn made clear through a traditional shot/reverse shot pattern between himself and the locals. However, in *La Chute de la maison Usher* there is a 'curious reversal and denial of POV [and spatial] expectations' (Abel, 1984: 465). Rather than introduce the inquiring figure into the basic plot with coherent editing and compositions, Epstein distorts physical space through oblique framing and blocking, with 'unanswered' looks and movements occurring in a non-delineated locale. The narrator-figure remains mysterious, almost ghostly, positioned at indirect angles within the frame like a 'revelation … continually denied or deflected' (465). He is variously displayed with his back to the camera, or his body turned just enough so that his face remains unseen.

With this sequence, Epstein displaces the first-person narration of Poe's 'Usher', while retaining and stressing that narration's perceptual unreliability. Throughout Poe's story the narrator repeatedly questions what he sees, hears or experiences. Through a visual logic of spatial displacement that disallows consistency with regard to the characters' specific physical locations within the film, Epstein is able to portray this same sense of uncertainty: as in Poe, only sensations, not senses, can be trusted.

In this way, the film's point of view is 'approximate', offering oblique visual 'impressions' meant to invoke the instability of Poe's prose through an indefinite perspective. There are numerous shots in the film seemingly composed to imply a specific point of view, yet the perspective taken cannot possibly be that of the characters. Is it, perhaps, the experience and point of view of the house of Usher itself? In his short story, Poe describes the house as a living organism, personifying it as 'melancholy' and with 'eye-like windows' (Poe, 1975: 231). Are Epstein's oblique points of view meant to display what the house sees or feels? Is it intended to depict the animism of an inanimate consciousness? Or is the film suggesting its own consciousness, the 'consciousness of cinema' itself?

Such suggestions are essential to Epstein's 'investigation of cinematic specificity'. Although the world of the film may not abide by the 'laws' and 'logics' of standard conventional cinema, it does follow the specific 'laws' of Impressionist cinema, especially since Epstein not only alternates multiple perspectives, both animate and inanimate. In doing so, he invests each one with an individually elusive, evocative power.

Perceptual ambiguity extends throughout the film's diegesis. The exterior of the Usher house is depicted in very obvious miniatures, with artificial smoke and small, bare branches for trees. Although this visual iconography is ostensibly a replication of Poe's prose, the sudden inclusion of obvious artifice troubles spectatorial expectations. Just as the peasants at the inn appear uncertain as to who or what they are seeing, the vision of this 'insufferable gloom', rendered with such intentional artificiality, questions whether what we see is meant to be understood as 'real' or 'imaginary'. At the film's conclusion, when this miniature ignites and splits apart, this uncertainty becomes even more pressing: is the 'fall' of this artificial construction occurring within the consciousness of the characters (as the 'fall of Usher' appears to be in the original story) or is it actually happening? The objectification of the subjective forces the spectator into the same precarious subject position as the characters.

Although it is composed of full-size sets, the interior of the house does not provide a sense of physical certainty or spatial orientation. Epstein introduces these interior spaces inductively, beginning with a close-up of hands, followed by a close-up of a painter's palette, and then a close-up of Roderick in an undefined location. Finally the film cuts to an 'establishing' long shot, but the room is so massive that it remains difficult to determine the figures' positions. Such a process reverses traditional cinematic practices that seek to establish a locale before focusing in on crucial narrative details. The reversal delays and confuses the interpretation of the images. The spectator is obliged to wait for a clarification of meaning through subsequent montage, or to infer or create provisional interpretations of images until the full sequence secures meaning. Through allusive and abstract imagery, Epstein allows a discrete image to suggest sensations rather than clarify a stable meaning. A disconnected close-up of hands lowering into frame in slow-motion, for example, momentarily free of specific signification, nonetheless seems invested with an unnatural, evocative power.

Such suggestive images have their correlation in Poe's original prose. Poe's description of the house's 'stern, deep, and irredeemable gloom' (Poe, 1975: 234) is closely reproduced in Epstein's décor. The massive space of the central room renders the profusion of furniture sparse. Further, long shots trouble the depth of field, so that it becomes difficult to discern the furniture from the actors. What appears to be the entrance hall is an elaborate, multi-leveled theatrical construction with a vast, empty foreground and a strange ramp-like passage in the background leading downward to suits of armour. To the right of this is a staircase whose railing is composed of large posts, like stunted tree stumps, with iron chains slung between them. The effect is theatrical, expressionistic and medieval. Besides these 'rooms', there is also a hall with 'dark draperies hung upon the walls' (Poe, 1975: 241). This hall figures prominently in a number of scenes where it is used more for its evocative properties than as a practical structural locale. With the space unoccupied, the 'dark and tattered draperies'(Poe, 1975: 241) billow into ghostly shapes in both slow and fast motion, and the hall acquires that 'cinematic animism' so essential to Impressionistic *photogénie*. Yet just as these objects, images and architectures attain life, they begin to deteriorate, infected by the 'peculiar malady' disintegrating the House of Usher.

An exquisite affliction

In both Epstein's film and in Poe's original story, it is obvious that the 'House of Usher' encompasses more than just an architectural structure. Epstein retains the hereditary 'deficiency' (Poe, 1975: 232) that Poe makes explicit yet locates it within a specific cause. As an intertitle describes it: 'By a quirk of heredity, every male descendant of the Usher family devoted himself passionately to painting his wife's portrait.' Thus, in Epstein's film, the Usher malady is a near-biological impulse centered upon an 'exquisite' obsession to paint. The decisive place of Roderick within this strange heritage is made clear through another intertitle: 'The Usher family tree was as tormented as an old oak and threatened Roderick, the last of the line, with degeneracy.' The 'undeviating' sterility of the Usher line ultimately leads to Roderick and his fatal inability to renounce the painted representation of his wife in favour of the living person. In the film, what might be called the story's psychoanalytic complexities are sublimated in favour of this stressed examination on the nature of representation – specifically, what it means, or *can* mean, to represent a human subject, both in paint and on film. Traditionally, portraiture 'assumes some degree of difference between the portrait image and the person, otherwise they would be identical and no question of likeness would arise' (Brilliant, 1997 [1991]: 25). Due to the degenerated nature of Roderick's psyche, 'the psychodynamics of perception interfere with the comprehension of the [painted] image as something different from the image of the actual person' (24). Thus, negotiations between 'reality' and 'representation', between subject and object, deteriorate until the object becomes the subject and vice versa. Madeleine's portrait begins as an alternate or double which ends up replacing the original in the affections of the artist. In this way, the incestuous ramifications of Poe's story are refigured as the self-contained, decadent aesthetic pursuits of a cloistered aristocracy. Locked away in his decrepit mansion, Roderick embodies and ensures the final degradation of his familial line by exploiting the limits of his own hermetic, onanistic desires.

In *La Chute*, the portrait poses much more of a threat to Madeleine than to Roderick. The quasi-mystical experience of investing the portrait with the spirit of Madeleine herself involves keeping her (as an inter-title explains) 'in a state of strange seclusion' in the dark gloom of the mansion with only the candles keeping her company. Appropriately, candles become a primary associative motif for Madeleine and her ebbing strength. There are numerous crosscuts between Madeleine and dwindling candles, and the actress is often posed behind large candle stands, her waxy features drooping over the flames. At one point, the candles appear to drip onto Roderick's palette, and as he paints with the wax itself, multiple symbols conflate. Madeleine's frown 'drips' into the candles that dwindle and drip themselves onto the palette; and in a true transference of being, Roderick then literally applies the symbol of Madeleine, in the form of melted wax, onto the representation of her. The more Roderick paints, the lower the candles burn, and as Madeleine's strength diminishes, it becomes clear that Roderick is, in a very real sense, painting the life out of her. In Epstein's film, Madeleine undergoes a transubstantiation from 'flesh' to 'paint', 'real' to 'represented' (Abel, 1984: 467). As shots of Roderick at work on the portrait alternate with shots of Madeleine growing weaker, it is obvious that 'adding to the painted image subtracts from Madeleine' (466). Just as Roderick's act of painting transforms Madeleine from subject to object, it also forces her to move physically from presence to absence, sometimes embodying both at once. Indeed, throughout the film Madeleine's absence is felt *as* a presence and her presence as an absence. Often when she is present, Roderick disregards her completely, staring fixedly off-frame at either the portrait or his palette. As Madeleine floats through the room in ghostly distraction, it is as if she is already missing, her strength and life-force extracted from her and incorporated into the portrait.

Cinema may be the ideal medium for portraying Madeleine's predicament because it 'encourage[s] the viewer to concentrate on [an] immaterial appearance on the screen as the true sign of [a] presence' (Brilliant, 1997: 104). Madeleine is not quite there physically, yet her form is still visible, and so embodies 'that specific simultaneity of presence and absence which only the cinema can satisfy' (Cavell, 1979: 42). Within this ambiguous position, Madeleine also represents a kind of discarded muse-figure, the exhausted product of an obsessive temperament that latches onto a singular subject at the expense of all others. Long shots of Madeleine moving spectrally through the vast central hall express a Gothic vacancy while prefiguring certain features of some of Salvador Dali's landscapes, amidst whose barrenness remote figures or constructions stand out as the fixations of a neurotic mind. Due to the distance of the shots, the room achieves a sort of psychic aridity in which Madeleine and the black-draped portrait are situated as dual and dueling fixations, positioning for dominance over Roderick's consciousness.

In *La Chute*, it is the portrait's very 'life-likeness' that provides the film with its most obscure and, in Impressionist terms, *photogénic* element of décor. Initially the portrait is filmed from behind or angled slightly away from the camera, much like the 'denied and deflected revelation' of the visitor in the film's opening sequence. Likewise, early in the film, close-ups of the brush working on a small portion of the canvas reveal nothing of the complete composition. When the portrait is finally shown in full, the effect is even more ambiguous. As if mocking or exaggerating traditional painterly illusionism, the supposedly flat, two-dimensional canvas surface is actually a mirrored or superimposed film image of the actress portraying Madeleine. Cinema's innate representational capacities, its *photogénic* embodiment of materiality/immateriality, allow Epstein to literalise Poe's motif of the 'living' portrait, while narratively, ironically fulfilling Usher's repeated prophecy of 'It is *there* that she lives!' At times, the actress in the portrait visibly blinks her eyes and the 'psychological distance between [the portrait] and the viewer [is] closed' (Brilliant, 1997: 27). This 'film/ painting' contains the visual iconography of both cinema and portraiture. It is 'painted' in a style of what might be termed *decadent naturalism*. Since the figure in the painting *is* Madeleine herself, she is therefore rendered 'naturally' or 'realistically'; yet this 'naturalism' is infringed upon by dense shadows that threaten to submerge her figure. In this sense, the 'painted' image of Madeleine fulfills portraiture's standard function, which 'aims to capture ... and represent its subject as extended in time, even in the process of displaying a particular moment of its existence' (Scruton, quoted in Brilliant, 1997: 58). However, in traditional portraiture 'the correspondence between the original and the portrait must necessarily be incomplete [...] The more a portrait resembles its human counterpart, the more obvious and destructive of the illusion of comparability are the substantial differences between them' (Brilliant, 1997: 26). With the painting of Madeleine, the correspondence between the original and the portrait is complete; they are identically filmed images. Due to this identical likeness, 'the reception given to [the] portrait by the viewer ... conflicts with the normative function of a representation to produce something clearly distant and distinct from the person represented' (Brilliant, 1997: 23).

The portrait's singularity is continually stressed through its isolated position in dark – indeed, *black* – surroundings. With its easel draped in a black curtain, the portrait appears both suspended in and consumed by shadow, forced to provide its own obscure illumination. These images recall a specific passage from Poe: '[D]arkness, as if an inherent positive quality, poured forth upon all objects of the moral and physical universe in one unceasing radiation of gloom' (Poe, 1975: 236). In Epstein's film, gloom infiltrates the portrait like an infection, threatening to consume the 'life-like' image of Madeleine. In this way, both Madeleines – the 'real' and the 'represented' – are trapped in Usher's 'undeviating' patrimony.

The portrait's hypnotic obtuseness is also emphasised through Epstein's disruption of conventional continuity editing, and the fluid, almost levitating movements of both the camera and the actors. Often, as characters move forward to admire the painting, the camera tracks behind or in front of them, as if the camera/portrait itself is pushing or luring them onward. Later, these advancements toward the painting will be countered with dolly shots pulling away from the portrait, as if the portrait retreats elusively with a supernatural evasiveness all its own. The often-confusing movements of the actors themselves mirror these fluid, trance-like shots. At one moment, a POV shot seems to establish the friend's position as behind the easel, approaching Roderick from the front as he paints. Yet in the following shot, the friend emerges from behind Roderick – that is, from the completely opposite direction. Also, during Madeleine's final sitting, shots of Roderick looking off-camera while he paints, as if referring to his actual subject, alternate with full shots of Madeleine collapsing in slow-motion. Even when her figure lies inert on the floor, Roderick continues looking in her direction, as if she were still sitting for him. Throughout this sequence, the two characters are framed individually, as if existing in separate locations that are only tangentially linked.

Often the portrait seems to have its own point of view. Over-the-shoulder shots of Roderick at work on the painting alternate with close-ups of his intent face as he applies brushstrokes directly toward the camera – almost as if we, the viewers, are within the portrait, inhabiting the same 'psychological space' (Brilliant, 1997: 15) as the painted image. Yet the point of view is circumscribed, restricted by both the floral frame surrounding the 'canvas' and the cinematic frame itself. In this way, despite its 'life-likeness', the portrait also becomes a kind of tomb. From the restricted depths of the frame, as if buried alive, both the spectator and the painted Madeleine can only gaze, in close-up, as Roderick struggles over the brink of a hysterical obsession.

While Madeleine's slow demise is expressed through the visual motif of melting candles, Roderick's madness is depicted through associative editing patterns. During the sequence of Madeleine's final sitting, close-ups of Roderick's face are intercut with an obscure close-up of his hands painting a dark corner of the canvas, followed by shots of the palette. These images occur in increasing rhythms, with shots of shorter and shorter duration, eventually giving way to the unhinging of Madeleine in those double and triple exposures. The precise formalism of this sequence creates a kind of musical phrasing or notation. Bordwell observes a similar 'musical notation', albeit in an earlier sequence in which shots of Roderick strumming his guitar alternate with exterior landscape shots, each of various predetermined lengths (Bordwell, 1980: 205–6). In that sequence, the 'strict tempo' (205) created by the 'musical' patterning of shots may be said to explicitly represent Roderick's song through the only means available to silent cinema: montage. In the sequence of the final sitting, the strict repetition of identical shots at varying lengths articulates the treacherous tension of Roderick's compulsive painting and his continued blindness to the lethal effects such portraiture has on Madeleine.

Such sequences represent a cinematic exteriorisation of consciousness, with displaced visual patterns imitating or even inducing extreme psychic states. Epstein evokes and sustains moods and sensations by suggesting Roderick's inner psychological state through an assemblage of images and optical effects: the pendulum of a grandfather clock swinging in empty space; a mass of books tumbling in slow-motion from a fissure in a black-curtained wall; tracking shots of leaves blowing across a barren floor. However provisional such interpretations may be – assuming a shared spectatorial reading – there is no doubt that, like Poe, Epstein intends a correspondence between the house of Usher and the 'House of Usher', that is, the body or mind of Roderick. So images of apparently random points throughout the mansion signify the dark corners of Roderick's deteriorating psyche – haunted, haunting and black as night.

Just as the richly suggestive, melancholic prose of 'Usher' is meant to imitate or induce the *state* of melancholy into the mind of the reader as a traceable facsimile of a psychological breakdown or 'fall', *La Chute* attempts the cinematic equivalent of a multidimensional, conceptual fragmentation of reality as an expression of the true movements of the mind. The film seeks 'impressions of incoherence' (Flitterman-Lewis, 1987: 118) in order to stress the dislocations of its own self-contained world. In Poe's 'Usher', these dislocations are the product of a psychological disorder affecting the visual and experiential faculties of the characters themselves. In *La Chute*, this disordered psychological space and point of view is adapted into something solely and specifically cinematic.

Imitation of grief

Perhaps the sequence in which Epstein achieves his most specific example of a purely cinematic conception is that of Madeleine's funeral and burial. Indeed, with the funeral procession in particular Epstein creates an alternate spatial-temporal universe that is not so much 'inner' as 'other'. The sequence has painterly values as well as cinematic and dramatic ones, with layered or textured images expressing a different sort of 'film/painting' than the portrait. The entire sequence is a meticulously orchestrated progression of cinematic effects, with multiple exposures, abstract imagery, slow-motion photography and dramatic camerawork all operating in conjunction with the melodramatic movements of the actors to create a textured imitation of dazed mourning and grief.

The sequence begins with a complex image of multiple exposures. On one level, there is an extreme long shot of Roderick, the friend, a physician and a servant carrying Madeline's coffin down a tree-lined path. Superimposed over this image are two towering columns of candles. While the candles are obviously meant to recall Madeleine, their superimposition over the landscape, conflating the natural with the funereal, creates an imposing processional aisle like an exterior Gothic cathedral. Underneath these images is a third exposure of what appear to be gilded leaves falling or spinning mobile-like against a black background. The film then cuts to various shots of the actors' legs or oblique close-ups of their faces, triple-layered with the same candles and leaves, creating a richly-textured, gauze-like effect. The sequence is even more ponderous due to the conflated movements of the actors and the camera. As the characters struggle with the coffin over the marshy terrain in highly-stylised synchronised movements, the camera imitates their motions, swaying up and down with the ominous regularity of a pendulum, to create a plodding, dirge-like effect. There is an overriding dissonance between the ambiguous and, at times, indecipherable superimpositions and the camera movements accompanying each one. Just as one image gains prominence – for example, the candles becoming more visible – it is overtaken and obscured by another. Together the multiple exposures have the visceral quality of tissue, each individual image solid enough to be visible yet opaque enough to see through. The viewer must visually discern the individual images before deciphering or interpreting their 'meaning'.

Each of these superimposed images – pallbearers, falling leaves and candles – stands on its own, each layer invested with its unique, unusual import. Yet what happens when these images combine? Is there a breakdown in signification or a deepening? Taken together, the three images create a new symbolic or metaphoric (even metamorphic) 'geography' representative of Roderick's grief and, consequently, the disintegrating 'House of Usher'. Close-ups of Roderick's face show him struggling, much as the spectator does, to decipher the meaning of events and to separate one sensation from another. Yet for Roderick, such an endeavour is nearly impossible; like the dark layers of a grief-stricken consciousness, these images are fundamentally interconnected.

Ultimately, this layering of images signifies not only a re-creation of a psychological state, but an attempt at the inducement of that state within the consciousness of the spectator, impressing upon the viewer associative sensations of melancholy, madness or grief. Indeed, the fragmentary discord and chaotic indecipherability of the compounded images of the funeral procession enact an identical chaos within the viewer, until one is as stunned and confounded as Roderick himself appears to be by the film's end.

The final eruption and ostensible resolution of this chaos occurs upon Madeleine's return from the grave. The doors of the Usher house crash open, revealing Madeleine's tortured figure framed by the blackness of the doorway. As this shot is echoed by a full shot of the framed portrait of Madeleine, hung in blackness, the dual implications of Madeleine's burial become obvious. Besides burying her alive in the tomb, Roderick has also buried her 'alive' in the portrait; only with the true death of one Madeleine, can the other survive. Whereas earlier in the film 'the sign function of the portrait [was] so strong that it seemed to be some form of substitution for the original' (Brilliant, 1997: 40), here the roles are reversed. As the 'painted' Madeleine blinks, expressing the same rigid dismay as the re-animated Madeleine, flames engulf the three-dimensional 'canvas'. Amidst flames and swirling smoke, only the living characters stumble from the increased wreckage of the house.

Yet while the characters of *La Chute* seem to escape the 'fall' of the 'House of Usher', the house itself does not. We see an obvious miniature exterior of the house, whose 'barely perceptible fissure ... extending from the roof of the building ... down the wall in a zigzag direction' (Poe, 1975: 233) now 'rapidly widen[s]' (245). As the miniature bursts into flames and splits apart, a 'tree of lights' or 'stars' forms optically in the dark sky. Is this an indication of Roderick's salvation, the redemption of his 'family tree'? Is Roderick saved from being an Usher and the 'passionate desire' to paint? The film seems to resolve these ambiguities in its own peculiar manner. In a way, the reanimated figure of Madeleine functions almost as a macabre sort of *deus ex machina*, arriving just in time to save Roderick and his friend from the burning house. Yet the artificiality of the exteriors seems to locate the entire end sequence as occurring within the consciousness of the characters, an internal location once again implying containment or entrapment. Can one escape one's genealogy, let alone one's already disintegrated consciousness? Despite the apparent escape of the figures at the film's end, they seem no more free or safe from the restricting confines of the Usher 'madness' or from the specifically cinematic realm of *La Chute de la maison Usher.*

Conclusion

While the funeral sequence is characteristic of the palimpsestic nature of *La Chute* – the moment at which the layers of aesthetic influence are reflected and reinforced through the cinematic image itself – in truth the entire film is a 'tightly-fitted Chinese box-like construction' (Abel, 1984: 437) that requires a viewing process akin to the unravelling of a puzzle. The film's textual, thematic and formal conjunctions, as well as its appropriation of numerous diverse aesthetic trends, allow one to trace its avant-garde trajectory from Edgar Allan Poe's nineteenth-century 'early modernism' into early twentieth-century modernism. Through its synthesis of disparate traditions, *La Chute de la maison Usher* advances a purely cinematic representation of reality, which, in Clement Greenberg's words 'determine[s], through operations peculiar to itself, the effects peculiar and exclusive to itself' (quoted in Clark, 1984: 11). Jean Epstein's film not only stands as a classic of the 'first avant-garde' but as the culmination and adaptation of many avant-gardes.

The unfilmable? H. P. Lovecraft and the cinema

Julian Petley

> It was in the hot autumn that I went through the night with the restless crowds to see Nyarlathotep; through the stifling night and up the endless stairs into the choking room. And shadowed on a screen, I saw hooded forms amidst ruins, and yellow evil faces peering from behind fallen monuments. And I saw the world battling against blackness; against the waves of destruction from ultimate space; whirling, churning, struggling around the dimming, cooling sun. Then the sparks played amazingly around the heads of the spectators, and hair stood up on end whilst shadows more grotesque than I can tell came out and squatted on the heads.
>
> *Nyarlathotep*. H. P. Lovecraft.

Considering the immense impact of H. P. Lovecraft's stories on modern culture, it might seem at first sight surprising how few of them have been filmed. Lovecraft wrote around sixty stories and three novellas, but only ten of these have served as the actual basis of feature films. Indeed, Dan O'Bannon has called Lovecraft 'an unconquered film category' (quoted in Migliore and Strysik, 2000: 110). But is this in fact the case?

The Lovecraft stories which have been credited as movie sources are:

'The Case of Charles Dexter Ward': *The Haunted Palace* (Roger Corman: 1963); *The Resurrected* (Dan O'Bannon: 1992).
'The Colour Out of Space': *Die, Monster, Die!* (Daniel Haller: 1965); *The Farm* aka *The Curse* (David Keith: 1987).
'The Shuttered Room': *The Shuttered Room* (David Greene: 1967). (This is based on a story which claims to have been written by Lovecraft and August Derleth but is in fact almost wholly the latter's work.)

'The Dreams in the Witch House': *Curse of the Crimson Altar* (Vernon Sewell: 1968); *Dreams in the Witch House* (Stuart Gordon: 2005).
'The Dunwich Horror': *The Dunwich Horror* (Daniel Haller: 1969).
'Herbert West – Reanimator': *Re-Animator* (Stuart Gordon: 1985); *Bride of Re-Animator* (Brian Yuzna: 1990).
'From Beyond': *From Beyond* (Stuart Gordon: 1986).
'The Unnamable': *The Unnamable* (Jean-Paul Ouellette: 1988); *The Unnamable Returns* (Jean-Paul Ouellette: 1992), which is also based on 'The Statement of Randolph Carter'.
'The Lurking Fear': *Lurking Fear* (C. Courtney Joyner: 1994); *Bleeders* (Peter Svatek: 1997).
'The Rats in the Walls', 'Cool Air', 'The Whisperer in Darkness': *Necronomicon* (Brian Yuzna, Christopher Gans and Shusuke Kaneko: 1994).
'The Outsider': *Castle Freak* (Stuart Gordon: 1995).

The situation is complicated, however, by the presence of films which, whilst not being based on actual Lovecraft stories, either draw on specifically Lovecraftian elements or radiate a peculiarly and distinctly Lovecraftian aura. The most significant of these generically heterogeneous films include: *Dark Intruder* (Harvey Hart: 1964); *Alien* (Ridley Scott: 1979); *City of the Living Dead/Paura nella città dei morti viventi* (Lucio Fulci: 1980); *The Beyond/L'aldila* (Lucio Fulci: 1981); *The Evil Dead* (Sam Raimi: 1981); *The Thing* (John Carpenter: 1982); *Aliens* (James Cameron: 1986); *Evil Dead II: Dead by Dawn* (Sam Raimi: 1987); *Cast a Deadly Spell* (Martin Campbell: 1991); *Army of Darkness: Evil Dead III* (Sam Raimi: 1991); *Alien³* (David Fincher, 1992); *Alien Resurrection* (Jean-Pierre Jeunet: 1997); *Phantoms* (Joe Chappelle: 1998). The fact that many of these are far more Lovecraftian than certain films which claim to be based directly on his work, for example *Curse of the Crimson Altar* or *Lurking Fear*, is ample testament to just how profound the influence of Lovecraft has been on the contemporary cinema. As Guillaume Foresti puts it in his fascinating study of Lovecraft and Roger Corman:

> Just as on the literature which succeeded it, Lovecraft's oeuvre has had a major and widespread influence on the cinema of the fantas-

> tic, as much on its subject matter as on its form, and the fundamentals laid down by the writer have never ceased, sometimes in part, sometimes wholly, to act as a formidable well of inspiration, a sort of reserve of horrific concepts from which film-makers can draw notions, ideas and atmospheres with strong visual potential in order to shape them to their own conception and give them visual form. The occurrences of the Lovecraftian presence in films of the fantastic are thus multifarious and can be found across all its periods and to different degrees. However, direct adaptations of his stories are few indeed in number. It is more a matter of ambiance, notions, themes, indirect and indeed unfaithful adaptations, drawn from Lovecraft's universe. From this angle, the makers of these films place themselves in a lineage analogous to that of Lovecraft's literary disciples, working at a formidable continuation of a particular and singular mythology, a permanent and perpetual adjournment of reality, in order to redefine the contours of the fantastic and of horror. (Foresti, 2002: 31–2)

Before proceeding further, however, we need to define precisely, albeit briefly, what is meant by the term 'Lovecraftian'.

Maurice Lévy, one of the first scholars to take Lovecraft seriously, succinctly described his outlook as 'a bizarre synthesis of ancient mechanistic philosophy, German pessimism, and the most rigorous positivist materialism' (Lévy, 1988: 30). More recently, and more colourfully, the novelist Michel Houellebecq has summed it up as 'absolute hatred of the world in general, aggravated by an aversion to the modern world in particular' (Houellebecq, 2005: 37). He also states that: 'Few beings have ever been so impregnated, pierced to the core, by the conviction of the absolute futility of human aspiration' (32).

Evidence of Lovecraft's profoundly pessimistic worldview is not hard to find, both in his stories and in his other voluminous writings. For example, Lovecraft refers to human beings as 'miserable denizens of a wretched little flyspeck on the back door of a microscopic universe' (quoted in Joshi, 1996: 208) and as 'momentary trifles bound from a common nothingness toward another coming nothingness' (Lovecraft, 2001: xv), elsewhere stating that:

> Humanity with its pompous pretensions sinks to complete nothingness when viewed in relation to the unfathomed abysses of infinity and eternity which yawn about it. The entire period of existence of mankind, or of the sun and solar system, or of the visible universe itself, is but an inconsequential instant in the history of the whirling

> spheres and ether currents that compose all creation; a history which has neither beginning nor ending. Man, so far from being the central and supreme object of Nature, is clearly demonstrated to be a mere incident, perhaps an accident, of a natural scheme whose boundless reach relegates him to total insignificance. His presence or absence, his life or death, are obviously matters of utter indifference to the plan of Nature as a whole. Even the vast universe we behold is but an atom in the absolutely unlimited expanse which stretches away on all sides. (Quoted in de Camp, 1975: 81)

Or again:

> All my tales are based on the fundamental premise that common human laws and interests and emotions have no validity or significance in the vast cosmos-at-large. To me there is nothing but puerility in a tale in which the human form – and the local human passions and conditions and standards – are depicted as native to other worlds or other universes. To achieve the essence of real externality, whether of time or space or dimension, one must forget that such things as organic life, good and evil, love and hate, and all such local attributes of a negligible and temporary race called mankind, have any existence at all. (Quoted in Joshi, 1996: 402)

From such a perspective springs Lovecraft's complete lack of interest in 'characters' in the conventional fictional sense, which is one of the most striking features of his stories and may well be one of the main reasons why they have proved resistant to cinematic adaptation. As he himself puts it:

> I could not write about 'ordinary people' because I am not the least interested in them. Without interest there could be no art. Man's relations to man do not captivate my fancy. It is man's relation to the cosmos – to the unknown – which alone arouses in me the spark of creative imagination. The humanocentric pose is impossible to me, for I cannot acquire the primitive myopia which magnifies the earth and ignores the background. (Quoted in Joshi, 1996: 319)

This too explains why so many of the stories consist largely of description. As Lovecraft avers: 'The only "heroes" I can write about are *phenomena*' (Lovecraft, 2001: xv, original emphasis). Consequently:

> My natural – and only genuine – form of imagination is that of passive witnessing – the idea of being that of a sort of floating, disembodied eye which sees all manner of marvellous phenomena

> without being greatly affected by them. I am constitutionally unable to see anything interesting in mere *motions* and *events*. What absorb me are *conditions*, *atmospheres*, *appearances*, and things of that kind. (Quoted in de Camp, 1975: 348, original emphasis).

As Michel Houellebecq states, Lovecraft perceived

> the futility of all psychological differentiation. His characters no longer required it; all they needed was functional sensory equipment. Their sole function, in fact, would be to *perceive*. It might even be said that the deliberate banality of his characters contributes to reinforcing the compelling nature of Lovecraft's universe. A more obtrusive psychological brushstroke would have only detracted from their testimony and diminished its transparency; we would have left the domain of material horror to enter that of psychological horror. And Lovecraft did not wish to describe psychoses, but repugnant realities. (Houellebecq, 2005: 68)

Lovecraft himself described his work as a form of 'non-supernatural cosmic art' (Lovecraft, 1999: xvi) and the foremost Lovecraft scholar S. T. Joshi uses the term 'cosmicism' to describe the sensations described in and evoked by Lovecraft's stories. He defines this as 'the aesthetic crystallisation of that burning and inextinguishable feeling of mixed wonder and oppression which the sensitive imagination experiences upon scaling itself and its restrictions against the vast and provocative abyss of the unknown' (Joshi, 1996: 488), and as

> at once a metaphysical position (an awareness of the vastness of the universe in both space and time), an ethical position (an awareness of the insignificance of human beings within the realm of the universe), and an aesthetic position (a literary expression of this insignificance, to be effected by the minimising of human character and the display of the titanic gulfs of space and time). (319)

One of the most striking expressions of cosmicism in Lovecraft's work is to be found at the start of the story 'Facts Concerning the Late Arthur Jermyn and His Family':

> Life is a hideous thing, and from the background behind what we know of it peer daemoniacal hints of truth which make it sometimes a thousandfold more hideous. Science, already oppressive with its shocking revelations, will perhaps be the ultimate exterminator of our human species – if separate species we be – for its reserve of

> unguessed horrors could never be borne by mortal brains if loosed upon the world. (Lovecraft, 1999: 14)[1]

Similarly, in 'The Call of Cthulhu' Lovecraft writes:

> The most merciful thing in the world, I think, is the inability of the human mind to correlate all its contents. We live on a placid island of ignorance in the midst of black seas of infinity, and it was not meant that we should voyage far. The sciences, each straining in its own direction, have hitherto harmed us little; but some day the piecing together of dissociated knowledge will open up such terrifying vistas of reality and of our frightful position therein, that we shall either go mad from the revelation or flee from the deadly light into the peace and safety of a new dark age. (139)

One of the key means which Lovecraft employed to express his cosmic vision was the Cthulhu mythos, which plays a central role in a dozen of his stories, crops up in others, and also features in his 'History and Chronology of the *Necronomicon*' and the poem 'Fungi from Yuggoth'. It is, however, extremely important to understand that it is in absolutely no sense a pseudo-religious mythology (indeed, in a story such as 'The Dunwich Horror' it can be read as a grotesque and blasphemous parody of certain aspects of Christian mythology), that Lovecraft was not always consistent in his use of the mythos, and that the term was invented not by Lovecraft himself but by August Derleth, one of the many Lovecraft aficionados who helped to develop the mythos both during and after Lovecraft's lifetime. As Joshi has argued, the mythos is best understood as a series of plot devices which help to facilitate the expression of Lovecraft's philosophy of mechanistic materialism on the cosmic scale. These devices, he argues, can usefully be organised into three general groups: 'A wide array of extraterrestrials (deemed "gods" by their human followers); an entire library of mythical books containing the "forbidden" truths about these "gods"; and a fictionalized New England landscape analogous to Hardy's Wessex or Faulkner's Yoknapatawpha County' (Joshi, 1996: xvii). Foremost amongst the extraterrestrial 'Old Ones' is Cthulhu, and amongst the books the *Necronomicon*.

In terms of the literary form in which Lovecraft chose to express his vision, it might at first sight seem strange to make a claim for realism, but like so many creators of the fantastic, such as Arthur Machen, M. R. James and Nigel Kneale, Lovecraft understood the dramatic importance of rooting the unknown and strange firmly in the soil of the known and familiar. As he himself explained:

> To make a fictional marvel wear the momentary aspect of exciting fact, we must give it the most elaborate possible approach – building up insidiously and gradually out of apparently realistic material, realistically handled. The time is past when adults can accept marvellous conditions for granted. Every energy must be bent toward the weaving of a frame of mind which shall make the story's single departure from nature seem credible – and in the weaving of this mood the utmost subtlety and verisimilitude are required. In every detail *except* the chosen marvel, the story should be accurately true to nature. (Quoted in Carter, 1975: 14)

Or as Lévy puts it, Lovecraft

> creates the strange, he excites fear, by *turning the world inside out*. For Lovecraft, writing is the making oneiric and wrong side of things appear, substituting the nocturnal for the diurnal, replacing the reassuring image of the Waking World by the alienating ones of the great depths. The world of the surface has in his work no other raison d'être than provisionally and imperfectly to cover up the abyss. (Lévy, 1988: 71, original emphasis)

This is what Houellebecq calls Lovecraft's 'oneiric precision' (Houellebecq, 2005: 74), citing one of the author's finest creations, the novella *At the Mountains of Madness*, as a key example. But it is actually in Lovecraft's numerous stories set in New England that his method of combining the realistic and the fantastic can be seen at its most effective.

As Lovecraft himself writes in 'The Picture in the House':

> The true epicure in the terrible, to whom a new thrill of unutterable ghastliness is the chief end and justification of existence, esteems most of all the ancient, lonely farmhouses of backwoods New England; for there the dark elements of strength, solitude, grotesqueness, and ignorance combine to form the perfection of the hideous. (Lovecraft, 1999: 34)

Like Thomas Hardy's Wessex, Lovecraft's New England is an imaginary landscape conjured from real places, with towns such as Arkham standing in a similar relation to Salem as Casterbridge to Dorchester. It is a landscape whose terrible Puritan witch-hunting heritage plays much the same role here as medieval myths in the original Gothic novels. As Lovecraft put it:

> Only in New England do I feel that odd undercurrent of sinister and unholy life in the brooding fields and woods, and the little huddled farmhouses. Elsewhere I find *antiquity*, but never *concealed terror*. Terror is the legacy of a long Puritan heritage with its unnatural philosophy – the heritage of Salem, Endicott, and the Mathers – and only these visible symbols closely connected with this system possess the terror element to a complete degree. (Quoted in Lévy, 1988: 127, original emphasis)

Or as Lévy himself avers:

> These imaginary places form, in the real topography of New England, a zone of shadow, a zone of mystery, a *dream-zone*, which spreads little by little to the rest of the countryside, contaminating the diurnal space of the maps and charts and giving it suddenly a different aspect. The familiarity of places is blurred, leaving the weird to take its place. (Lévy 1988: 37)

Arkham and its surroundings are 'the fault through which the bizarre, the horrific, the disquieting, the morbid, and the unclean spread' (Lévy, 1988: 37) and 'the landscapes, the cities, the dwellings of New England lose their pleasant, picturesque, diurnal aspect, to become lunatic sites, nocturnal images, degraded images in a demented dream' (41). In the Lovecraftian topography, then, this corner of New England is, to neighbouring America, and to misquote the title of a Lovecraft story, the horror on the doorstep.

As already noted, Lovecraft's influence on modern culture has been, and continues to be, immense, even though in his own lifetime his work was barely known outside the readership of the pulp magazine *Weird Tales*. Fritz Leiber described him as 'the Copernicus of the horror story. He shifted the focus of supernatural dread from man and his little world and his gods, to the stars and the black and unplumbed gulfs of intergalactic space' (quoted in Smith, 2006: 3). Lovecraft's imagination, and especially his ability to conjure bizarre landscapes and weird atmospheres, was prodigious, and it is this which, above all, constitutes his enduring legacy to horror fiction. In this respect, Houellebecq talks of 'this extraordinary ability to create a universe, this visionary power' (Houellebecq, 2005: 25) and argues that his oeuvre can be compared to a 'gigantic dream machine, of astounding breadth and efficacy' (42). Stephen King has said that Lovecraft's stories 'make us feel the size of the universe we hang suspended in, and suggest shadowy forces that could destroy us all if they so much as grunted in their sleep' (King, 1993: 80); and Colin Wilson's remark that the effect of the story 'The Shadow Out of Time' is 'to produce an authentic impression of awe and mystery, resting on the evocation of vistas of time and space' (Wilson, 1976: 116) applies equally well to Lovecraft as a whole. In his masterly essay *Supernatural Horror in Literature*, Lovecraft himself wrote: 'The one test of the really weird is simply this – whether or not there be excited in the reader a profound sense of dread, and of contact with unknown spheres and powers; a subtle attitude of awed listening, as if for the beating of black wings or the scratching of outside shapes and entities on the known universe's utmost rim' (Lovecraft, 1973: 16). At their best, Lovecraft's own works excite this sense to an almost unbearable degree, but the most powerful testimony to the extraordinary depth and breadth of his singular vision is the manner in which it has continued to inspire so many others in every field of modern culture.

Nonetheless, we can now perhaps begin to understand why it has often proved difficult to adapt Lovecraft's stories directly for the cinema: short on 'characters' (especially female ones) and 'action' as conventionally understood, no sex (except occasionally – and only implied – in the back-story, and then between degraded humans and unspeakable monstrosities), heavy on description, sometimes only a few pages in length, underpinned by a complex and not always coherent mythos, and informed by a philosophy of the bleakest pessimism, their cinematic potential is not immediately obvious. Even ardent Lovecraft aficionados agree that his work is not easy to adapt. For example, John Carpenter: 'Once you start reading it, you realise it's in his language. He describes things that are indescribable, the indescribable horror. Some of his best stories are just impossible to visualise' (quoted in Mitchell, 2001: 7). Or Stuart Gordon, who observes that his work is full of 'implications imagined instead of tangible and action-oriented' (quoted in Migliore and Strysik, 2000: 65). Similarly Brian Yuzna notes: 'Lovecraft has this convoluted way of weaving stories that is so vague, because he never writes so-and-so went there and did this. It just doesn't work that way. It is very much in spinning the mood' (quoted in Migliore and Strysik, 2000, 96). Similarly, apropos the extraordinary architectural descriptions which are such a feature of 'The Shadow Out of Time' and *At the Mountains of Madness*, Houellebecq argues that: 'Reading these descriptions is at first stimulating, but then discourages any attempt at visual adaptation (pictorial or cinematographic). Images graze the consciousness but none appear sufficiently sublime, sufficiently fantastic; none come close to the pinnacle of dreams' (Houellebecq, 2005: 63–4).

This does not mean, however, that no films have succeeded in transferring Lovecraft's vision, or at least aspects of it, to the screen. Lovecraft himself judged films based on literary works solely according to their fidelity to their source, concluding that: 'Generally speaking, the cinema always cheapens and degrades any literary material it gets hold of – especially anything in the least subtle or unusual' (quoted in Joshi, 1996: 581). Dismissive as he was of his own work, and detesting as he did most aspects of popular culture, one suspects that he would have thoroughly disliked all of the films based on or inspired by his work. However, in the following pages, fidelity to the letter of their literary sources will not be the criterion used to analyse the films under discussion, but, rather, fidelity to the particular spirit of Lovecraft, and the extent to which these films radiate a distinctly Lovecraftian aura.

In terms of conjuring up a Lovecraftian milieu, *The Haunted Palace* is particularly successful. Though sold by AIP as part of Corman's Poe cycle, the film is quite closely based on 'The Case of Charles Dexter Ward' and tells the story of a New England warlock who returns to life in the body of a descendant in order to carry on evoking dark forces. Daniel Haller's sets strikingly conjure a hermetic, self-enclosed universe, particularly in Ann Ward's oneiric wanderings through the palace, and the scenes in Arkham's streets and graveyard which recall Lovecraft's evocation of the town in 'The Unnamable', with its 'crumbling slate slabs, the patriarchal trees, and the centuried gambrel roofs of the witch-haunted old town' (Lovectaft, 2005: 83). Conversely, in 'Dagon', a real Spanish fishing village is used as an effectively convincing location for the bizarre story of a community (Innsmouth in the original) which has abandoned Christianity for faith in a god of the deep, becoming ever more piscine in the process. Equally, Lucio Fulci in *City of the Living Dead* makes atmospheric use of Savannah, Georgia, to evoke another of Lovecraft's fictional New England towns, Dunwich. Although the film includes Christian tropes quite alien to Lovecraft – a priest commits suicide in the run-up to All Saints Day, which threatens to open the gates of Hell – it nonetheless contains enough elements, such as the setting, the *Book of Enoch* (which is mentioned in *Supernatural Horror in Literature*) and the idea of a portal to another dimension, to endow it with the aura of Lovecraft. Meanwhile in *In the Mouth of Madness* (John Carpenter: 1995) which, though not based on any Lovecraft story, is highly Lovecraftian, the eruption of the fantastic into the real is played out in the little town of Hobb's End.[2] This is imagined into existence by the horror writer Sutter Cane as the site for opening the gates to the Old Ones and thus destroying the world; neat but largely deserted, the place is inexplicably eerie, made all the more so by the black Byzantine church which dominates it. The film's title obviously references *At the Mountains of Madness*, with which John Carpenter's *The Thing* shares the same Antarctic setting and, more importantly, the same meticulous attention to creating a convincingly realistic setting for its later scenes of shape-shifting horror. It has to be admitted, however, that although quite a number of Lovecraft films are set in Arkham and feature its Miskatonic University, a really Lovecraftian New England milieu still awaits its screen debut.

The *Necromicon* and other *grimoires*, both real and imagined, feature in many of the films mentioned at the start of this chapter. Like the story on which it is based, *The Dunwich Horror* quotes from it at some length, and it plays a particularly significant role in *The Unnamable Returns*, the (original) wraparound story of the portmanteau film *Necronomicon*, and the *Evil Dead* trilogy, although in the first film of the trilogy it is referred to as *The Book of the Dead*. In the *Evil Dead* films, and in *Dreams in the Witch House*, the book is rendered especially sinister by being bound in human skin. It also forms the basis for *Cast a Deadly Spell*, set in a 1948 Los Angeles where magic has become part of daily life, and in which private eye H. P. Lovecraft is engaged to recover a stolen copy. Part latter-day *film noir*, part horror movie, the film, if not entirely successful throughout, shows just how flexible is the Cthulhu mythos as a signifying device.

The main role of the *Necronomicon* in the stories and films alike is to summon forth Cthulhu and the other 'Old Ones'. As in all horror, the creation of monsters carries with it the danger that they will not be horrifying enough (a danger that Lovecraft frequently circumvented by falling back on words such as 'indescribable') and the films vary in how effectively they translate his pantheon of vast, slimy, tentacular beings to the screen. The most effective visualisations are generally the briefest – such as the tantalising glimpses which we are vouchsafed in *In the Mouth of Madness*, and the sudden eruption of the eponymous monster from a well in *Dagon*. *The Dunwich Horror* opts for a Lovecraftian solution by barely showing the monster at all, giving us instead shots from its point of view and showing the effects of its passage on the natural environment; the latter communicates the monster's power remarkably effectively, but the POV shots are rather dated by their 'psychedelic' quality and certainly lack the absolutely maniacal power of those in the first two *Evil Dead* films, which absolutely radiate a Lovecraftian sense of utterly malign and destructive power. The most striking monster in these films, however, is not an 'Old One' but the grotesquely deformed Alyda Winthrop in the otherwise routine *The Unnamable* – winged, horned, fanged and hooved, she is, thanks to remarkable costume design, make-up and acting, a creature quite unlike anything imagined by Lovecraft, terrifying and repulsive, yet also pitiable and indeed fascinating.

Returning now to Lovecraft's mechanistic view of human life, it might at first sight seem surprising to cite the *Re-Animator* films as reflecting that view, as their mixture of sex, gore and humour has not endeared them to all Lovecraft aficionados. However, it is worth pointing out that the six-part story on which they are based was written for a humorous magazine, *Home Brew*, and, as its original title, *Grewsome Tales*, suggests, was actually a parody, albeit a dark-hued one, of supernatural fiction of the more lurid kind. Its body horrors were, in fact, notably more explicit than those of most of Lovecraft's other work, and Herbert West's rhetorical question in *Bride of Re-Animator* – 'What are people, over and above a collection of living body parts?' – faithfully reflects the blackly anarchic spirit of the original, as well as Lovecraft's own mechanistic view of life. Certainly the treatment of and attitude towards the human body in these two films is nothing if not profoundly and radically materialist. Indeed, it is a quite literal illustration of Houellebecq's observation that: 'Implacably, HPL destroys his characters, evoking only the dismemberment of marionettes' (Houellebecq, 2005: 32). Equally unremitting in this respect is the unflinching portrayal of the hideously tortured body of madman-in-the cellar Giorgio in *Castle Freak* and the skinning alive of the last remaining human inhabitant of the Spanish port in *Dagon*.

Lovecraft's crushingly pessimistic wider worldview is clearly more difficult to convey in a commercial medium, even in the horror genre. That said, *Dreams in the Witch House* resolutely eschews a 'happy end', finishing on the bleakest of notes. But it is actually in Lovecraft-inspired films, as opposed to adaptations of his stories, that we occasionally glimpse that all-important sense of 'cosmicism': in *Alien* (co-written by Dan O'Bannon, who directed the best 'straight' Lovecraft adaptation, *The Resurrected*, and featuring a monster designed by Lovecraft illustrator H. R. Giger) with its extremely powerful sense of mankind adrift in the cosmos and at the mercy of forces utterly indifferent to its fate; in the vast cosmic canvas which is glimpsed as Ash is sucked through the astral gate at the climax of *Evil Dead II*; and finally at the end of Lucio Fulci's *The Beyond* when, after witnessing the most unspeakable horrors, the leading characters suddenly find that they have passed through one of the seven gates of Hell (as described in the *Book of Eibon* – an invention of Lovecraft aficionado Clark Ashton Smith) and are marooned in the Sea of Darkness – an immense, grey, skeleton-strewn Lovecraftian emptiness, like a scene from the last days of the planet.

Imperfect geometry: identity and culture in Clive Barker's 'The Forbidden' and Bernard Rose's *Candyman*

Brigid Cherry

> Like a flawless tragedy, the elegance of which structure is lost upon those suffering in it, the perfect geometry of the Spector Street Estate was only visible from the air.
>
> 'The Forbidden', *Clive Barker's Books of Blood*, V, 1.

> The pain, I can assure you, will be exquisite. As for our deaths, there is nothing to fear. Our names will be written on a thousand walls. Our crimes told and retold by our faithful believers. We shall die together in front of their very eyes and give them something to be haunted by. Come with me and be immortal.
>
> The Candyman to Helen Lyle, *Candyman*, DVD chapter 17.

> I have always enjoyed the imagination of Clive Barker because he takes a very obvious joy in the supernatural, the macabre and the downright weird. His plots have always twisted and turned forcing the reader/viewer to follow him further and further into the myths he creates. I have never seen anyone else create quite such a variety of monsters. Some are ugly, some are beautiful, they are happy, confused and sad just like human beings. On the whole they all have one thing in common, they all enjoy being monstrous, one way or another, and it is very much up to the viewer whether to like them or not. I like them all and I enjoy watching Clive Barker films for the dubious pleasure of their company.
>
> 35-year-old artist and horror fan

Each of these epigraphs suggests that no matter how terrible or horrific a thing might be, if viewed from the correct angle its beauty will emerge. The first two – the opening of the short story

'The Forbidden' in volume five of *Clive Barker's Books of Blood* (1985) followed by a line of dialogue from the film *Candyman* (Bernard Rose: 1992), an adaptation of this story – provide a telling parallel to the spectatorial pleasures expressed in the third – a quote from a female horror fan with a particular love for Barker's work. In terms of its aesthetics (and this is true of both written word and image), the horror genre is frequently both repellant *and* enthralling. Furthermore, the horror text itself, often assumed to be masculine by dint of its generic classification alone, and requiring stereotypical male traits such as a strong stomach and bravado to view, can contain aspects (as reflected in the response of the female viewer) which are clearly feminine. The 'dubious pleasures' promised in Barker's fiction have strong appeals for the feminine spectator, and female viewers respond accordingly – with both terror and delight.

This linkage between text and responses to text highlights a particular appeal of horror, namely that horror texts do not always – or only – horrify. They also excite, amuse, fascinate and arouse. The horror genre offers pleasures alongside its pains in the complex interplay of aesthetics and modes of emotional affect at work in these texts. In this respect, certain films (or types of films) offer specific sets of pleasures (both visual and narrative) picked up on by different audience segments; importantly these pleasures may be at odds with the genre's dominant modes, and modes of affect.[1] Clearly, the audience for the genre is not homogenous, and the various audience segments privilege different patterns of emotional affects, as well as textual and aesthetic features in the various horror subgenres or styles. In particular, studies of the female audience[2] suggest that there are significant differences between female horror film viewers and the primary male audience in terms of their responses to the text, the affects they seek out and the specific films they prefer. The findings of such research into the preferences and responses of the female horror film audience[3] suggest a feminine aesthetic of horror that includes: appealing images alongside (or even as) horrific ones; alluring, sympathetic and even sexually-attractive monsters; representations of strong or sexually-dominant women (whether they be villains, monsters or heroines); believable plots, characters and settings; and, most importantly, a range of emotional affects other than shock and disgust. On the whole, female viewers do not reject masculine forms of the genre, but where gore and splatter effects are present, these viewers prefer them as subservient to story, characterisation and *range* of affect. In order to explore these links further, this chapter undertakes an analysis of 'The Forbidden' and *Candyman*, highlighting the feminine aesthetic of horror and how this is played out with respect to transformations of identity within horror film and fiction. It is proposed that this form of comparative analysis – that is, of the main elements of horror in a British short story and its 'Americanised' Hollywood film version – can underscore the gendered dimensions of, and reactions to, horror narratives.

During the aforementioned study of female horror fans, the participants were invited to name up to ten of their favourite horror films. The most popular (that is, the most frequently named) were ranked according to the number of times they were listed.[4] This list illustrates that these horror fans enjoy an extremely diverse group of texts drawn from a very broad range of horror sub-genres and cycles. As such, this list provides an appropriate guide to the aesthetics of horror and the narrative conventions which the female viewers prefer. These films, then, provide a set of valuable case studies which can contribute to a definition of feminine forms of horror cinema and illustrate the aspects of horror that are most appealing to the female audience. The prevalence of films associated with Clive Barker on the list cannot be ignored.

As a prolific horror *auteur*, working in theatre, literature, film, art and comic books, Barker is an important figure in the recent history of horror and his work holds strong appeals for female fans. He is mentioned frequently by female fans both during discussion of their overall attraction to horror and also in reference to the specific films that they enjoy, many naming Barker's films as particular favourites.[5] *Hellraiser*, adapted and directed by Barker from his novella *The Hellbound Heart*, is the most frequently mentioned film, named by 33 participants.[6] *Nightbreed* (again adapted and directed by Barker from his novel *Cabal*) is named by 13 participants and appears in 13th place on the list. In addition, two *Hellraiser* sequels – *Hellbound* and *Hellraiser 3* (both written by Barker's friend and collaborator Pete Atkins and directed by Tony Randel and Anthony Hickox respectively) and *Candyman* (adapted and directed by Bernard Rose) are also on the list at 14th, 25th and 32nd place, with 13, 12 and 6 mentions respectively.[7]

In addition, horror literature is as important for this fan community as horror cinema. The majority of the fans (86 per cent) read horror literature, often as their main reading material. Horror is the most popular genre read, with fantasy and science fiction also read by over half the fans; Stephen King and Clive Barker are particularly popular, but vampire fiction, psychological thrillers or melodramas, and historical or Gothic fiction are also a key part of the taste profiles. A substantial number of the favourite films are based on literary works of horror; in addition to the five associated with Barker, the list also contains 16 literary adaptations.[8] Whilst there is little to indicate that the fans like these films because they also like the books (or even that the books came first for them – in fact, several fans state that they discovered the *Books of Blood after* having enjoyed *Candyman*), it does suggest a strong literary bias to their tastes and a clear link between film and fiction within their overall patterns of consumption. This suggests that an analysis of these works might valuably contribute to a definition of the feminine aesthetic of horror.[9]

In many respects, *Candyman* is a key text. Fans mention the strong female lead, the erotic appeal of the monster, their delight in the horrific imagery and themes, and a narrative that makes the viewer think. Since these are not necessarily universal responses, in a number of respects short story and film are both polysemic texts offering a range of potential understandings and pleasures for various groups of readers and viewers.

Since the types of film liked by the fans *are* so wide and varied, approaches to genre theory and even established accounts of horror sub-genres in terms of broad (and thus reductive) psychological processes would seem counterproductive in this context. There are, however, strong links between the visual aesthetics of horror and the preferred underlying textual features of the favourite films which have a gendered dimension.[10] Horror, and the Gothic tradition in particular, has a long history of female consumption.[11] Barker's work contains features which can potentially be read as feminine and queer, positioning them within the traditions of the Gothic, the melodrama and the fantastic (primarily in the shape of the fairy tale).[12]

Candyman has already been subjected to multiple readings. In particular the theme of race horror in the film has been productively explored.[13] Gender and sexuality have not been so thoroughly examined, though Andrea Kuhn provides valuable insight into female subjectivities in the film (Kuhn, 2001). Clearly, the short story and film both offer multiple and oppositional readings to the audience and this can be observed in the responses of the female horror fans. Rather than approaching an analysis of the film in terms of the relation between the semiotic and the symbolic as Kuhn does, however, this account is directed by fan responses to the film with a particular focus on gendered audience positions.[14]

The female horror film spectator is often assumed to be a cringing victim of the genre. This, however, has not been borne out by the research. Though the overall tastes of the female viewers suggest clear preferences for vampire films, supernatural films and psychological horror, as well as an overall dislike of slasher films and gore, body horror or splatter cinema (and the favourites list generally reflects this), these fans can overlook these broad generic tastes in cases where the films contain other elements they privilege. *Candyman* (which, significantly, shares key features with other films on the list) incorporates elements of the romance narrative. It draws on the modes of emotional affect familiar to this generic form, as well as the more established horror affects. The horror is largely built on atmosphere and suggestion; the narrative is centered around aspects of domesticity and male–female relationships, drawing on the conventions of the Gothic, the melodrama, and, in the case of *Candyman*, the fairy tale. It also contains a representation of aberrant femininity and sexuality, not least in the erotic appeal of the monster (who is an integral part of the romance). These elements are more important to the female viewers than any absolute generic classification or the level of gore or violence. Nevertheless (and a small number of female fans dislike the film because of this), *Candyman* can be described as a splatter film in that it contains a number of instances of violence and gore.

The latter is not particularly evident in 'The Forbidden'. Barker's early work (including his first novel, *The Damnation Game* (1985)) has the reputation of being explicit and graphic. In both 'The Forbidden' and *Candyman*, however, the main signifiers of horror are urban deprivation. The main themes of the short story – poverty, slums, class difference and folk culture – are easily mapped onto the film adaptation, replacing class with race as the main locus of the horror. The atmosphere of British social realism in 'The Forbidden', however, is transposed in the film into a much deeper concern with (urban) folkloric and historical versions of the Candyman figure – and these tap into aspects of the slasher and body horror sub-genres. There is a higher level of violence in the film, with Helen brutally assaulted by the Cabrini Green gang members, and Bernadette, the psychiatrist, and Anne-Marie's dog all being bloodily slain (in the short story, only Anne-Marie's child dies – he is saved in the film). Taken together with the signifiers of abjection in the form of the Candyman's hook hand and nest of bees, *Candyman* shares conventions in common with the dominant (masculine) forms of the genre.

This tension between splatter and subtle atmosphere illustrates an important opposition within Barker's work. Several of Barker's short stories have become an accepted part of the splatterpunk sub-genre of horror literature,[15] and his films, recognised for their gore content, frequently interest predominantly male readers/viewers. Writing on the splatterpunk genre, Louis J. Kern describes its 'exploitative use of spectacle' (Kern, 1996: 56). In discussing Barker's 'Midnight Meat Train' (in volume 1 of the *Books of Blood*), Kern asserts that:

> The technique of descriptive gore reinforces the reader's humanity by linking him viscerally to the victim as it underscores the fragility of morality. At the same time that such violence offends and repulses what we most treasure as human in ourselves – our rational minds, our compassion – it attracts us as a reflection of the repressed, the darkly instinctive level of human experience. (Kern, 1996: 49)

But this human experience appears, at least here, to be gendered male. The 'exploitative use of spectacle' (Kern, 1996: 56) and 'macho, in-your-face' stance (55) assumes a young male readership. This, however, belies the broad scope of his appeals and the differences of gender and sexuality Barker explores. These factors arouse interest amongst a range of audiences, including queer as well as female viewers. The female audience who might popularly be expected to reject such explicit horrors[16] embrace Barker's work for wholly different reasons (many of the female fans dislike gore and splatter for being unsubtle, boring or unimaginative, rather than explicit or offensive).

Rather than belonging definitively to the splatterpunk genre, the stories in the *Books of Blood* are all deliberately very different in tone, style and format, and many of the individual stories are subtle (or at least not particularly graphic). Certainly, 'The Forbidden' is at the other end of the scale from 'Midnight Meat Train' and thus does not invite the label 'splat lit' to the same extent. Reliant more on the concept of taboos and the allure of breaking them (as opposed to any explicitly violent or gory imagery), Barker's biographer Douglas E. Winter believes 'The Forbidden' to be 'one of the more self-conscious, and perhaps the most self-reflexive, of Barker's early stories' (Winter, 2001: 363). Nonetheless, the story contains several moments of horror which, whilst not explicit, allow the imagination to concoct gruesome images, and invite strong reactions. The moments of body horror in the text include second-hand references to a bloody murder in which the victim's eyes were put out and the castration of a mentally-handicapped boy. In addition, and central to the story, is the killing of Anne-Marie's baby. Each of these is described in a rather perfunctory fashion, the first two relayed in conversation by unreliable witnesses and probably deriving from versions of urban myths. The details necessary to convey the horror of the event are given, but these are not excessive and cannot be described as explicit. Even in the third instance, where Helen sees the body of the child herself, the description remains vague; 'his body showed everywhere signs of the fiend's attentions' (Barker, 1985: 32), but the exact nature of the wounds must be assumed. Some of the female fans prefer horror literature to explicit films, since this allows them to more easily self-censor what they experience.

In the place of overt body horror, 'The Forbidden' principally explores the real-life horrors of poverty and urban blight on a run-down estate. It is only in the descriptions of, firstly, location and, secondly, seduction by the monster, that the horror becomes overt. This satisfies the female fans in terms of imaginative horror combined with strong, believable storylines. Barker also evokes a horror aesthetic in the sights, sounds, smell and feel of the place:

> The maisonette wasn't that large, but the windows had been boarded up throughout, and as she moved further from the front

> door the dubious light petered out altogether. The smell of urine, which had been strong at the door, intensified too, until by the time she reached the back of the living room and stepped along a short corridor into another room beyond, it was cloying as incense. This room, being furthest from the front door, was also the darkest, and she had to wait a few moments in the cluttered gloom to allow her eyes to become useful. This, she guessed, had been the bedroom. (Barker, 1985: 5–6)

There are though no indicators of specific locale; the city in 'The Forbidden' is unnamed. The above passage could well describe any economically deprived urban area – a rundown estate of blocks of flats, many vacant and boarded up, marred by graffiti and grime. Though the fans commonly assume it is either Liverpool (Barker's home town) or London (characteristically British), this is a recognisably horrific environment even if the reader has not experienced it first hand. In this sense, the text allows the reader to picture a city with which they are most familiar and find believable. For example, one fan suggested it 'took place in a rather frightening area of London', thus imbuing the story with her own experience and memories. This brings to mind social tensions within British social structures and can as easily work for readers of other nationalities. Certainly, there is a continuum here with the film, offset as the horror is onto race.

In terms of this horror, it is with the higher level of gore and violence that *Candyman* first diverges from 'The Forbidden'. The first two instances of horror in the story continue to be relayed as hearsay and urban myth in the film, though newspaper evidence is available on the murder in one of the flats (the sex of the victim has been changed in the film), and a typical babysitter urban legend is added at the start of the film to introduce the mirror motif.[17] Furthermore, Anne-Marie's dog's decapitation substitutes for the murder of her son, as discussed below. The horror comes, rather, from embellishments of Helen's role in the narrative, which in turn adds to the romance theme (Helen's seduction by the Candyman and the revelation that she is his lover in the past and present of his legendary existence). The horror in *Candyman* is thus located within a series of atmospheric 'numbers' (the term Cynthia Freeland employs to describe scenes of horror (Freeland, 2000)) which reinforce viewer identification with Helen. These splatter numbers include: Helen's exploration of the public toilets and the beating she receives from the false Candyman; the aftermath of the baby's kidnapping and the killing of Anne-Marie's dog when Helen, drenched in blood after seeing the Candyman for the first time, comes to in Cabrini Green; the appearance of the Candyman in Helen's apartment and the subsequent sight of Bernadette's bloodied body; the slaughter of Dr Burke when Helen calls for the Candyman in the psychiatric hospital; and Helen's revenge at the very end of the film when Trevor calls for her after her funeral. There is clearly a feminine subjectivity at work here. Significantly, the only murders actually shown on screen are the psychiatrist's, which Helen observes after she has consciously called up the Candyman to free her – prior to this she was mesmerised and unaware of the murders – and Trevor's, when she has become the monster herself. Furthermore, the horror in these scenes is suggestive and there are few moments of excess in terms of gore; although quantities of blood and the result of injuries are shown, these are depicted in relatively brief shots. More importantly, these atmospheric numbers are interspersed with almost erotic sequences which add to the pleasures one can gain from the film. These sequences concern the Candyman's seduction of Helen: the flashes she has of his painting when mesmerised, his appearance in the car park, his words as she is driven away in the police car, his floating above her in the hospital, his taking of the promised kiss in his Gothic lair. Although the gore adds to the overall impact of the film, it is the atmosphere which lends the film a feminine aesthetic.

On yet another level, both story and film also locate elements of horror in the gender power imbalance one experiences in a relationship with a serial philanderer (Trevor's frequent affairs are spelt out in the story, implied in the film) and within academia. The gender theme is continued in the emphasis on emotion within the text. Helen is driven not just by her desire to complete her thesis (on graffiti in the story; on urban legends in the film), nor simply by curiosity – though this plays a part in the character motivation. Rather, it is Trevor's (and Purcell's) attitude towards her and her desire to belittle him (and male-dominated academia generally). As the story puts it, 'when her courage faltered she thought of Trevor, and how badly she wanted to silence his condescension' (Barker, 1985: 5). The story, unlike the film, stops just short of Helen's fatal attraction to the Candyman, which leads to outright revenge. Helen observes Trevor from within the bonfire as he searches for her:

> Poor dupe, she thought, following his antics. She willed him to look past the flames in the hope that he might see her burning. Not so that he could save her from death – she was long past hope of that – but because she pitied him in his bewilderment and wanted to give him, though he would not have thanked her for it, something to be haunted by. (Barker, 1985: 37)

Isabel Pinedo believes that there is 'some pleasure and sense of power to be gained, at least by female and black audience members, from seeing the power in these violent figures' (Pinedo, 1997: 131), namely in the form of abused women who kill and aggressive black men. For Pinedo, *Candyman* 'lends itself well to this subversive reading strategy' (Pinedo, 1997: 131). This is borne out by the responses of the female horror film fans. For these viewers, a major dimension of the film is the substantially increased revenge element which sees Helen become the new form of the Candyman and actually destroy Trevor. One 28-year-old secretary, for example, likes the film for the fact that Helen 'becomes a mythic figure of vengeance'. In this way, the morbid fascination exhibited by the female fans is satisfied: Helen crosses the boundary not only of class (or race in the film), but of life and death. She becomes an abject figure, but one of feminine power – although her hair, a signifier of femininity, is lost, she appears exquisitely beautiful in death.

Whilst both texts are thus concerned with boundary crossings and the resulting transformations of the body, some of the major differences between the texts are ones surrounding nationality and culture. Most obviously, as hinted at above, the film version depicts racial difference as a site of horror, substituting for the class differences in the story. There are, however, other key indicators of nationality and culture inherent in the short story which bring a sense of intimacy to readers familiar with Britain's history and recent past. On a number of subtextual levels 'The Forbidden' taps into both folk and high culture. As regards the former, the events in the story take place in the week leading up to Bonfire or Guy Fawkes Night. Traditionally celebrated to commemorate the foiling of a Catholic plot to blow up parliament, effigies of the conspirator Guy Fawkes are burnt on a bonfire. Typically, the effigy would be made from old clothes, often pyjamas, stuffed with old newspapers and surmounted by a cloth face or mask.[18] Though his status and origins are left somewhat open, the Candyman in the short story resembles such a being, a rag-bag figure, garish and exaggerated:

> He was bright to the point of gaudiness: his flesh a waxy yellow, his thin lips pale blue, his wild eyes glittering as if their irises were set with rubies. His jacket was a patchwork, his trousers the same. He looked, she thought, almost ridiculous, with his blood-stained motley, and the hint of rouge on his jaundiced cheeks. (Barker, 1985: 32)[19]

As the personification of a 'guy', the Candyman becomes the figure in a terror tale used as a warning against challenging the dominant hegemony (the anti-Catholic flavour of the event originally had effigies of the Pope being burnt). For Helen, this defiance of the dominant culture takes the form of her straying outside of her social class, and in the film it is represented through miscegenation. There is, notably, a hint of subversive respect for Guy Fawkes's audacity. The children's rhyme exhorts celebrators to 'Remember, remember the fifth of November, gunpowder, treason and plot. I see no reason why gunpowder treason should ever be forgot' – this song keeps alive the belief in, and grudging admiration for, the 'monster'. When she finally encounters the Candyman, Helen (who has failed to remember or believe) realises 'there was a *monster* here, beneath this fetching display' (Barker, 1985: 32). The appeal of the monster, and Helen's realisation that 'this *was* a seduction' (Barker, 1985: 33), are facets of the romance genre and add a sexual dimension to the text. This carnal tone is substantially developed in the film.

In Bernard Rose's script[20] the Candyman is described as 'a tall, dark silhouette', and when he speaks, 'his voice is rich and sonorous'. His appearance in the film is also far more appealing than in the story:

> He speaks, murmuring so softly that seduction might be in the air.
> MAN: No need to leave yet.
> HELEN: (wary) I'm late ...
> He moves towards her and light falls on his face. Helen freezes. The fine cheekbones, the sparkling eyes. She has seen this face before.

> MAN: You were not content with the stories, so I was obliged to come . . .
> He is finely dressed, his dark suit an antique cut. His right hand hidden in his coat pocket.
> He pulls his hand out of his pocket. The hand has been crudely sawn off. A butcher's hook rammed into the bloody stump.
> CANDYMAN: Be my victim . . .

The Candyman is still dangerous, monstrous and attractive, but his fascination now has a far more exotic allure. As Rose describes him, he has a sense of the aristocratic about him, especially evidenced by the antique cut of his fine suit, the fine cheekbones and sparkling eyes. He is the tall, dark, handsome foreigner of feminine horror, but here the mysterious European aristocrat of *Dracula* (and the Gothic in general) is transformed into the tragic figure of the oppressed African-American male and, thus, taps into a different history – that of the West's involvement in slavery and racism.

For a white women such as Helen, the African-American male is a both a dangerous menacing figure (personified in the gang leader who assaults her) and a potent – and undeniably beautiful – sexual lure (the talented son of a slave who becomes an object of desire for the white woman he paints).[21] Since the 'guy' figure of 'The Forbidden' is almost entirely and intractably Other, he seems almost unemotional – sterile even, whilst the relationship between Helen and the Candyman in the film version (especially Helen being the reincarnation of the artist's lover as hinted at in the painting in the Candyman's lair) is the emotional heart of the film. *Candyman* is, at least in part, a romance and a romantic melodrama lies at the heart of the narrative: lovers, torn apart, strive to be reunited. As the Candyman says, 'It was always you, Helen.' This invention for the film brings yet another strong feminine aesthetic into the basic plot, exacerbated by the taboo of miscegenation in the historical version of the legend; it is a forbidden and thus dangerous romance.

The appeal for some female viewers is the simultaneously attractive and abject figure of the monster and the strong identification with the heroine. Certainly, the Candyman is a striking visual and aural presence in the film, and he is linked to Helen throughout. As Purcell retells the historical version of the legend over dinner, he pauses as he is about to describe the 'terrible revenge'. At this point Phillip Glass's romance-themed score is reprised in conjunction with the sounds of the lynching. The shot/reverse shot sequence of Purcell speaking and Helen listening is replaced at this point by a slow zoom in on Helen as she seems overcome and mesmerised by the story. This sequence concludes with a sound bridge as dialogue, music and sound effects are played over the subsequent scene of Helen back at Cabrini Green taking photographs of the Candyman painting in the ruined apartment. Later, in the car park sequence when the Candyman first appears to Helen, a similar sequence of shots is accompanied by the Candyman's 'rich and sonorous' voice and Helen's fluttering eyelids, both of which suggest sexual arousal. This becomes a repeated motif, providing the fans with a series of shiver moments (one fan echoed Helen's response by stating that these sequences 'made me feel quite overwhelmed').

These sequences further emphasise the romance subplot. Whilst the female fans do not indicate any strong liking for the romance genre itself, this aspect nevertheless appeals to female viewers and is a further factor in the film's popularity. A 38-year-old teacher enjoys the film 'for the anti-heroine and demon, [they] blur good and evil and the characters are ambiguous'. As a tragic figure, the Candyman elicits sympathy. One fan explains this by suggesting that 'tragic hero figures' such as Heathcliff or Lord Byron are similar to the 'magnetic vampire characters' of the horror genre. Many of the female fans find monsters attractive. A 28-year-old florist puts this down to 'the power that these creatures wield to change your life forever'. There are parallels here to the brooding hero of romance and Gothic fiction.

Further aspects of melodrama and romance emerge through the linking of sweets to the Candyman via both the offerings in his shrine and the bees nesting in his body cavity (in the film he feeds the baby with their honey). In the short story, though, these are not simply straightforward signifiers of romance: they provide a link (albeit a somewhat tenuous one) to high culture, and these in turn draw on morbid sexual curiosity and the attraction of death and forms of monstrosity (all aspects which are evident amongst the female fans). In 'The Forbidden', Barker draws attention to Shakespeare as a source text through Helen's musings:

> '*Sweets to the sweet*' it read. She was familiar with the quote, but

> not with its source. Was it a profession of love? If so, it was an odd location for such an avowal. Despite the mattress in the corner, and the relative privacy of this room, she could not imagine the intended reader of such words ever stepping in here to receive her bouquet. No adolescent lovers, however heated, would lay down here to play at mothers and fathers; not under the gaze of the terror on the wall. (www.clivebarker.info\candyman.html, paras 1–18)

Significantly, since the phrase is taken from the lines Gertrude speaks as she throws flowers onto Ophelia's coffin in *Hamlet* (Act V, Scene 1), Helen refers to flowers, not candies, as the sweets of the quote. The Shakespearean connection is never made entirely clear, though Helen questions its origins on two further occasions (it is never once considered in the film). We might, of course, expect Barker – as a playwright – to be deliberately signposting this phrase for knowing readers. In fact, Barker draws parallels between Shakespeare and horror, and, in conversation with fellow horror writer Dennis Etchison,[22] alludes to a Shakespearean dimension in his work. Barker claims that fear and anxiety are constants of the horror genre and had 'great literary value in the past' (Barker, quoted in Jones, 1991: 61). He goes on to say that 'nobody calls *Hamlet* a horror story, yet it's got ghosts and murders and poisonings … ' and that 'the future will either condemn me or discover that I did have a little bit of *Hamlet* buried in there' (Jones, 1991: 65). In 'The Forbidden', 'sweets to the sweet' can be taken as referring to suicide. The room, in this sense, is a tomb, not a bedroom. Indeed, later in the story it is here that Helen finds the body of Kerry, Anne-Marie's child, along with a handful of chocolates and caramels and a dozen razor blades (the latter signifiers of suicide).

The textual landscape is thus one of doomed romance and death. In this way, the locale of the story (and of the film, though through a slightly different route) stands in for the Gothic space:

> The territory of the estate behind her was indisputably foreign, sealed off in its own misery, but the rooms in front of her were more intimidating still: a dark maze which her eyes could barely penetrate. (Barker, 1985: 5)

Both the external spaces of the estate itself (the Gothic's foreign lands) and the internal spaces of the flats (the disorientating Gothic castle) offer feminised Gothic spaces (the perfect geometry of the estate is, from ground level, maze-like). The estate of the story is also a feminised space in that it is literally inhabited solely by women and children (Anne-Marie and her son, the two middle-aged women, the older boy who acts as her guide). Despite the class difference, by the end of the story Helen feels that she is coming home – significantly at a moment when 'death had brought the estate to life' (Barker, 1985: 29).

The Candyman's lair in the film is an equally maze-like – and thus Gothic – space. It transgresses the boundaries of the individual apartments (even – in a clear use of the doppelgänger trope – becoming one with Helen's mirror-image condo) and is a variation of the house-within-the-house motif common in Gothic novels. It is also, like Spector Street, almost deserted, but in *Candyman*'s Cabrini Green, the external spaces are coded as masculine and inhabited by male gang members. It is only once inside the flats that Helen enters a feminised space. It is both a place of safety (from the real world's 'racialised' threat) and a place of forbidden sexual encounters (with the otherworldly Gothic monster). The Candyman's world, in both the story and film, offers terrors *and* delights.

This aesthetic, and the responses it elicits, serves to highlight the appeals of the horror genre for its female audience, appeals and responses which may significantly contradict those of the dominant male audience (an imperfect geometry perhaps). The cultural and aesthetic dimensions of *Candyman* (and its relation to 'The Forbidden') draw attention to moments of heightened emotion in the text that clearly evoke the female Gothic, the melodrama and the romance. The aesthetics of *Candyman* – particularly in terms of its overall atmosphere and the seductive eloquence of the monster – taken together with a loosening of traditional cultural and identity differences in post-modern horrors (such as those created by Clive Barker) indicate that feminine horror remains a significant strain of horror literature and cinema. Whilst there are scenes of gore in the film and moments of heightened shock and disgust typical of the genre, these frequently serve to highlight the objects of morbid (and sexual) fascination with monstrosity and death. Additionally, they highlight the strong contrasts between the beauty and repulsiveness of the images, mirroring the 'aberrant' romance (not only in terms of miscegenation, but certainly reflected through it) central to the discourse of the film. Candyman's eponymous tragic figure incorporates an eroticised and racialised Other, thus introducing a gendered look which offers possibilities of pleasure through gendered spectatorship, though as in other areas of the horror genre, this is fraught with tensions. The subject positions suggested by the consumption and appropriation of the horror text by heterogeneous groups of fans (divided along lines of gender, sexuality and nationality) can – as here – indicate that the horror genre is a site of struggle. The recognition of the existence of oppositional cultural participation raises issues that are pertinent to the study of fan cultures and film audiences in general, as well as the understanding of horror texts specifically.

Part II

Re-imaginings and re-articulations: thematic adaptation in contemporary horror cinema

Out from the realist underground; or, the Baron of Blood visits Cannes: recursive and self-reflexive patterns in David Cronenberg's *Videodrome* and *eXistenZ*

Steffen Hantke

When the Canadian Film Development Corporation, and Universal Pictures in the US, released *Videodrome* in 1982, its director David Cronenberg was little known outside a hardcore fan community. Apart from a few student film productions, Cronenberg had made *Shivers* (1975) and *Rabid* (1977), which had advanced him from film school projects to professional filmmaking, followed by *The Brood* (1979) and *Scanners* (1981), which had established him as one of the new up-and-coming directors of low-budget horror films. Although he had received funding from the Canadian government for his films, Cronenberg was clearly operating outside the cinematic mainstream. Known as a genre director of a particularly visceral and unpleasant type of horror film (one of the nicknames at the time had him pegged as 'Dave "Deprave" Cronenberg'), his reception by the media during those years was often less than friendly. In an overview of reviews published mostly in British newspapers, Ian Conrich has shown that, because 'Cronenberg's early low-budget horrors [were] more identifiable as part of exploitation cinema' (Conrich, 2000: 36), they were 'subjected to considerable hostility from the British press' (37). Some critics 'accused Cronenberg of reveling in gore and maximizing the special effects moments', while others charged his films with 'being too unbelievable, and weak in narrative and characterization' (38). Conrich underlines the hostility of critics by quoting from particularly acerbic, or even outright hostile reviews by Arthur Thirkell in the *Daily Mirror* and

Nicholas Wapshot in *The Times*, who called Cronenberg's films 'sickening' (38), and a headline from the *Sunday Mirror* which, in reference to the infamous 'exploding head' signature shot of *Scanners*, 'screamed "OFF WITH HIS HEAD!"' (38).

By the time *eXistenZ* was released in 1999, Cronenberg seemed to have had the last laugh on his detractors. In the light of the thematic and stylistic consistency of the six feature films he had made since *Videodrome*, it looks like Cronenberg prevailed by way of sheer stubborn persistence.[1] This is not to say, as Jonathan Crane reads the arc of Cronenberg's career, that, once upon a time, Cronenberg '*was* a horror film director', but now, 'as Cronenberg's career has developed, his recent films cannot be so handily corralled' (Crane, 2000: 50, emphasis added). Later films, like *Naked Lunch* (1991), may have 'reconfigured' or 'severely muted' the 'grisly fancies and obvious hallmarks of the genre', though they still qualify as special effects extravaganzas. But Cronenberg has most decidedly not 'abandoned' his interest in subjects many consider beyond the pale of polite filmmaking, or his willingness to articulate these interests with visual frankness (50). Instead of a 'mainstreaming' of Cronenberg, Crane's description speaks, perhaps unwittingly, of a paradigm shift within the popular and critical reception of Cronenberg's work.

This shift took place as 'the majority of reviewers [who] could not be forced to change their aesthetic sense' began to be outnumbered by an even vaster majority of reviewers who were willing to embrace Cronenberg as 'a committed auteur' (Conrich, 2000: 39). The paradigm shift – from being dismissed as an exploitation filmmaker, to being accepted within the framework of *auteur* theory – took place within a discursive field given validity by 'the degree to which high culture trades on the same images, tropes, and themes that characterize low culture' (Hawkins, 2000: 3). That is, critical opinion shifted from the perception that Cronenberg was trying to push the envelope of genre, to the recognition that Cronenberg was pursuing an idiosyncratic personal vision outside of genre. Significantly enough, this recognition also retroactively affects critical assessment of Cronenberg's earlier films, which now appear in a new light as well. Chris Rodley, perhaps the critic with most direct access to Cronenberg himself, has succinctly pointed out that Cronenberg's reputation profited most from the opportunity that the passing of time afforded his critics to see that Cronenberg's films showed a consistent vision at work. 'As one film followed another,' Rodley argues, it 'became clear that Cronenberg is an *auteur* [...] Cronenberg continued to work on the same project, which was becoming increasingly complex, refined and highly achieved with each film he made' (Rodley, 1992: xv–xvi). The market followed suit. One home video distributor, for example, started listing Cronenberg's films 'under the heading "Canadian Cinema", with the following catalogue note: "David Cronenberg has matured from his early B-movie period into a filmmaker whose films transcend the horror genre"' (quoted in Hawkins, 2000: 220, n30).

The shift in the critical reception of Cronenberg's work was accompanied by the outward trappings of success. While his earlier films, up to *Videodrome*, had primarily been Canadian productions – shot in Canada, with an eye first on the Canadian market, and with funding from Canadian sources – his films starting with *The Dead Zone* (1983), which was produced by Dino de Laurentis and distributed by Lorimar, received wider distribution in the US. Cronenberg's films became a staple at international film festivals, especially with the controversy surrounding *Crash* in 1996. Having appeared in brief cameos in other directors' films, Cronenberg further established a public persona in 1999 when he served a turn as president of the jury at the Cannes Film Festival – a form of public recognition unthinkable for the man who had been dubbed the 'King of venereal horror' and 'Baron of blood' in the early years of his career (Rambaldi, 2004). In 1987, his film *The Fly*, by way of Chris Walas' special effects, even made its way into the Academy Awards, and Cronenberg himself was to receive a Genie Award for best direction in 2002 for *Spider*. This was after *Crash*, *Naked Lunch*, and *Dead Ringers*, respectively, had had a strong showing at the Genie Awards in the years of their release.[2] In other words, after sixteen years, the time that passed between *Videodrome* and *eXistenZ*, David Cronenberg had arrived. Often compared to David Lynch, or younger Japanese directors like Miike Takashi, Cronenberg had shed the label of genre director and secured the status of serious *auteur*. At the time he made *Videodrome*, he had been a relative novice, with merely four horror films under his belt; by the time he made *eXistenZ*, he was an accomplished and respected, even distinguished, professional in the North American film industry.

In this overview of Cronenberg's career, I have deliberately chosen *Videodrome* and *eXistenZ* as crucial turning points for several reasons. First and foremost, both films are not only directed by Cronenberg, but are based on his original screenplays. The films in between are adaptations of material by other authors, which suggests continuity between the two bookends despite their temporal distance.[3] Though the films are separated by a considerable period of time, they are likely to express Cronenberg's vision as an artist more directly and succinctly than films in which Cronenberg must first shape and rework the material produced by another author before it will fit his own vision. More importantly, both films share a host of thematic interests that extend beyond the scope of authorial consistency most critics are willing grant all of Cronenberg's films, even those not based on an original script by Cronenberg himself. Granted, *Videodrome* and *eXistenZ* feature many of Cronenberg's signature themes and motifs, most prominently an 'ongoing concern with "masculinity in crisis" [...] frequently dramatized through an impossible vision of male interiority' (Williams, 1999: 32); the 'literalization of organs emerging outside the bounds of organic pragmatism' (Bronfen, 1996: 402); an 'invasive social order – especially its medical and media technologies' (McLarty, 1996: 231); and the 'insidious corporate takeover or [...] the dangerous vision of a solitary, venomous imagination' (Crane, 2000: 51). Were it not for the elements in both films that do *not* recur in other Cronenberg films with the same centrality and urgency, the two films could easily be integrated into a larger interpretive framework in which they figure as examples of *auteurist* style, or as belonging to the thriller or science fiction genre.

However, the similarities between the two films are, in fact, so pervasive that I will consider the later film as a kind of remake, an adaptation, of the earlier one. Other critics have pointed the way toward such a reading. Walter Chaw, for example, points out that, in many ways, 'Cronenberg's *eXistenZ* continues the auteur's fascination with protagonists seeking to redefine their corporeal and existential realities' (Chaw, 2004: para 91) which was already a central theme in *Videodrome*. But while Chaw sees *eXistenZ* as a stepping stone in the 'evolution for the filmmaker that will reach maturity in the quiet, devastatingly economical eloquence of *Spider*' (Chaw, 2004: para 91), I consider the film as a kind of plateau, a still point from which Cronenberg looks back over his previous work, assesses his development as a filmmaker, and reflects on the larger context of his career in which this development has taken place. David Thomson singles out *Videodrome* when he argues for the emergence of a self-reflexive turn in Cronenberg's films. It is the first of Cronenberg's films in which he incorporates 'his response to all the controversy', films 'in which he seems ready to educate us in how to watch him' (Thomson, 2002: 190).[4] Xavier Mendik concurs: 'The requirement for a "reflexive" theory of the director's cinema is made all the more important by the fact that Cronenberg is so clearly a filmmaker who actively *engages* with the theory that surrounds his work' (Mendik, 2000: 169).

Let me start by outlining one major difference between *Videodrome* and *eXistenZ*. *Videodrome* is a city film, it thrives on tropes of noir urbanity. Its *mise-en-scène* is cold and bleak; because of its 'lack of summer scenes' Chris Rodley calls it typical for 'what became known as "the tax-shelter production"' (Rodley, 1992: 69).[5] Its hardboiled qualities also show in some of the locations – the condemned ship in the harbour where Max Renn, the protagonist, hides at the end of the film, or his stylish yet cavernous apartment. While later Cronenberg films like *The Fly* sustain the noir overtones, *eXistenZ* abandons noir visual influences altogether. To the puzzlement of many reviewers attuned to the cyberpunk visuals of *The Matrix*, warm browns and greens dominate the look of *eXistenZ*; crickets chirp, trees are swaying in the breeze, and there is a lot of *Twin Peaks*-like wood-panelling. But these rural settings do not signal backwardness; they are modelled on Silicon Valley, a central bucolic trope of post-Fordism. The woods are crawling with game designers. Like the ski boot that serves as a handbag and the omnipresent SUVs the characters drive, the ski chalets that do double duty as game pod laboratories are illustrations of what has been called 'sunshine industries', making good on 'the postindustrial prophecy of an imminent synergy of labor and leisure spheres' (Latham, 2002: 151). When *eXistenZ* was made, however, the prophecy had already had its utopian legs cut out from under it by the shipwreck of many of the startups in the late 1990s. Similarly, Cronenberg makes sure to counterbalance First World privilege by showing the grubby Dickensian sweatshop of the trout farm setting as its early industrial or Third World complement. Noir might be gone from the film's *mise-en-scène*, but it lives on in its depiction of economic exploitation and sense of moral ambiguity.

While the setting in *eXistenZ* has been updated to create a uniquely Canadian version of the 'sunshine industries', the theme of corporate paranoia appears relatively consistent from the earlier film to the later one. The 'invasive social order' that, according to one critic, features so prominently in many Cronenberg films, appears in both films as a variety of media technology (McLarty, 1996: 231). Corporate paranoia is articulated through structures of the thriller, in which vast conglomerates or organisations are engaging in clandestine or open warfare with each other. Each organisation comes with its corollary antagonist. In *Videodrome*, the principle of free competition plays itself out in the battle for the hearts, minds, and wallets of North America as waged between Barry Convex's organisation Spectacular Optics and Brian O'Blivion's media guerilla. Things get slightly more complicated in *eXistenZ*: Antenna Research gives rise to its business rival Cortical Systematics; both of these components, in turn, necessitate the emergence of the Realist Underground, which opposes the technology both Antenna Research and Cortical Systematics manufacture and distribute. Lastly, both *Videodrome* and *eXistenZ* chronicle the adventures of their respective protagonist through the labyrinth of plot and counterplot, allegiances and betrayals, secrets and discoveries.

While *Videodrome* explores the narrative and dramatic structures of the thriller in good faith, *eXistenZ* articulates them self-consciously. The film cites or re-iterates thriller conventions by embedding them in a multi-layered plot that is scripted, in an ironic *mise-en-abyme*, by characters and events on at least one (maybe more) superseding ontological level . As characters travel through the 'architecture' of Allegra Geller's game, their adventures reflect and echo those in which the actual creator of the game, Yevgeny Nourish, is involved. 'Paranoid temporality', or 'haecceity', as Patrick O'Donnell calls it, sets in as 'reality thickens, experience accrues, and control increases' with each repetition of events or doubling of experiences (O'Donnell, 2000: 3). What follows is a 'molecularization of temporality' in which 'there is no past and no future beyond the diurnal present' – all of which, according to O'Donnell, are hallmarks of the paranoid thriller (O'Donnell, 2000: 3). By presenting a specific author of this paranoid narrative – Allegra Geller, the creator of the game – Cronenberg insinuates an intertextual link between *Videodrome* and *eXistenZ*. The earlier film functions analogously to the embedded narrative of the game 'eXistenZ', while the later film provides its frame. From the superior position of this frame, or through the interplay of frame and embedded narrative, Cronenberg can now critically comment on his earlier work and outline a position for himself for the present.

The character who stands in for Cronenberg himself is the protagonist at the centre of each film's paranoid plot. This figure is a small-scale entrepreneur, a loner, self-employed yet interacting with a large and complex business world that revolves around the fabrication of images. In *Videodrome*, this figure is Max Renn (James Woods), a cynical, glib operator and one of three partners who own and run a cable access television station. A master shot early in the film shows the building that houses Max's station inconspicuously sandwiched by two- or three-storey residential brownstones, with the Toronto CN Tower looming in the background, an urban metaphor suggesting the disproportion among competitors in the same marketplace. To hold out against these monolithic giants, Renn's station specialises in material just within the limits of social acceptability. 'Yeah, but can we get away with it?' is the question that typifies his business practices. Always in search of material that will push the envelope, he objects, for example, to an offer of Japanese softcore pornography as 'too soft, too nice'. Aside from a minimal degree of personal investment in the material he broadcasts, Renn's entrepreneurial spirit is shaped by ruthless competitiveness. Questioned about his business ethics on a talk show, he explains that he has staked his claim in the market by broadcasting material that the competition is afraid to touch. Of course, this answer is self-serving, even self-aggrandising, and perhaps not entirely truthful; the material in question may simply be beneath contempt, as are the covert acts of video-piracy he has one of his employees commit. This employee facetiously calls him 'patron', as if to highlight the exploitive nature of their relationship.

But the ambiguity suggests that Renn himself is perhaps not so much a seeker of extremes, as he wants others to believe, as he is an individual whose business and media ethics are in a state of development. James Woods skillfully projects the subtle unease Renn experiences whenever he is put at risk to reveal his personal investment in the pursuit of transgression. The capitalist credo the character reiterates throughout the film, which provides him with functional but not terminal values, figures as a kind of non-philosophy, an ethical void. Ultimately, Max Renn is not a dangerous man, even if he wanted to be, because he does not have 'a philosophy', as Masha, one of his business associates, tells him. Though the profit motif seems to suggest a rigidly maintained agenda, Renn suffers from a lack of ethical finish or maturity. It is this softness, this flexibility, that make him susceptible to the machinations of the two opposing conspiracies as they try to gain control over him and his station. In the course of the mental and bodily transformations Renn undergoes, Cronenberg's script reworks what starts out as a socially dubious character – someone whose morality does not extend beyond the bottom line – into a genuine force of social change.

In *eXistenZ*, sixteen years later, Cronenberg has written a similar character, but with a twist. Allegra Geller (Jennifer Jason Leigh) is a famous game designer signed on by Antenna Research, one of the two major competitors for a lucrative gaming market. Geller has designed the game that gives Cronenberg's film its title – the least subtle of hints that Cronenberg recognises himself, or at least aspects of his professional persona, in his protagonist. What makes Geller reminiscent of Max Renn is her economic independence. Like Renn, she is a freelancer, a hired gun, an isolated figure dependent upon larger economic and social structures, interacting with them from what she erroneously perceives as a safe distance. Like Renn, whose social relations are on the whole exploitive and shallow, Geller comes with a decidedly solitary inclination, bordering at times, as Leigh's performance insinuates, on pathological forms of autism. This solipsistic streak in her character corresponds to an ambiguity in the technology in which she deals. Cronenberg's game-pod technology brings to mind William Gibson's famous phrase of cyberspace as 'consensual hallucination' (Gibson, 1984: 5); it is intersubjective and social by nature, as players connect to each other via pods and 'umbi-cords'. But it also serves as an escape from unpleasant realities outside the game; Geller tends to retreat into 'eXistenZ' especially when she is bored. Given the eroticised shape and handling of the technological devices, Cronenberg suggests that there is a masturbatory element even in the interaction with others – a decidedly postmodern eroticism that cuts across the classificatory boundaries of conventional sexuality and requires new concepts of 'the social'.

Geller's withdrawal from social relations also functions as a psychological defence mechanism because, unlike Max Renn and his shady dealings, Geller is a public figure, a star, a celebrity. While Renn might be known within industry circles, Geller is the 'game goddess' or 'the demoness', depending on one's point of view. Cronenberg has written scenes in which she is recognised by friends and foes, many of which bring to mind the fan community devoted to his own person.[6] One of her fans, a gas station attendant aptly named Gas (Willem Dafoe), falls to his knees and kisses her feet because, as he says, 'She changed my life.' Ted Pikul, Geller's bodyguard (Jude Law), points to Gas's shabby workplace and asks, 'If she changed your life, what was it like before?' This ironic refraction does not, however, extend to the church setting in which the game itself is presented. It suggests, somewhat more seriously, that media celebrities have taken the place of religious icons. When the church pews materialise at the end of the game, as the test group emerges from its collective trial run of the game, it is also no coincidence that they look like the seats of a cinema. Allegra Geller, the game goddess, is also David Cronenberg, the director as celebrity, adored by fans and despoiled by critics like the one in the *Sunday Mirror* who screamed 'OFF WITH HIS HEAD!' – a headline too close for comfort to the slogan of the Realist assassins 'DEATH TO THE DEMONESS ALLEGRA GELLER!'

Geller is Renn's alter ego, sixteen years down the road, not only when it comes to their respective levels of stardom, but also with regard to their personalities. While Renn is hesitant to enter into further exploration of technology, Geller is a competent, fearless explorer. Renn must still *become* a hybrid creature, part human and part technology; his transformation is largely the story of the film. Geller, meanwhile, starts out as a specimen of 'the new flesh'. She is tech-savvy, comfortable with ambiguous ontologies, and comfortable in her pursuit of technological pleasures. She comes to us as her cyborg self, fully fitted with 'a bioport', that ambiguous orifice that allows players to interface directly with the film's fictional gaming technology. Whatever anxieties about technology's invasiveness and unpredictable effects are latent in Cronenberg's script are projected onto the character of Ted Pikul, Geller's bodyguard and gaming partner ('Look, I've been dying to play your games, but I have this phobia about having my body penetrated surgically'). Pikul is Max Renn, narratively atrophied into a secondary character. He serves as Geller's double, nervously frittering over his lack of technological comprehension. Even when Geller, in the final plot twist of the film, is revealed to be just another gamer – one of the faceless consumers rather than the 'game goddess' – she does not lose her ease around technology. Again, this may appear like a deliberate irony on Cronenberg's part, because Geller-the-player turns out to be one of the arch enemies of gaming technology. But this is, in fact, Cronenberg's point: terrorists share essential skills and convictions with the institutions and structures they oppose, and vice versa. There is a thin line between 'Know your enemy' and 'Become your enemy'.

In the closing scene of the film, Cronenberg focuses on questions about the conditions and possibilities of political action in the context of celebrity culture. What makes Geller, and her 'real-life' equivalent Yevgeni Nourish, targets of the opposing side and its assassins are their public visibility, their status as celebrities. Two groups function as opponents: inside the game, Geller is chased by Cortical Systematics, the rival of Antenna Research. As the players exit the game and Geller is revealed as just another player, the frame narrative presents the designer of the game, Yevgeni Nourish, as the target of two assassins from the 'Realist Underground'. Cronenberg himself has mentioned that the theme of 'open season on the artist' was inspired by an interview he conducted with Salman Rushdie.[7] The *fatwa* against Rushdie was to have served as the model for the 'Realist Underground', the zeal with which epistemological fundamentalists plan to assassinate Nourish as punishment for the sacrilege he has committed by crossing the boundary between reality and simulation.[8] *eXistenZ* seems to suggest that matters of corporate rivalry are really not about economic objectives after all – an idea that is in keeping with Max Renn's emptiness as a character before he acquires 'a philosophy'. What really matters are rivalries of a more philosophical nature that only incidentally adhere to the technologies that transport them. This is also suggested by the fact that economic rivalry dominates in the embedded narrative, while a more profoundly philosophical rivalry dominates the frame. The embedding of the trope of corporate rivalry also emphasises its origin as 'authored'. Presented in this way, the trope openly announces its origins in, for example, the cyberpunk world of William Gibson's *Neuromancer* or Murakami Haruki's *Hard-Boiled Wonderland and the End of the World*; it is indebted to the futuristic thriller that extrapolates American capitalism into dystopian scenarios of omnipotent zaibatsus and global conspiracies. The trope of fundamentalist terrorism of one brand or another, eerily enough for a film made in 1999, belongs to a world far more recognisable as our own; historical events after 2001 have provided a new interpretive frame of reference so that earlier films seem eerily prescient. But even our ability to recognise these settings does not afford the comfort of ontological certainty. Having gunned down Nourish, the two assassins face another cowering victim who poses the question which is to remain unanswered and unanswerable since Cronenberg ends the narrative here: 'Are we still in the game?'

To answer the question, which stands in the way of assessing Cronenberg's politcs in this instance, it is important to pay attention to the eccentric capitalisation of the games' titles (*eXistenZ* and *transCendeZ*). Analogous to the beginning and end of each word poignantly not coinciding with its first and last letter, there 'is no point at which the film's action originates in an unambiguously established reality, and no such point to which it unequivocally returns' (Grant, 2000: 15). Significant is also the heavy-handedness of the closing scene, on which many critics have negatively commented, but which I read as deliberately stilted, transparent and artificial.[9] The characters are no less 'game characters', driven by the dictate of 'game urges' and formulaic requirements of genre, than the ones inside the corporate conspiracy plot. This is not bad acting on the part of Sarah Polley or Ian Holm, but a clue that they are speaking words and performing action scripted for them by yet another imperfect author. Grant is correct about the absence of an equivocal point of origin, but this ontological uncertainty is exactly the film's point. The ending is a doorway into infinite regress or continued gaming. At the expense of more radical possibilities of ambiguity, *eXistenZ* argues that another imagination, as culturally specific and intersubjective as that of Allegra Geller, is at work in the writing of the ending.

This means that, politically, *eXistenZ* weighs in on the flipside of the same question Cronenberg was already pondering in *Videodrome*. How are we to conceive of political action in an arena in which the lines between sign and referent, signifier and signified, are not clearly drawn? How broad or narrow is the margin of political action *not* being symbolic? What constitutes subversion or transgression in a media-driven postindustrial culture? In *Videodrome*, Cronenberg answers these questions by chronicling the process of politicisation of his protagonist; in this sense, the film is a kind of cybertechnological *Bildungsroman* or political *education sentimentale*. Regardless of the effectiveness of Max Renn's suicide in the closing shot, which would be potentially meaningless if he were operating from within a personal hallucination, his willingness to sacrifice himself in the fight against Videodrome is what counts. Existential self-assertion *is* political action.

eXistenZ casts similar doubts upon the effectiveness of the assassination of Nourish as an act of political insurrection against an overpowering regime of image production and consumption. But now, seventeen years later, the technological saturation of the political environment has caught up with the existential dilemma in *Videodrome*. One might speculate, along with Fredric Jameson's periodisation of contemporary culture, that *eXistenZ* marks the shift toward a fully accomplished or finalised process of postmodernisation. While technology in *Videodrome* is still seen as a force of alienation, and thus as a reservoir of modernist resistance to postmodernisation, technology is *eXistenZ* has no such effect on Geller. It is Pikul, revealed as a member of the Realist Underground and an enemy of 'eXistenZ', who represents traces of modern alienation. The modernist ambiguity about technology missing from *eXistenZ*, also registers in the irony that appears in *Videodrome* whenever the film shows the complicity between forces ostensibly operating on opposite sides of the technology question. When Rena King attacks Max Renn for his exploitation practices, it happens on a television talk show that is itself a means of exploitation.

In *eXistenZ*, the necessary precondition for such irony no

longer exists because Cronenberg construes the film's imaginary media technology as collective. Unlike the video hallucinations plunging Max Renn into solipsism and alienation, game-pod technology is intersubjective. As Nourish remarks to his aide, one single person with an 'anti-game sentiment' will steer the narrative in his or her direction and thus shape the gaming experience for the entire group. Whereas the media technology in *Videodrome*, with its disturbance of clear cognitive categories, makes its consumers susceptible to political manipulation (Renn is being 'programmed' as an assassin by having a tape inserted into his body), in *eXistenZ* it is designed to enable collective hallucination. While *Videodrome* argues for a rending of the perceptual veil, *eXistenZ* recognises that the technology, as subtly alienating as it might be, also serves the social nexus; to leave the consensual hallucination means removing oneself from the social and political arena. One might take this as a sign in both films that political action, mired in cognitive uncertainty, is compromised, perhaps even negated, because of this complicity between conformity and resistance. But if we are willing to recognise the gravity of symbolic action, we might also see this situation as an incitement to political action, albeit in a sense that requires an adjusted definition of 'action'. Foucault's model of power as a decentralised network of social relations precludes the possibility that one death, strategically planned, will bring about a collapse of the network. This essential ineffectiveness constitutes the assassination of Nourish as a symbolic act. But in order even to register as a symbolic act, armed resistance must be integrated within the same cultural matrix that also harbours and validates its ideological other. Both sides in the corporate conspiracy plot of the game 'eXistenZ' and the formula of the thriller are locked in an inescapable dialectic, which means that the symbolic nature of the act is not the source of its weakness or the reasons for its futility, but the precondition of its strength.

While Cronenberg may have modelled the figure of the persecuted artist on Salman Rushdie, the aspect of the artist as celebrity also points back to the director's own emergence as a public figure since the days of *Videodrome*. Geller is not only the author of 'eXistenZ', the game, just as Cronenberg is the author of *eXistenZ*, the film. Despite Geller's repeated withdrawal from social interactions, she is also part of the product herself. Her creative vision is co-opted into a 'signature style', which is then used as part of the marketing of the product by Antenna. The film's opening and closing scene each show the author, somewhat uneasily, shmoozing the members of the focus group assembled by Antenna's marketing division. Geller/Nourish are in attendance to sell their product, and the audience has come to see them as much as play the game. As the nature of postmodern stardom has it, Geller/Nourish are simultaneously producer and product, author and text, just as the audience we see in the film – the focus group assembled by special invitation – is simultaneously a group of consumers (the game is available at a special pre-release discount in exchange for their filling out of questionnaires) and a mechanism of production/distribution (situated somewhere between distribution and consumption).

In *Videodrome*, the economic front lines were drawn more clearly. While Allegra Geller has collapsed the modern distinction between production and consumption, Max Renn is a distributor, not a creator. The process or act of actual creation is conspicuously absent from the film. We see the two Japanese businessmen peddling their wares out of a cheap hotel room, and even Renn's old acquaintance, Masha, as she presents him with a clip of her latest softcore epic, is presented more as a distributor than a director. Obviously, the makers of the eponymous Videodrome remain in the shadows, and when they finally do emerge, in the figure of Barry Convex, they are contextualised first and foremost as businessmen. The fact that Cronenberg virtually eliminates the creative artist from his depiction of economic and social exchange in the film suggests, on one level, that media technology is more important that the content transported by this technology. This is not yet the hardware/software dichotomy that computer technology has brought into widespread circulation and that we see literalised in *eXistenZ* years later. Rather, Cronenberg struggles with the McLuhanesque mantra that 'the medium is the message'. In other words, the hardcore violence of *Videodrome* is an inevitable product of a technology that is essentially indifferent to any aspect of content other than spectacle.

If we were to read Max Renn as a self-portrait of David Cronenberg at an early stage in his career, then the most striking feature of this portrait would be the intense self-loathing. Before the process of Renn's politicisation sets in, by way of his entanglement in the Videodrome conspiracy (imagined or real), his creative authorship over the material he distributes is nil. Image production, as far as it concerns him, manifests itself as the repetition of formula. 'Sex and violence' is the shorthand for the material Max Renn peddles to his viewers, a shorthand strongly evocative of the horror film genre. Subjugated to the demands of the genre, its fans and its formula, the creative author occupies a position closer to that of a distributor than a creator. This is not to say that Cronenberg reinvents the independent filmmaker with Allegra Geller as the original Romantic genius, a possibility Chris Rodley seems to consider a valid interpretive option ('In the Cronenberg Project, the creation of art must ultimately free itself of specific – and potentially paralysing – political, social and cultural concerns' (Rodley, 1992: xxiii)). Geller does not represent a pure and autonomous force of creativity that transcends the marketplace altogether. She is a celebrity author, complicit in the processes of commodification from which, by personal inclination more than strategic reasons, she tries to keep herself at a safe distance. That is, even with Geller, Cronenberg remains alert to the mechanisms surrounding the creative artist. But the depiction of Geller is somewhat more optimistic. If we were to speculate on the reasons why Cronenberg re-wrote the autobiographical character sixteen years later as a woman, we might, yet again, come upon questions of how Cronenberg conceives of artistic creation within a commercial context. The feminisation of Max Renn's body in one of *Videodrome*'s signature special effects scenes, could be seen as the beginning of an arc that ends with Allegra Geller, a female author who refers to her product as 'my baby'. This is a far more intimate and organic metaphor of creativity than the 'invasive social order – especially its medical and media technologies' (McLarty, 1996: 231), with its brutal domination and insidious colonisation of the imagination – that haunted earlier films like *Videodrome*. Perhaps this is a sign that Cronenberg the respected *auteur* is more in control of his production, which means that he is also more at ease with the commercial mechanisms of the film industry and more guardedly hopeful about the political functions of cinema than he used to be when he was still 'the Baron of Blood'.

‘These children that you spit on’: horror and generic hybridity

Andy W. Smith

The decade of the 1990s was characterised by a range of science fiction, fantasy and horror films that constituted a revival in the respective genres, both in terms of critical acclaim and box office takings. The development of cinematic effects during this period, with regards to creating fantastical worlds and gruesome monsters, led to the eventual dominance of computer generated imagery (CGI) in Hollywood cinema by the turn of the millennium. Between 1993 and 2003, a glut of blockbuster movies and cult films systematically and radically changed the viewing expectations of its target audiences. The spectacle of advanced special effects (arguably starting with James Cameron's *Terminator 2: Judgement Day* in 1991 and reaching its zenith with *The Matrix* in 1999), coupled with the concomitant rise of DVD technology, resulted in a series of movies that engaged directly with the epistemology of technology in a way not seen since the development of Technicolor in the 1930s.

Starting with Spielberg's *Jurassic Park* (1993), the accumulation of effects-laden cinema coincided with ‘event’ movies that sought to break previous box-office records in an endless cycle of one-upmanship: *Independence Day* (Roland Emmerich: 1996), *Titanic* (James Cameron: 1996) *Men In Black* (Barry Sonnefeld: 1997) and the gargantuan *Lord of the Rings* cycle (Peter Jackson: 2001–2003) all took over 500 million dollars world wide. Of the top twenty grossing movies of all time, only one was made before 1993: Spielberg's *ET: The Extra Terrestrial* (1982).[1] The development of DVD players, with which viewers could access bonus features, slow down scenes and control the viewing experience in multiple formats, also led to film studios offering the consumer/spectator a transparent insight into the movie-making process. Indeed, it has become common practice for film magazines to rate DVD extras and bonus materials in the same way that films are given ratings for their content. This technologically literate spectatorship is very different from the uninitiated viewer whose 'suspension of disbelief' is necessary for the old fashioned 'smoke and mirrors' effects to function; one of the (accidental) consequences of CGI is that it has become so commonplace as to be almost banal, especially within fantasy and science fiction film-making. These films cater to an audience raised on CGI; these spectators are also able to reference generic codes and conventions in a highly sophisticated way.

Horrality

In his essay 'Horrality', Philip Brophy argues for reading post-1975 horror films as a 'saturated genre' in a constant process of referencing itself as a textual object (Brophy, 2000). Brophy uses the term 'Horrality' to describe the conjunction of a number of disparate elements: 'horror, textuality, morality, hilarity'. Brophy argues that the modern horror film is composed of virtuoso technical set pieces and visual effects that stimulate the spectator (through fear and laughter) whilst offering the reassurance of a self-perpetuating cycle of known tropes:

> The contemporary Horror film *knows* that you've seen it before; it *knows* that you know what is about to happen, and it knows that you know it knows you know. And none of it means a thing, as the cheapest trick in the book will still tense your muscles, quicken your heart and jangle your nerves. It is the *present* – the precise point of speech, of utterance, of plot, of event – that is ever of any value. (Brophy, 2000: 279)

Brophy's argument is even more relevant for an analysis of 1990s horror/science fiction cinema than when it was first written in 1983. In particular, a spate of movies that engaged in a constant process of self-referencing were endemic in the late 1990s, a 'movement' that the film journal *Sight and Sound* described as 'teenage postmodern horror'.[2] These films included *The Craft* (Andrew Fleming: 1996), where a group of schoolgirls form a witches' coven, described by one of the male characters as 'the bitches of Eastwick'; *Scream* (Wes Craven: 1996), in which a series of killings are committed according to the known plot devices of teenage 'slasher' films; *I Know What You Did Last Summer* (Jim Gillespie: 1997), in which a group of teens are pursued from beyond the grave by the victim of a hit-and-run car accident; *Scream 2* (Wes Craven: 1997), a follow-up to the phenomenally successful *Scream* and which references the penchant for horror sequels; *I Still Know What You Did Last Summer* (Danny Cannon: 1998), which, unlike *Scream 2*, is a less self-aware but still-knowing nod to sequels; and finally *The Faculty* (Robert Rodriguez: 1998), perhaps the most intriguing film to come out of this loose collection of sub-generic films. Apart from *The Craft*, all these films were scripted by Kevin Williamson, an unusual status given to a writer in an industry more accustomed to the director as *auteur*.

All of the films mentioned above deal with generic patterns that can be detected in the iconography of the 'slasher' sub-genre made famous by John Carpenter's *Halloween* (1978). The protagonists are all teenagers on the cusp of sexual and emotional maturity. The films are based in or around US high schools, which, in Carol Clover's analysis of 'slasher' films, would stand in for the 'terrible place', the site of terror and obliteration by the Other (Clover, 1989: 101). In particular, the 'slasher' trope of post-coital death scenes and the survival of the 'Final Girl'[3] are key self-reflexive comments in the *Scream* films; as Kim Newman writes: 'This approach allows for likable cheap jokes, like Randy's "I never thought I'd be so grateful to be a virgin" as he survives the climax and Sidney's quickfire reaction when Randy says, "and this is the obligatory moment when the killer comes back from the dead for one last scare"' (Newman, 2002: 198).

What the *Scream* films demonstrate is the generic identification between audience and the subject matter. The film nerd Randy is, in effect, one of the audience members transplanted into the film's diegesis; he knows the plot contrivances, the technical effects and the underlying structural mechanisms of the sub-genre. It is this 'knowing' audience that best exemplifies the direction that 'postmodern horror' has taken between 1975 and 1995. As Carol Clover writes:

> The fact that the cinematic conventions of horror are so easily and so often parodied would seem to suggest that, individual variation notwithstanding, its basic structures of apperception are fixed and

> fundamental ... The 'art' of the horror film, like the 'art' of pornography, is to a very large extent the art of rendition, and it is understood as such by the competent audience. A particular example may have original features, but its quality as a horror film lies in the ways it delivers the cliché. (Clover, 1989: 94)

What terror/pleasure is left for a genre that has seemingly parodied itself into extinction? Or is it only Brophy's point of 'present/presence', its 'Horrality', that has any value left for the genre and its vertiginous offshoots?

The politics of terror

The generic components of cinematic horror tend to focus around four key areas: audience identification; sensual gratification; the build up of suspense (usually through performance, cinematography and sound); and, finally, the release of primal fears through the explication of the monster. Its tradition is drawn from a wide range of historical and ideological contexts; indeed, one of the reasons why the horror genre has been so actively analysed and dissected by critics and academics is precisely because of its metonymic powers; the ability of the monster to 'stand in' for something else – an idea, a feeling, a concept, a belief – is one of its most potent elements, and why the genre remains one of the most robust of cinematic forms.

The genre's ability to re-fashion itself and attract a new audience is also one of its attractions for cultural historians. From the classic Universal 'monster' pictures of the 1930s, which set down the *tabula rasa* for the genre through *Dracula* (Tod Browning: 1931), *Frankenstein* (James Whale: 1931) and *The Wolf Man* (George Waggner: 1941) through to the Cold War bodily invasion paranoia of *The Thing* (Christian Nyby and Howard Hawks: 1951) and *Invasion of the Body Snatchers* (Don Siegel: 1956), the horror film has continually responded to cultural pressures and ideological processes that resulted in new, mutated forms of the genre. The critical and popular success of films from the 1970s which dealt with 'Satanic' offspring[4] can equally be read as an appraisal on the processes through which US families are socialised into the norms and values of a consumerist, repressive culture. The zombie films of George Romero (*Night of the Living Dead*, 1968; *Dawn of the Dead*, 1978; *Day of the Dead*, 1985;

Land of the Dead, 2005) have been analysed as both political critiques of Vietnam and the rise of the extreme right wing in American mainstream politics in the late 1970s.[5] Faced with the creative output and extraordinary commercial success of underground/independent film makers like Romero, Wes Craven (*The Last House on the Left*, 1972), Tobe Hooper (*The Texas Chainsaw Massacre*, 1974) and John Carpenter (*Halloween*, 1978), Hollywood films in the late 1970s came up with a structural melding of horror tropes with the dystopian visions of contemporary science fiction.

Hybrid genres

The critical and commercial success of *Alien* (Ridley Scott: 1979) and *The Terminator* (James Cameron: 1984) established the rise of the 'sci-fi/horror hybrid' defined by Stephen Neale as being 'obliged by the conventions of generic verisimilitude to establish narrative equilibrium and disequilibrium, diegetic order and disorder, in terms of differences between, on the one hand, "the human" and "the natural" and, on the other, the "non-human", the "unnatural" and the "monstrous"' (Neale, 1989: 214).

This separation into 'difference' imbues the hybrid genres with consistent codes of comparison and elicitation; the viewer 'elicits' readings through the constant juxtaposition between what is 'normal' and what is 'monstrous', allied to the fantastical worlds of science fiction and their emphasis on utopian/dystopian futures. In *The Terminator*, for example, the everyday technology (phones/cars/machinery) of the diegetic world becomes a prescient commentary on the future war between man and machine that lies at the centre of the film's time-loop paradox. However, as with other 'hybrid genre' films, the separation out of its constituent binary elements is not as clear-cut as it first seems. As Constance Penley writes, 'the film, moreover, does not advance an "us against them" argument, a Romantic opposition between the organic and the mechanical, for there is much that is hybrid about its constructed elements' (Penley, 1989: 199).

This 'hybrid construction' is most obviously realised in the figure of the Terminator himself; a cyborg, a walking embodiment of the post-human, is made up of human tissue and machine parts able to replicate any human voice. In *Alien*, the threat to the crew of the *Nostromo* comes from four distinct points that problematise distinctions between 'human' and 'monster': the alien creature itself; the computer on board called 'Mother', whose secret mission is to capture and bring the alien life form back to earth; the post-human Ash, revealed as a robot in league with 'Mother'; and, finally, from within the crew itself, as the alien is 'born' through the stomach of Kane in a 'horrifying confusion of the sexual-gynecological with the gastrointestinal' (James H. Kavanaugh, 1980: 93–4).

But there are other, non-narrative elements that emphasise the unique melding of hybrid genre forms. The use of the roving steadicam to approximate the Alien's and the Terminator's point of view is a common device in horror films. Likewise, Sarah Connor's and Ripley's survival of, and triumph over, their tormentors replicates those of Clover's 'Final Girls'. Lastly, the remorseless resurrection of the Terminator/Alien mimics the horror trope of the killer/monster that refuses to die. As Neale writes, 'the genres of the fantastic often deal with issues of difference – especially the boundaries between the human and the monstrous' (Neale, 1989: 222). These 'issues of difference' also appear in another sub-genre that has seen a rise in popularity in the 1980s and 1990s: that of the 'teen movie' and its appropriation by other generic forms.

1980s teen cinema: 'Don't you forget about me'

The opening of John Hughes' 1985 teen film *The Breakfast Club* begins with an on-screen quote from the David Bowie song 'Changes':

> And these children that you spit on,
> As they try to change their worlds
> Are immune to your consultations.
> They're quite aware of what they're going through.

This epigraph acts as a commentary on a film that portrays the gradual self-realisation of a bunch of American high school kids as they sit through a Saturday detention. There is no doubt whose sympathies Hughes is playing on; apart from the parents we see dropping off and picking up their children, the only on-screen adults are a teacher and a janitor. Both characters are mostly depicted from the teens' perspective and fulfil their generic stereotypes: the teacher, Mr Vernon, is a strict disciplinarian who nonetheless becomes an object of derision for the 'breakfast club'. When ridiculed by the rule breaker Bender, the janitor, Carl, lets the teens know exactly who has the power in an institution designed to regulate social behaviour in a model of Bentham's Panopticon:

> You guys think I'm just some untouchable peasant? Peon? Huh? Maybe so, but following a broom around after shitheads like you for the past eight years I've learned a couple of things ... I look through your letters, I look through your lockers ... I listen to your conversations, you don't know that but I do ... I am the eyes and ears of this institution my friends.

The teens in *The Breakfast Club* are introduced one by one at the start of the film in a voiceover that places each of them within a generic 'type': 'You see us as you want to see us ... in the simplest terms and the most convenient definitions. You see us as a brain, an athlete, a basket case, a princess and a criminal.' The film then proceeds to dismantle these stereotypes with surprising consequences: the 'basket case' Allison is paired off with the 'jock' Andrew; the delinquent rebel, Bender, ends up with the 'prom queen', Claire. Meanwhile, the 'nerd', Brian, is left to write the class essay that details their refusal to conform to the image demanded of them by an adult society composed of parents and teachers. Boundaries of class (but, crucially, not race) difference are broken down in a rather egalitarian ending, which finishes on the still-frame image of Bender walking across the football field with his gloved fist raised in triumph.[6] This film points up the 'issues of difference' between 'types' that results in a process of change; each student comes to recognise the limitations placed on them by adhering to their social definitions. As the final voiceover letter reveals: 'But what we found out is that each one of us is a brain and an athlete and a basket case and a princess and a criminal. Does that answer your question? Sincerely yours, the Breakfast Club. '

As Timothy Shary writes, 'the ways in which school characters are portrayed may offer an index of identifiers and signifiers for the young viewers who are presumably meant to relate to one or more of these types, and thus the films can be seen to "teach" the proper mannerisms of each school persona' (Shary, 2002: 32). *The Breakfast Club* stands as a good example of the type of genre film that is aimed at a specific demographic: the teens watching the film will identify with the problems and situations presented on screen. This is particularly applicable to the raft of 1980s teen dramas, known as the 'Brat Pack' films, because they adhere in form and content to the diegesis of a 'real world'.[7] Only *Ferris Bueller's Day Off* (John Hughes: 1986) breaks this convention of realism through a radical style of direct address, which works as a form of self-enabling commentary on teen mores and attitudes. The teen genre works through the processes of audience self-identification, perhaps more so than any other form of genre. This connection is intensified when combined with other genres to create another hybrid form: the teen/horror/science fiction film.

The remainder of this essay will examine how the film *The Faculty* combines the tropes and stylistic conventions of teen movies, gothic horror and science fiction to effectively create what the critic Thomas Kent has identified as a 'supergenre': a process in which the spectator/reader can observe a 'shift ceaselessly from one set of generic conventions to another' (Kent, 1986: 22). This self-reflexivity is one of the main ways in which different generic conventions can be adapted and transformed.

'I'm not an alien. I'm discontent. ' (Stan, *The Faculty*)

Robert Rodriguez's *The Faculty* (1998) has a cover version of David Bowie's 'Changes' playing over the closing credits. Indeed, 'these children that you spit on' are more than 'immune' to the vagaries of teenage life; after all, they have just saved the world from being taken over by parasitic aliens. As noted earlier, *The Faculty* was written by Kevin Williamson, who also wrote the *Scream* trilogy, and Rodriguez's film falls into the cycle of 'teenage postmodern horror' that was prefaced by the *Scream* films in the late 1990s. It is also one of the most interesting and gratifying films of the sub-genre in the way it references films like *Alien*, *Independence Day* and *Men In Black* and acknowledges its debt to *The Breakfast Club*. As in the latter film, *The Faculty* introduces each of its main characters by their teen stereotype. But before we even get to that point, the film offers up a series of scenes that transparently outlines its shifting of genres and film contexts.

The first image we see in the film is of a football spiralling through the air. The setting is a football field, a common location in countless US teen films. The irate coach is berating his recalcitrant and sullen players. The film's location has an immediate resonance, especially with US audiences (and, by extension. European audiences acclimatised to US signifiers). As the players depart, the coach is confronted by an off-screen figure. The film then cuts to the faculty staff room in the school at night, following a meeting where the unpopular Principal Drake refuses all requests the teachers make for school trips and special events, with the exception of the football team. What follows is a radical shift in genre as Drake, locked alone in the building, is attacked and then chased by Coach Willis through the deserted corridors in a sequence that borrows heavily from 'slasher' movies. Just as Principal Drake thinks she has escaped from the coach by getting out of the school, she finds herself attacked and presumably killed by the English teacher Mrs. Olsen.

So from the very first moments of the film it is clear that we are in the territory of a horror film set in a high school, complete with expected witticisms: as the English teacher stabs Principal Drake, she comments 'I always wanted to do that', imitating what Coach Willis says when he first attacks Drake. This opening places the film's generic conventions in an ambivalent context; whilst adhering to horror's cinematic techniques, the teacher's placement as the *source* of that horror creates a scenario rich in self-reflexive commentary. This is demonstrated by two different advertising 'taglines' for the film's US release: 'The students at Herrington High will not only question authority ... they'll have to destroy it' and 'You will not be disrespectful this school year!' The adaptation of American high school drama with fantasy/horror/science fiction/comedy formats has already been well documented in US television shows from the 1990s, in particular *Buffy The Vampire Slayer* (1998–2003), *Roswell* (1999–2002) and *Smallville* (2001–2006).

In *The Faculty*, the school's teaching staff are progressively infected by a parasitic alien life form using their bodies as hosts (referencing the two *Invasion of the Body Snatchers* films from 1956 and 1978). A group of disparate teenagers find ways of combating this alien invasion, and in doing so deconstruct the stereotypes placed upon them by the expectations of the genre, the school and, by proxy, the spectator. In effect, the teachers' physical mutations are subsumed within the alien species, acting as a metonym for the wider transmutation of generic signifiers that occur during the course of the film. Each main teenage character in *The Faculty* is introduced as a specific 'type' within the social context of high school, drawing upon the template of *The Breakfast Club*, where the fixed identity of archetypes like 'the rebel', the 'nerd' or the 'jock' are progressively questioned within the school's stultifying power structures. Rodriguez's film takes this questioning of authority even further by cross-referencing the generic horror/science fiction fear of the 'Other' with the deliberate destabilising of these 'fixed archetypes' in the high school film.

The student 'types' are introduced through actions and still frames. Their names are then superimposed over the freeze to emphasise both their generic role in the film and their importance to the narrative. So we have the school 'nerd' Casey being shoved legs first into a flagpole; Stokely, the 'weirdo' with a penchant for wearing all black, reading sci-fi novels and having no friends; Delilah, the cheerleader/popular girl who is dating Stan, the football team's quarterback; Mary-Beth, the new girl who bears an uncanny resemblance to the character of Sandy in *Grease* (1978); and finally the delinquent rebel dope peddler Zeke. Of course, the structural relationship to *The Breakfast Club* is not exact, as *The Faculty* introduces a sixth 'type', that of the new girl Mary-Beth. This apparent difference from *The Breakfast Club* and its collection of *five* types (brain, athlete, basket case, princess and criminal) is part of the film's shifting generic conventions: Mary-Beth is, in fact, the 'mother alien' whom the others must destroy to free the whole town which, by the end of the film, has been taken over by the alien parasites. Her opening line therefore has an added ironic texture: 'I'm feeling very alien myself today. I'm Mary-Beth Louise Hutchinson. I just moved from Atlanta. I'm new here. '

From the introduction of the 'types' forward, the film engages in a continual process of meta-textual commentary where audience expectations of generic signifiers are constantly reversed. Stan, the 'jock', gives up his place on the football team to concentrate on his studies, much to the disgust of his girlfriend Delilah: 'The accepted social order is that head cheerleader dates star quarterbacks, not academic wannabes!' The 'rebel', Zeke, when he is not selling his homemade 'scat', displays an acute intelligence and sensitivity in two separate classroom scenarios. It is Zeke who discovers that it is his drugs (which he makes from a sophisticated laboratory in his house) which kill the alien species. The 'nerd', Casey, is the one who discovers the alien life form on the football field, and it is he who, with Delilah, infiltrates the faculty staff room and discovers the alien plot. Finally, is he who destroys the mother alien at the end of the film. As Delilah says to him, 'Casey, when did you become Sigourney Weaver?', referencing the *Alien* films and unknowingly commenting on Casey's role as the 'Final Girl'. In fact, the students actually work out how to defeat the alien invasion by drawing upon their knowledge of cultural referents, from science fiction literature through to contemporary films: Casey makes the point that 'If you were going to take over the world, would you blow up the White House, *Independence Day* style, or sneak in through the back door?' Zeke insists that Casey sniffs the drug when they are the only two left that have not been assimilated: 'I leave for five minutes and when I come back everyone's a fucking alien. Don't make me fucking *Men In Black* your ass, you're gonna fuckin sniff it!' Peter Matthews, in his review of the film, suggests that the postmodern referencing makes for a vacuous experience for the viewer:

> As in the *Scream* films, specialist knowledge of movie clichés becomes a survival tactic: here sci-fi nerd Stokely deduces the existence of a queen-bee alien by remembering *Alien*. Unsurprisingly, the Ur-text is *Invasion of the Body Snatchers* (1956), and Williamson even pilfers one of its key lines of dialogue: 'It's so much better. There is no fear or pain.' However, *Body Snatchers* belonged to a world where cultural anxieties found metaphorical expression in pulp. Rodriguez and Williamson have gone beyond all that. Their version of pop cinema cheerfully dispenses with sub-text. (Newman, 2002: 205)

Rather than dismiss *The Faculty* as '1990s pastiche-land', as Matthews does, it would be constructive to see the genre shifting and self-reflexivity as a development on Brophy's 'Horrality'. At play in the film is a complex signification denoted not only by generic conventions and cinematic techniques but also by the actors' status as genre icons. In particular the actor Robert Patrick, who plays Coach Willis, is familiar to science fiction film fans as the shape shifting Terminator T-1000 from *Terminator 2:*

Judgement Day. His main 'identity' in that film is as an LAPD policeman tracking down the twelve-year-old John Connor, a referent to the teen fear of authority figures and graphically positioned in opposition to Schwarzenegger's iconic biker-garbed Terminator. His subsequent television/film roles have also positioned Patrick in relation to the remediation of science fiction/horror crossovers: notably FBI agent John Doggett in seasons eight and nine of *The X-Files* (2000–2002), and also David Scatino, the gambling addict school friend of Tony Soprano in season two of *The Sopranos* (2000). This last role is perhaps his most interesting, cast against type as the 'victim' prey to the horrors of the Mob. Piper Laurie is another actor in the film who has had a distinguished career in cult horror film and television, having played the fanatically religious mother in *Carrie* (Brian De Palma: 1976) and also appearing in David Lynch's television series *Twin Peaks* (1990–1991).

As a film, *The Faculty* is defined by the cultural assimilation of genres, contexts and conventions that connects both the characters and audience, resulting in a pleasurable experience of self-identification for the viewer, with attendant social-political side effects. The hatred and willed destruction of authority, only vaguely expressed in *The Breakfast Club*, is allowed to flourish within the parameters of fantasy. The alien species brings order and control to the school; the teaching staff, once unmotivated and cynical, become paragons of pedagogy; the English teacher, Ms Burke, is transformed from a dowdy spinster into a literal *femme fatale* as she attempts to infect Zeke in a sexual/parasitic metaphor. The students become disciplined and controlled, demonstrated most clearly in a witty classroom scene that shows every hand raised to answer the teacher's question. The Friday night football game[8] sees Herrington High annihilate the local opposition in every sense of the word: both on the field and by infecting them with the parasitic alien during the game. This combination of hybrid genres creates a film that offers both parody and homage to its antecedents: *The Breakfast Club*, *Alien* and *Invasion of the Body Snatchers*. This tribute is further embodied in the speech Mary-Beth/mother alien delivers as she faces Casey for the climatic showdown:

> You were lost and lonely, just like me. And I thought that maybe I could give you a taste of my world. A world without anger, without

> fear, without attitude. Where the underachiever goes home at night to parents that care. The jock can be smart, the ugly duckling beautiful, and the class wuss doesn't have to live in terror. The new girl – well – the new girl she can just fit right in with anybody. People who are just like her. You see, Casey, even Mary-Beth's feelings can be hurt by a bunch of pathetic, lost, little outcasts who truly believe that their disaffected lonely life is the only way they can survive. I can make you a part of something so special Casey, so perfect, so fearless ... Don't you want that, Casey?

The film's conclusion suggests a re-ordering of generic conventions: like *The Breakfast Club*, the ex-jock Stan is romantically paired up with the basket case Stokely; the nerd-turned-hero-turned-media celebrity Casey ends up dating the prom queen Delilah; and the eternal rebel/drug dealer/scientist Zeke ends up playing for the football team, wearing the numbered football uniform that so often denotes social conformity in the high school scenario. Unlike Bender in *The Breakfast Club*, who raises a clenched fist on the football field in defiance of conforming to the normative value system, Zeke is assimilated into the culture of conformity. But the film finishes on an image of transmutation, as Casey photographs a butterfly. It is an apt metaphor for a film where everything changes – and everything remains the same.

'Our reaction was only human': monstrous becomings in Abel Ferrara's *Body Snatchers*

Jay McRoy

> 'They're here already!
>
> *Invasion of the Body Snatchers* (1956)

> 'They're all part of it, all of them!'
>
> *Invasion of the Body Snatchers* (1978)

> 'Where're you gonna' go? Where you gonna' hide? Because there's nobody like you left ...'
>
> *Body Snatchers* (1993)

Approximately one-third of the way through Abel Ferrara's 1993 film, *Body Snatchers*, army doctor Major Collins (Forest Whitaker), concerned about a recent influx of patients, questions EPA (Environmental Protection Agency) representative Steve Malone (Terry Kinney) about the toxicity of chemicals stored on the military base at which he is stationed:

> Can they interfere with chemoneurological processes? Can they foster psychosis, paranoias, narcophobias? ... Simply, can they alter a person's view of reality ... I'm seeing people at the infirmary who are exhibiting extreme delusional fixations. People afraid to sleep. People afraid to deal with family members. Afraid of family members. Exhibiting paranoia about others, about other people's identities. People afraid of themselves. All of a sudden I've got a camp full of very displaced people.

The use of the term 'displaced' is particularly noteworthy here, because corporeal, historical, economic, and narrative displacement are central themes in Ferrara's re-imaging of the 'Body Snatcher' motif. However, unlike Don Siegel's and Philip

Kaufman's *Invasion of the Body Snatchers* (1956 and 1978 respectively), in which the 'invasion' of the films' titles functions simultaneously as a patriotic call to arms against the looming 'menace' of communism *and* as a critique of conformity (McCarthyist or New Age), Ferrara's *Body Snatchers* takes place in a post-Desert Storm, late industrial US landscape very much removed, at least on its glossy transformational surface, from the strict 'us' versus 'them'motif. In fact, in a cultural landscape defined by economies of modulation in which, as Brian Massumi suggests, 'every boundary is present everywhere potentially' and where there are only fields of 'exteriority, a network of more or less regulated passages across thresholds' (Massumi, 1993: 27), Ferrara's *Body Snatchers* no longer requires the term 'invasion' in its title. The 'horrors' in this text are dispersed and multiple, and the greatest moments of dread in the narrative arise not so much from the fear of what one might become as from the process of *becoming* itself. These instances of corporeal transformation and ontological anarchy link the fluidity of late capitalist socio-economics with alternative (and often 'dangerous') matrices of desire and power, revealing a myriad of post-humanist, and specifically post-Desert Storm, cultural anxieties. In the end, however, *Body Snatchers* recuperates, albeit tenuously, a modernist politics of cohesion. As the film's teenage heroine and narrator, Marti Malone (Gabrielle Anwar), asserts while the helicopter in which she is riding destroys a convoy of supposedly pod-laden military transport vehicles, 'In the end, it had to happen ... our reaction was only human.'

Produced during the forty-plus years of capitalist panic known as the Cold War,[1] both Siegel's and Kaufman's cinematic interpretations of Jack Finney's novel, *The Body Snatchers* (1955), reflect a cultural preoccupation with the corporeal and ideological integrity of the American social and economic body. Furthermore, both texts have been the focus of numerous critical studies,[2] with Siegel's film receiving the most attention from film and cultural studies scholars. Given the climate of anti-communist paranoia into which his text was released (a political dis-ease to which the Hollywood film community was far from immune), it is not surprising that Siegel's *Invasion of the Body Snatchers*, like Kaufman's re-make, has been understood as participating in a tradition of alien invasion narratives that posit extra-terrestrial invaders, with their anti-individualist inclination towards the formation of aggregate collectives,[3] as a threat to the 'American' way of life. As Adam Roberts states in his sweeping, predominantly historical investigation of science fiction:

> During the latter 1950's, American society was convulsed with a paranoid campaign against communism, led by Joseph McCarthy: people were publicly condemned for not embracing 'American values' with enough zeal. McCarthy believed that agents of the old Soviet Union were åinfiltrating American society, and turning, as he saw it, 'good' American citizens into secret 'evil' communists. This climate of political paranoia, with its fearful conformity and obsessive focusing on the Alien as Enemy, fed directly through into SF [Science Fiction] imaginations. (Roberts, 2000: 79–80)

This sentiment is echoed by James Combs who, in his essay, 'From the Great War to the Gulf War: Popular Entertainment and the Legitimation of Warfare', argues that throughout the Cold War, the Pentagon and Hollywood maintained a relationship predominantly characterised by a climate of 'stable ... cooperation.' Indeed, he contends, the US military was 'able to count on ... [Hollywood] to say and image the right thing on screen' (Combs, 1993: 70). This is not to suggest that Cold War science fiction and horror films provide a platform for 'the wholesale anti-communist demonization of the Soviet Union' (Hendershot, 2001: 246). Indeed, some Cold War science fiction films, like *The Day the Earth Stood Still* (Robert Wise: 1951) and *Close Encounters of the Third Kind* (Steven Spielberg: 1977), advocate a more tolerant politics of acceptance and integration. Other works, as Cyndy Hendershot demonstrates in her essay, 'Anti-Communism and Ambivalence in *Red Planet Mars*, *Invasion USA*, and *The Beast of Yucca Flats*', are less specific in their anti-communist agendas, targeting 'American weakness and decadence in the social disasters they imagine' (Hendershot, 2001: 246). Nevertheless, it is undeniable that anti-communist rhetoric, with its paranoiac, and frequently hyperbolic, discourse of invasion found a familiar and, at times, willing host within the body of genres like science fiction and horror, particularly in speculative, if not outright spectacular, narratives.

Alien invasion tales like *Earth vs. the Flying Saucers* (Fred Sears: 1956), *Invaders from Mars* (William Cameron Menzies: 1953), *The Blob* (Irvin S. Yeaworth: 1958) and *War of the Worlds*

(Byron Haskin: 1953) likewise contribute to this cinematic tradition, but it is motion pictures like Siegel's *Invasion of the Body Snatchers*,[4] with its 'human-seeming monsters' (Benshoff, 1997: 128), that are particularly effective at creating dread through the collapsing of the illusion of 'self' vs. 'other'. Given the invaders' ability to hide in plain sight, anybody may be an alien. Furthermore, everybody is susceptible to invasion, and once the 'pods' have established a presence within a given locale, whether it be a non-descript Los Angeles suburb in the Siegel's 1956 version or the 'New Age' San Francisco of Kaufman's 1978 rendition, they spread 'like a virus' (Benshoff, 1997: 128), replacing entire families and communities in a fantastical realisation of the 'domino effect' theory mobilised as a means of justifying increases in military spending and the continued presence of US forces in so-called 'international hot spots'. To be 'human' in these films is to uphold the standards and traditions of Western capitalist culture, maintaining hierarchical structures and performing conventional gendered roles. Ironically, 'human' identity in these films is exposed not as a significant force against which alien forces must struggle, but rather as a fragile construction in need of policing through an almost perpetual culture of surveillance. Indeed, in all three cinematic interpretations of Finney's novel, 'invasion' occurs when one is not fully conscious. As James Twitchell notes, it is while slumbering that humans are particularly vulnerable; 'to be in a state of sleep is', he argues, 'to surrender one's identity' (Twitchell, 1985: 5).[5]

To claim that the 1956 and 1978 versions of *Invasion of the Body Snatchers* are exclusively conservative narratives, however, would be reductive. Critics from Harry Benshoff to Stephen King[6] have understood these films as illustrative of both a fear of 'mindless U. S. conformity and communist infiltration' (Benshoff, 1997: 128). In other words, they function simultaneously as critiques of the threat(s) to, and the dangers of, capitalist culture. Additionally, critics of these films have read these 'invasion' narratives as hyper-allegorical works that engage, as Marty Roth suggests, 'the entire range of modernism' (Roth, 2000: 109), from the zombifying momentum of consumer culture and the correlation of monstrous embodiment with disease and biological contamination, to the alien form as emblematic of apocalyptic annihilation or variably resistant to the medical and psychiatric community's panoptic gaze. Thus, while it is possible to read the Siegel's and Kaufman's *Invasion of the Body Snatchers* as reactionary tales that reify traditional capitalist master-narratives, one can also recognise their roles as 'left-wing liberal satire[s]' of right-wing conformity (Hendershot, 2001: 80). As Roth (following Andrew Sarris) notes, Kaufman's 1978 film version of the 'Body Snatcher' motif engages a culture preoccupied with alternative lifestyles, pornography, anti-choice activism, self-help seminars, and other modes of cultural and environmental cross-'contamination' (Roth, 2000: 111; Sarris, 1978: 46). Indeed, one may read Kaufman's 1978 film as a work interrogating late 1970s culture as a social and political landscape ripe for the seeds (or pods) of 'un-American' activities, as well as a potentially progressive lifestyle endangered by the encroachment of conservative ideals. From the film's earliest scenes, in which Elizabeth Driscoll (Brooke Adams) finds an underdeveloped pod that she believes to be a '*grex*' – a 'completely unique' and extremely durable floral life form created when two different species cross-pollinate – Kaufman advances the notion of late 1970s culture as a kind of ideologically 'devastated ground' ripe for a multiplicity of hybridizations and invasions.

Abel Ferrara's *Body Snatchers* differs from the 1956 and 1978 versions of *Invasion of the Body Snatchers* in that, while the earlier films reproduce 'allegorical readings' that engage virtually 'the entire range of modernism' (Roth, 2000: 109), Ferrara's film interfaces with ranges of postmodernism in its thematics of displacement and in its exploding of the very concept of sociocultural organicity. Its setting is the post-Cold War, post-Desert Storm US, a bastion whose economic structure, as David Harvey reminds us, is far removed from Fordist systems of social and economic organization in its privileging of models informed by logics of flexibility and transformation. The film's action takes place, then, within a cultural landscape in which capitalist disciplinary power functions as a 'constantly revolutionary force' that perpetually reshapes itself while its underlying logic of accumulation, with its tendency towards crises, continues to exist. Operating discursively throughout Western culture, this model informs the socio-political climate in which Ferrara's text emerged, allowing for a multi-faceted critique that addresses cultural anxieties quite distinct from those attended to in the earlier cinematic incarnations of Finney's vision. These concerns evoked by Ferrara's film advance the theme of displacement that runs through all three 'Body Snatcher' narratives. As we shall soon discover, however, Ferrara reveals a cultural plasticity distinct to contemporary modes of socio-political organisation.

From its opening moments, *Body Snatchers*' narrative, coupled by Ferrara's careful direction, is purposefully ambiguous and provisional. We are never fully certain, for instance, if the uncanny events taking place throughout the world of the film are the result of an alien invasion, or paranoid hallucinations brought about by the military's complicity in the improper disposal of toxic waste. Thus, unlike Siegel's and Kaufman's film versions, in which the pod invasion narrative steadily assumes dominance, Ferarra's film resists defending or discounting a single dominant scenario. Consequently, *Body Snatchers* frustrates audience attempts to arrive at an absolute explanation for the events on the screen. Contrasting hypotheses as to the possible causes of the strange events in the film follow close upon one another, and although a thematics of environmental contamination and paranoia can be read into the 1956 and 1978 adaptations of Finney's novel, no solitary or thoroughly convincing explanation for the events in Ferrara's film emerges. Rather, viewers are left with multiple explanations that contradict, compliment, and erase one another. In other words, contrary to J. Hoberman's contention that the ecologically charged, toxic waste story line is a 'red herring' (Hoberman, 1994: 31), Ferrara's film is a narrative hatchery in which attempts at determining an absolute 'truth' behind the 'invasion' are subverted and stymied at every turn.[7] Even the film's opening title sequence negates the possibility of a stabilised narrative. Unlike the beginning of Kaufman's film, in which the audience witnesses the pods escaping their dying planet and being transported to earth via solar winds, the opening of Ferrara's film disallows any stable signifiers upon which viewers may anchor their gaze. Indeed, given the often contradictory and self-effacing explanations that soon emerge during Ferrara's *Body Snatchers*, the orange, nebulous mist drifting slowly across a star-filled screen during *Body Snatchers*' title sequence can be read in two ways. First, the mist can be understood as extraterrestrial in origin. Optically transposed over a field of stars, the orange mist may be comprised of the spores from which the initial pods develop. Or, given the contesting hypothesis that develops throughout the earlier stages of the film, one may interpret the mist as a visual representation of some vague 'airborne toxic event', to borrow the media catch-phrase from Don Delillo's novel of postmodern paranoia, *White Noise*. We can, in other words, read the mist as an alien life form or as a chemical or biological agent that literally infects those unlucky enough to encounter the military base or the soldiers stationed there, and that figuratively contaminates the audience's understanding of what we see and hear. Consequently, Ferrara's film displaces and contaminates its audience's expectations from the start.

Ferrara's intentionally oblique approach to *Body Snatchers*' diegesis positions the film as not simply a curious genre exercise, but also as a film that challenges the very practice of film spectatorship. Such a move is by no means anomalous to Ferrara's oeuvre. *King of New York* (1990) and *Bad Lieutenant* (1992) are complicated crime films that demand nuanced considerations of the works' eponymous anti-heroes. Similarly, Ferrara's subsequent films continue his interest in genre deconstruction. *The Addiction* (1995) re-invents the vampire film through philosophically-charged dialogues that daringly challenge audience complicity in the violence they elect to view and re-view, while *New Rose Hotel* (1998) adapts a short story by cyberpunk author William Gibson into a film that elides depictions of conventional science fiction conceits in favour of an interrogation of both 'seeing' and 'memory' as multi-layered subjective phenomena. As such, although Ferrara scholar Nick Johnstone dismisses *Body Snatchers* as a 'poorly thought out' example of 'big-budget crap' (Johnstone, 1999: 160) and faults the work's lack of clear-cut, if over-determined metaphors to which viewers may cling, Ferrara's film might be better comprehended as a vital contribution to the science fiction and horror genres, as well as an aesthetically vital moment of divergence in his filmmaking career. What Johnstone describes as a destructive strain of narrative ambiguity that leaves Ferrara wandering 'aimlessly in search of meaning' (160) might ultimately evidence Ferrara's development of a serious director concerned with expansive, rather than obvious and pointed, critiques. In this sense, it marks a profound meta-filmic engagement with the very grammar and syntax of cinema itself. In other words, the ambiguity Johnstone decries in *Body Snatchers* is one of the work's most interesting components and major themes.

Ferrara's selection of a US military base as the film's primary setting certainly seems designed to push his adaptation of the 'Body Snatcher' motif in important directions. A self-contained community complete with its own day care centre, the location of so much of our culture's 'basic training', the military base is an intriguing and ironic locale at which to stage a film about invasion. 'Military' is, after all, hardly antonymous with 'invasion' or 'conformity', a point perhaps never more painfully felt in our post-9/11 world. Additionally, if one elects to view the film as an 'invasion' scenario in which the pods aim to create a uniform societal collective, a selection of a military base setting is a curious one. It is, after all, a location far more renowned for discipline and order than the rural small town of Siegel's film and the urban San Francisco in which Kaufman set his remake. Hence, the military base setting functions on several levels. Plot-wise (and, remember, the film's narrative stability remains contingent at best), the pods' immediate intention would certainly be harder to detect, enabling the extraterrestrial life forms to get a solid foothold and providing an effective allegorical critique of the US military and other repressive social and ideological apparatuses. However, despite increasing suspicion that all may not be right at this military establishment, the military's chain of command remains firmly intact. Despite the base's non-commissioned residents' apparent complicity, the commander is still quite obviously the individual in command, barking orders as he directs supposedly pod-filled trucks to other military bases.

Furthermore, given the post-Cold War and post-Desert Storm social and political climate during which Ferrara's film emerged, the choice of a military base is also exceedingly appropriate for other reasons. Rather than being mobilised to stop the invasion, as was the case in the 1956 version, the military in Ferrara's film can be viewed, on one level, as seemingly facilitating the distribution of the pods; this is, of course, if one adopts to privilege the 'invasion' scenario. Such a gesture evokes comparisons to Kaufman's more conservative 1978 film version, in which the conspiracy theorist (played by Jeff Goldblum) fears that the government may not be able to stop the invasion, especially if they have already been replaced by the pods. Additionally, given the post-Desert Storm climate into which the film was released, the possibility of government involvement in an ambiguous invasion certainly raises questions as to the extent to which the US military acts in the 'best interests' of the US populace. At the very least, the military in Ferrara's film might be responsible for a toxic spill affecting the physical and mental health its own troops. The EPA representative in the film has, after all, been commissioned to search for dangerous chemicals, a task that is met with some resistance by the base commander and with anxious curiosity, as the quote in this chapter's first paragraph illustrates, by the military base's top physician. Indeed, if one reads the film's spectacular events as hallucinations resulting from chemical exposure, then scenes of leaking barrels and soldiers working knee-deep in eerily phosphorescent swamps assume even greater thematic importance, further exploiting the film's narrative variability through a disavowal of a single, unequivocal reading of the movie's plot.

What's more, such scenes have distinct political overtones, especially given the emergence in the early 1990s of Gulf War Syndrome, an ambiguous ailment characterised by a multiplicity of seemingly unrelated symptoms and without, according to historian Steve Yetiv, a single identifiable cause 'such as war-time exposure to biological or chemical weapons' (Yetiv, 1997: 188). These metaphorical implications increase when one considers that, as a contagion, Gulf War Syndrome is 'comparable to AIDS' (Miller, 1996: 108), a parallel that may in fact be a bit of an understatement given that some scientists feel that Gulf War Syndrome may be passed through 'sweat' or through that most amorphous of substances, 'the air' (108). Thus, understanding the film's action as, at least in part, a metaphor for the dangers of Gulf War Syndrome reveals cultural and political anxieties over corporeal integrity in an increasingly fluid and variable political and cultural landscape. Lacking a stable origin and capable of a plurality of manifestations, Gulf War Syndrome mirrors popular constructions of the post-Desert Storm political arena. Namely, it resembles a cultural paradigm in which threats to personal and national security are increasingly depicted as coming not from established nation-states, but rather from re-configurable pockets of localised, if ultimately non-locatable, resistance. Here, too, Ferrara's film seems eerily prescient, resonating with contemporary audiences all-too-familiar with the US military's latest assault on human rights: the so-called 'war on terror'.

In a post-Cold War culture without a seemingly antithetical adversary against which to easily define one's cultural ideology, a substantial portion of the allegorical momentum that drove the earlier films, namely the threat of a perceived communist menace, is absent, replaced by a plurality of new cultural anxieties. Thus, rather than positing the illusion of a discrete 'enemy', displacement and contingency are revealed as the operant modes of existence. Matrices of desire and power are revealed as conditional; the locus of fear and dread is diffusive. In short, *Body Snatchers* exposes the artificiality of the ideological and ontological boundaries that imprison as effectively as they 'protect'. Ferrara demonstrates how, in Brian Massumi's words, 'any bounded space … simply does not exist as an effectively self-enclosed, self-identical entity' (Massumi, 1993: 27). *Body Snatchers* illuminates '"bounded" social spaces' as merely 'fields of variation'. Of course, when the boundaries move, the '(im)balance of power moves with them' (27). The enemy is not 'out there', the film suggests, nor was it ever; 'Once again, "we" are it [the enemy]' (26).

Given Ferrara's revelation of the social and cultural logics at work in US millennial culture, it is only fitting that the most pronounced moments of cinematic horror in *Body Snatchers* arise not from the fear of what one may become, but from the very act of *becoming* – the process of transformation. This is not to say that in the earlier film versions the prospect of being 'body snatched' did not elicit dread or fear from the audience. The image of indeterminate physiologies, of bodies not quite fully formed and, thus, abject or monstrous in their *not quite doneness*, appear in both the 1956 and 1978 versions. Kaufman's adaptation is particularly graphic in this regard. Thin, web-like tendrils cover mucous-coated bodies; heads readily split open like overripe melons when struck with the blade of a shovel. However, Ferrara's *Body Snatchers*, more than the previous translations of Finney's novel, revels in ambiguity and the spectacle of the body in transition. In this sense, it participates in the body horror tradition best represented in the films of Clive Barker and David Cronenberg.[8]

Put simply, Ferrara's *Body Snatchers* is about the terror of bodies in transition, be these forms political (a post-Cold War US military), social (the Malone family is in transit, seemingly moving from one southern military installation to another), or familial (the Malone family, though conforming to traditional gender roles, are hardly the ideal nuclear family the 1956 film celebrates and whose loss the 1978 film bemoans). Furthermore, Ferrara deploys representations of transitional bodies in ways that both exceed and contain any humanist underpinnings spectators may discern within the narrative. In particular, Ferrara films the 'snatching' process as at once transgressive and recuperative, simultaneously seductive and repellent. Consider, for instance, the film's two most memorable 'snatching' sequences, both involving Marti, the film's teenage heroine. In each scene she is nude, a state that, coupled with the defenselessness implied by sleep, amplifies her vulnerability. In the 1978 film version, the female lead is also shown nude, but Ferrara's camera positions his audience in a more overtly voyeuristic role than Kaufman's. In scenes strategically lit and choreographed to maximise their potential to horrify and tantalise, Marti's 'imperiled' body is twice overtly eroticised and conspicuously construed as monstrous. In each scene, Ferrara's camera lingers as multiple translucent tendrils the size and consistency of spaghetti penetrate multiple orifices, translating Marti's corporeal specificity for her rapidly developing pod-body. This scene's power resides within conceptualisations of the human body, with its multiple openings and crevices, as a site for a myriad of potential penetrations, and this erotic and/or horrifying focus on corporeal invasion and permeability further distances Ferrara's vision from Siegel's or Kaufman's. It acknowledges the tenuousness of corporeal and, by extension, social identity. No body is safe; everything is open to legislation. Nothing is what it seems on the surface – not the military chain of command that regulates domestic and foreign policy; not the 'family unit'; not 'human' identity; and certainly not the narrative itself – whichever narrative one chooses to follow.

The confrontation between a consolidated 'human' body and a potentially 'alien' body-in-flux plays a substantial role in all three films, although these confrontations are much more graphic and explicit in the 1978 (Kaufman) and 1994 (Ferrara) versions. However, the confrontations between the 'fully human' and the bodies in a state of becoming also differ substantially in tone. Far more screen time is devoted to 'gazing' at these transforming physiques in the Kaufman and Ferrara adaptations. In addition, although the transforming bodies are far more gruesome in these incarnations, examining the reactions of the 'normal' characters to these bodies-in-progress exposes subtle, but important, changes in the connotations of these monstrous becomings. In the 1978 film, characters recoil far more violently than their counterparts in the 1956 version. One-upping Kevin McCarthy's momentary pitchfork frenzy, Donald Sutherland smashes his pod-double's head with a shovel, a scene that is by far the goriest moment in either of the first two films.

In Ferrara's *Body Snatchers*, the confrontation between consolidated and indiscrete bodies is even more immediate and visceral. One can even posit that the conflict, with its ideological underpinnings, is literalised through physical interactions that differ radically from the 1956 and 1978 versions' scenes of piercing or bashing of a prone and motionless pod with the tines of a pitchfork or the blade of a shovel. In *Body Snatchers*, these 'monstrous' becomings grab at your ankles, wrestle with you in the bathtub, and even attempt to seduce you with their 'sexuality'. This last strategy is one that differs significantly from earlier representations of the pod-bodies as members of a new species decidedly marked, through their lack of 'proper emotional responses', as non-'human' and, worse, non-'American'. In Ferrara's adaptation, monstrous becomings have an erotic potential absent from earlier cinematic incarnations of Finney's novel. While on a cot in the base's infirmary, Marti's pod-double raises chest-first and then reclines seductively, beckoning seductively to Tim (Billy Wirth), Marti's love interest. Such behaviour reveals, if only temporarily, the erotic possibilities of monstrosity. It advances the notion that, in addition to provoking fear, monstrous embodiment likewise possesses the capacity to 'produce astonishment and wonder' (White, 1995: 244). As Eric White notes in his explorations of the intersections between evolutionary theory and monstrous becomings in science fiction literature and film, monsters are liminal physiognomies that 'transgress the ontological categories and distinctions upon which the construction of a comprehensive and lasting representation of reality depends' (244). As a result, they can 'recall the libidinal economy of unconditional expenditure that Bataille thought he detected in potlatch rituals, or Artaud's body-without-organs'

(265). In other words, because monstrous bodies confound a myriad of traditional humanist ideologies, including those that circumscribe understandings of what it means to be 'human', they have the potential to uncover alternative economies of identity and desire.

Thus, the becoming-Marti that rises seductively from the cot advances the theme of displacement that permeates and informs Ferrara's film. However, it also occupies a precarious position, exhibiting behaviours that, while depicted as physically appealing (in the presence of the becoming-Marti's naked form, Tim pauses conspicuously before reacting), are ultimately posited as horrific. In particular, the film posits the becoming-Marti's erotic initiative – its *desire* – as threatening to Tim's corporeal and ideological integrity. As such, the becoming-Marti represents a sexual, and by extension, political economy of identity that is not sanctioned by conventional notions of gendered, 'human' behavior. One can further posit that it is, at least in part, the notion of female initiated sex without the 'proper' emotional or social context or intent (its *duplicity*) that is coded as monstrous. These attitudes lead Marti's military beau to save her human life by violently pulling the pod's lengthy tendrils out of her various orifices, an action that evokes an ambiguously orgasmic-yet-pained response from the becoming-Marti. Such a representation of sexuality (especially, but no means exclusively, *female sexuality*) as dangerous certainly links Ferrara's film with what many critics have read as the reactionary, patriarchal, pro-monogamy tenor of Siegel's and Kaufman's *Invasion of the Body Snatchers*. Both this scene and the earlier scene in which Marti's stepmother attempts to induce sleep by rubbing oil into her husband's back call to mind the critique of liberal 1970s San Francisco that has been read into Kaufman's film, as well as the numerous sexist attitudes blatantly present in Siegel's interpretation.[9]

Thus, while addressing a myriad of post-Cold War anxieties and, at times, revealing the very constructed-ness of narratives that allow for the circulation of disciplinary power in Western culture, Ferrara's *Body Snatchers* falls short of being a truly progressive horror text. In other words, the posthuman bodies in Ferrara's text fail to dismantle permanently 'the hegemony of culture and stereotype' and, thus, disallow for 'the development and availability of liberatory constructs and discursive practices that lead to freedom' (Mossman, 2001: para 31). In the end, whether we comprehend the invasion in Ferrara's *Body Snatchers* as real within the film's diegesis, or as the result of a chemically-induced hallucination, the film's conclusion prohibits the possibility of positing a political agenda that does not recuperate as much as it challenges. The corporeal and ideological integrity of a consolidated, 'human' body escapes pretty much intact; the status quo remains battered and bloody, but ultimately unbowed. In the end, the pods must be destroyed, even if it means obliterating the last shreds of that imaginary tapestry known as the traditional nuclear family. As Marti Malone states in the voiceover accompanying the images of a helicopter destroying military installations and troop transport vehicles with smart bomb accuracy: 'In the end it had to happen ... our reaction was only human.'

In their increasingly spectacular representation of the narrative, social, familial and corporeal body in flux, Siegel, Kaufman, and Ferrara's adaptations of Jack Finney's *The Body Snatchers* engage historically-specific cultures in transition. Just as the US has moved from a rigid 'us' vs. 'them' Cold War model of social and economic organisation to a post-Cold War political and economic structure that is, on the surface at least, flexible and transformational, one can trace certain changes and continuities throughout the three 'body snatcher' films. Always narratives of dis- and replacement, the locus of fear and dread in these films likewise becomes increasingly variable. Unlike Siegel's and, to a lesser extent, Kaufman's relatively straightforward allegorical narratives, in which the invading pods could be understood as either a metaphor for the danger of leftist politics or a parody of right-wing conformity, Ferrara's *Body Snatchers* is a work in which narrative instability paves the way for a complex exploration of a very different 'invasion', an invasion in which conspiracies are everywhere and in which the enemy was more than likely never 'out there' in the first place.

Part III

From avant-garde to exploitation: cinematic experiments as monstrous adaptation

Adapting the occult: horror and the avant-garde in the cinema of and Ken Jacobs

Marianne Shaneen

> Cinema consists of the eye for magic – that which perceives and reveals the marvelous in whatsoever it looks upon.
>
> Maya Deren

Haunted origins

Cinema has always been in league with the sorcerer's art. Magic, animism and the occult haunt its inception and history. In raising the dead and conjuring seeming materiality out of immaterial light and shadow, filmmaking resembles necromancy. Even the material substance of film itself is permeated with death; Kodak annually buys and processes eighty million pounds of bovine skeleton from slaughterhouses to make its emulsional gel. In other words, cinema enacts animal sacrifice to perpetuate the life of the image.

Indeed, *all* film is horror film.

American avant-garde filmmakers from Maya Deren to Harry Smith have followed this spectral path, illuminated by magic lanterns, Phantasmagoria spectacles and the magic of Georges Méliès. For Stan Brakhage, light, or *lumen*, held the status of a supernatural force. The last word in Brakhage's seminal book *Metaphors on Vision* (1976) is 'magic'; for Kenneth Anger, a disciple of and strongly influenced by Aleister Crowley, making film was the equivalent of 'casting a spell' (Rowe, 1974: 24–33). Through the avant-garde exploration of film's formal, non-narrative possibilities, avant-garde filmmakers revealed cinema as a numinous medium, a liminal conduit flickering between the realms of the living, the dead and the undead.

This chapter examines how contemporary experimental filmmaker Ken Jacobs adapts this legacy of magic. By formal, materialist means, Jacobs divines cinema's occult realms, exploding narrative, representation, and standard projection techniques in revolutionary ways. His astonishing spectral eruptions immerse the viewer in the enigmatic nature of perception and the haunting ineffability of materiality.

At first glance, Jacobs' work might seem a bit out of place in the context of the horror genre. However, adapting the interpretive framework of the horror film to experimental film can be very illuminating. Jacobs' filmmaking method is one of extraordinarily innovative adaptation, as demonstrated in his early film *Tom Tom the Piper's Son* (1969–71), and in his more recent 'Nervous System' and 'Nervous Magic Lantern' performances. In these efforts, Jacobs adapts the 'primitive' methods of proto- and early cinema to create unique projection apparatuses. In the process, he adapts easily recognisable images from early cinema to generate abstract visions that optically, physically, and psychically haunt and disturb.

Magic's ghost has persistently clung to the body of technology throughout the ages, as the history of film demonstrates. According to Harry Smith, the heretical Renaissance philosopher of occult sciences, Giordano Bruno, was 'the inventor of cinema' (quoted in Sitney, 1978: 235). Indeed, within the late medieval/early Renaissance cauldron, innovations in science, natural magic and optics bubbled along with alchemy, hermeticism and belief in the supernatural. It was here that proto-cinematic technologies, such as the magic lantern, came into being. Thus, cinema's origins are steeped in sorcery. Images produced by the magic lantern (or the 'Sorcerer's Lamp') were often believed to spawn from black magic and witchcraft. Macabre spectres, demons, and skeletons routinely flickered from what came to be known as the 'Lantern of Fear'. In the 1780s, the French polymath Etienne-Gaspard Robert (aka Robertson) experimented with innovative magic lantern techniques, producing the first large-scale public Phantasmagoria performances. These spectacles were wildly popular, until eventually superseded by the Cinematographe and the Vitascope motion picture camera. In spectacles of flamboyant necromancy, Robertson staged projections in dark crypts and other eerie environments, and engineered diabolical visitations from ghostly luminaries killed in the Great Terror following the French Revolution. Thus, projected images and the phantoms of death were inextricably linked in cinema's subconscious.

Embodiments of late nineteenth- and early twentieth-century magical ethos, Aleister Crowley, Georges Méliès and Sigmund Freud, were all in their thirties when Edison's Vitascope and the Lumière brothers' Cinematographe were first demonstrated publicly. Crowley's ritualistic, sympathetic magic was akin to the kinds of supernatural beliefs infusing Victorian Spiritualism, whilst Méliès' 'trick films', directly informed by his experience as a stage magician, recalled the 'natural magic' of the Renaissance, with effects resulting from natural, rather than supernatural, phenomena. Similarly, Freud's psychoanalytic theories evince the 'magic' of modernity, as the irrational world of symbolic affinities and hidden influences were decreasingly thought of as 'magical' and became increasingly subsumed under the psychological, the irrational, and the subconscious (Castle, 1995).

Cinema's very mechanisms, namely the motion picture camera and projector, played a key role in these transformations of consciousness, as they magically produced and populated the world with doubles. At the same time, the psychoanalyst Otto Rank's theories of the doppelgänger were influencing Freud's formulation of the uncanny. For Rank, the concept of the immortal soul as it arose in primitive cultures was the earliest appearance of 'the double', and its original function was an 'energetic denial of the power of death' (Rank, 1958: 66). For modern 'over-civilized' man, however, the double becomes symbolically inverted. Instead of displaying the desire for eternal life, the double as a recurring modern literary motif frequently assumes a terrifying form, functioning as 'a symbol of death', 'the announcer of death itself' (Rank, 1958: 66). Rank attributes this absolute reversal to 'a fundamental change ... from a naive belief in supernatural forces which (man) was certain could be influenced by magic, to a "neurotic" fear of them, which he had to rationalize psychologically' (Rank, 1958: 66).

Monstrous resurrections: Ken Jacobs' *Tom Tom the Piper's Son*

Enter Ken Jacobs. Instead of repressing the irrational as unworthy products of a rational mind, and rather than turning backwards in a reactionary, uncritical embrace of supernatural explanations for the mysterious, Jacobs formally delves into its material thickets. Ken Jacobs' cinematic conjurings pulsate with film's magical ability to mediate the forces of death and regeneration, as well as film's unique access to the unfathomable terrains of mind and matter. Jacobs demonstrates that life's spectacularly infinite mysteries reside not in the realms of the supernatural, but in material reality.

With his seminal film *Tom Tom the Piper's Son* (1969–1971), Ken Jacobs rescues a 1905 Biograph slapstick movie of the same name from cinematic oblivion. Pioneering the method of rephotography, he re-filmed the original Biograph production frame by frame, altering its speed and direction and often enlarging frames into abstraction. In this way, Jacobs radically adapts the appropriated source material, extending its original ten-minute life into a two-hour revelatory experience. Through formal manipulations, he illuminates the hermetic depths of the original, that otherwise would not be seen. Likewise, by slowing down, freezing and repeating the frames of the Biograph original, Jacobs establishes rhythm as a fundamental structural element, creating non-narrative dramatic tensions between light and shadow. Jacobs completely transforms the figurative body and the human form, as if alchemically dissolving and reconstituting it into its primal elements. At times, Jacobs enlarges various frames to zoom in on, and examine, the patterns of the film grain itself, revealing it as an impalpable whirling force with a secret life of its own.

Thus, Jacobs' *Tom Tom the Piper's Son* exhumes a forgotten film buried in the crypt of cinema's past and then re-animates it, effectively raising the original text from the dead. In doing so, he resurrects a particular moment of cinema history, but he also taps into perhaps the most uncanny of *all* cinema's occult powers: its inherent ability to revive the dead:

> Ghosts! Cine-recordings of the vivacious doings of persons long dead . . . each cold still [frame] . . . stirred to life by a successive . . . pattering on our retinas, the teeming energies elicited . . . to form the always-poignant-because-always-past illusion. (Jacobs, 2002)

Cinema marks the death of the recorded moment; every image is inherently a *memento mori*. Indeed, as Jacobs muses, 'These aren't mere images on a screen. Life took place in front of a camer' (Jacobs, 1997: np). Each frame captures and embalms a non-repeatable moment, and its projection magically re-imbues it with life. Every filmmaker (re)enacts a cycle of death and resurrection, and every darkened cinema shrouds the viewer in Night for an encounter with its Living Dead.

Jacobs screens both the 1905 Biograph version of *Tom Tom the Piper's Son* and his own filmic reimagining together. First, Jacobs shows us the source material, the original ten-minute slapstick film about the antics of a pig thief at a county fair. He then re-presents to us its double – its simulacrum – transmutated into a two-hour extravaganza of wondrous monstrosity. The earlier film's comedic actors appear utterly alien and almost unrecognisable in Jacobs' version. It is as if Jacobs has been let loose in cinema's Anatomy Theatre, opening the seamless surface of the familiar figurative body to reveal the dark material mysteries teeming beneath. Furthermore, his formal adaptations magically dissolve these doubles into endless depths of purely visual information. From a short film reel, Jacobs generates a near-eternity of visual life. While *Tom Tom the Piper's Son* ignites the wondrous pleasure of looking, it also provokes an undeniably disturbing encounter with an ungraspable and terrifying perceptual infinity.

In provoking perceptual horror, the doubles that assail the viewer in Jacobs' *Tom Tom the Piper's Son* function similarly to Rank's and Freud's 'harbinger(s) of death'. However, through Jacobs' 'primitive' means, these transmogrified doubles ultimately serve their original 'primitive' function – the denial of death's power: 'I meant for this work to be alive, above all, alive' (Jacobs, 1999).

His uncanny, unfamiliar doubles act as immaterial intermediaries ushering us back and forth between the stable world of figure and narrative, and the world of dissolved perceptual stability. They reveal their secret double life by guiding us into the depths of spectral variation and disturbing us into new ways of seeing.

In his 1927 essay *Sorcery and the Cinema*, Antonin Artaud proposes that film is inherently imbued with occult powers:

> In the cinema I have always distinguished a quality wholly peculiar to the secret movement and material of images ... even the ... most banal image is transformed on the screen. The smallest detail ... takes on a meaning and a life which is theirs alone, aside from the meaning of the images themselves ... which becomes increasingly independent and detaches them from their ordinary sense ... a leaf, a bottle, are imbued with a quasi-animal life which begs to be used. (Artaud, 1988: 49)

Artaud here illuminates film's uniquely 'inscrutable and mysterious' quality, that the projected cinematic image *itself* is infused with life of its own.

In a magical universe a mundane object can be imbued with extraordinary attributes, rendering it a fetish object used to assert influence over one's environment. Similarly, the moving projected image can be used fetishistically. The film image as a cipher possesses both wondrous and terrifying power, which can be potentially devastating. This is particularly so – as Walter Benjamin claimed and Leni Riefenstahl demonstrated – when transferred to the realm of politics and the perpetuation of dehumanising ideologies.

While Jacobs appeals to cinema's origins in magic, he does so with a critique of the deeply problematic ritual dimension of film, as illustrated when Harry Kreisler, in an interview, referred to Jacobs as a 'worshipper' of film, and then checked himself, asking Jacobs:

> INTERVIEWER KREISLER: 'Worshipper' ... I worried about that word, is it okay?
> JACOBS: No. I have many, many mixed feelings about it, including root fear. I think it's very, very powerful. Very dangerous.
> INTERVIEWER KREISLER: Film?
> JACOBS: Film, yes. Cinema. Essentially it's a way of thinking and it's a way of conducting the mind. So it can be very dangerous. (Jacobs, 1999)

Many critics have examined the quasi-religious/ritualistic aspect of film spectatorship: strangers gather together in a sanctioned, darkened space; a film projector's beams emit spiritual light in a modernist evocation of altar candles and ceremonial or sacrificial flames. Viewers experience immaterial 'visions', silently surrendering ourselves to immortal, almost god-like beings. In the cinema, we *believe*.

Progressive monstrosities: Jacobs' 'Magic Lanterns'

Cinema emerged in the late nineteenth century, accompanying capitalism's monstrous progeny: alienated production and the fetishised commodity. These spectres still haunt our 'rational' notions of progress in the twenty-first century. Ideological constructs informed by economic power relations buttress Hollywood's perpetuation of idol worship and conventional storytelling devices. The seductive power of the projected image reinforces perceptual patterns of cause and effect, heroic individuality, narrative resolutions, linear time, historical progression, the privileged position of the omniscient viewer and a 24 frames-per-second understanding of reality. As Benjamin prophesised, such power could be used and misused. Film, Benjamin posited, has the unique ability to show the masses their historical situation; a 'simultaneous collective experience' (Benjamin, 1968: 231), film thus has immense revolutionary potential.

For Walter Benjamin, the mechanical reproducibility of the film image strips it of its 'aura', rendering it unique among the arts in its lack of a ritualistic cult function, thus giving it enormous revolutionary potential. For Benjamin, to define film's extraordinary capabilities in ritualistic or supernatural terms, was reactionary.

This potential, however, can be hidden and undermined by capitalism. The interests of profit and power under capitalism, as under fascism, recuperate the medium's 'shriveling ... aura' (Benjamin, 1968: 231) by suffusing the medium with a new ritual; the embrace of the movie star as cult figure. The film industry uses the film image to cast the 'spell of the personality' which, for Benjamin, is 'the phony spell of the commodity' (231). Further, as the masses seldom control the system of film production under capitalism and fascism, they largely assume the role of the passive spectator. For Benjamin, this relationship has dire consequences: 'The violation of the masses, whom Fascism, with its "Fuhrer" cult, forces to their knees, has its counterpart in the violation of an apparatus which is pressed into the production of ritual values' (231). In cinema's cathedral, the passive image consumer becomes a devout worshipper.

Jacobs' work, like much of the American avant-garde, rages against the commodification of the image and its seemingly passive consumption. With some 'hair of the dog', Jacobs uses the magical properties of cinema to combat its magical power – to dispel the reactionary ritualisation of cinema and the power it wields over its spellbound audience. His works challenge the viewer and demand engagement. Jacobs taps into the occult miasma that clings to cinema, unleashing and reconfiguring the ghost in the machine to engage in mortal combat with alienated perception. In this way, his doubles provide a potent remedy for 'a century of cinema industrialized, standardized, economically determined and "rationalized"' (Jacobs, 2004).

Adapting the lens of the horror genre to Jacobs' 'Nervous Magic Lantern' and 'Nervous System' performances is particularly apt. Here Jacobs channels perhaps the most prescient symbol of the anxieties accompanying the transformations engendered by technologisation: Mary Shelley's Dr Frankenstein of 1818. Jacobs' live performances galvanise the corpses of forgotten footage, infusing them with the electricity to create spectacular cinematic monsters that reveal the human condition as only monsters can. Jacobs' 'Nervous System' performance expands upon his formal adaptations in *Tom Tom the Piper's Son*. Simultaneously running identical prints (films comprised of 'small discarded strands' of archival footage) (Jacobs, 2002) through two projectors, Jacobs manipulates the images by varying their speeds, running them backwards and then forwards, and even freezing on individual frames, thus 'pitting different frames of two prints of the same film against each other' (Jacobs, 2002) so that they move slightly in and out of sync. Jacobs also designed an adjustable shutter in front of the projectors to separate and superimpose the images. A propeller whirs between the projectors to strobe and flicker the images in a complex alternation in which 'the two images don't just vibrate against each other', but

> merge in very, very strange and mysterious ways. It's possible to create continuous movements with these two frames from the same film, one frame out of synch with the other, to merge them and make them do all kinds of things, make them move this way or that way, or up or down. And also, in many cases, to bring them into three dimensions. (Jacobs, 2002)

These subtle manipulations create a spellbinding, confounding and utterly compelling phantasmagoria.

Recalling the works of the early Renaissance magicians of

proto-cinema, many of whom were scientists deploying their optical toys toward the advancement of optics and understanding of vision, Jacobs' 'Nervous System' performances, like Robertson's Phantasmagoria spectacles, produce mesmerising images through formal experiments. What's more, Jacobs' works, as singular performances, recall Robertson's live manipulations of his magic lantern; for both artists, the engagement of the biological with the mechanical is central.

Many of Jacobs' 'Nervous System' performances, such as *Loco Motion* (1996), *Georgetown Loop* (1997) and *Disorient Express* (1995), are generated from some of the earliest footage of the locomotive, perhaps the turn of the nineteenth century's most conspicuous and celebrated symbol of technological transformation. Jacobs' train imagery directly recalls the Lumière brothers' train arriving at the station in La Ciotat, a cinematic moment that, perhaps more than any other, radically changed our understanding of space and time.

Jacobs' 'Nervous System' performances penetrate the depths of the connection between the genesis of film and locomotive technology. Saturated with these ghosts of cinema's earliest days, Jacobs' electrified spectral wonders are infused with a palpable sense of loss, evoking a cosmic dread of irretrievable connection to the past and uneasy millennial forebodings of the future. It is more than 100 years since the original Biograph *Tom Tom the Piper's Son* appeared, and anyone who might have seen it at that time, along with anyone who had any notion of pre-industrialised perception, is no longer alive. The train, once the ultimate symbol of the shock of the new, has now become the very image of the antiquated. As in birth, so in death: the twilight of the train is bound to that of the cinema as the digital sun ascends. One can almost see Benjamin's angel speeding along the rails, facing backwards as he's propelled into the future, in Jacobs' description of his 1996 'Nervous System' performance *Loco Motion*: 'We hurtle along going nowhere fast … with the land we're racing from impossibly gaining on us, overtaking us' (quoted in Schwartz, 1997: np).

Watching – or rather, experiencing – a Jacobs performance leads us into the recesses of our brain's processes of interpreting sensation and making meaning. Our normal perceptual sense-making systems are disrupted, and viewers become unhinged from habitual understandings of depth, figure and ground relations, scale, and temporal markers. Jacobs describes his *Loco Motion* as: 'The classic perspective train tracks gone berserk' (quoted in Schwarz, 1977: np). Living up to the pun in its title, (loco, crazy, motion) his cinematic investigations produce dizzying results. Similarly, Jacobs describes his *Celestial Railway* as creating 'a synaesthetic experience of celestial magnitude ... through immense unstable 3-D vistas ...' (quoted in Schwarz, 1997: np). He asks viewers of his *Disorient Express* to enter a state of expanded consciousness, to 'look for impossible depth inversions, for jewelled splendour, for CAT scans of the brain' (quoted in Schwarz, 1997: np). Familiar landscape scenes shot from passing trains in the first years of the nineteenth century, when relayed through Jacobs' 'Nervous System', produce near-hallucinogenic experiences.

To borrow a metaphor from Victorian fantasy, a 'Nervous System' performance leads the viewer down a bottomless rabbit hole into a bewildering perceptual wonderland where previous understandings of space and time no longer apply. In making film new and strange again, Jacobs harks back to the disorientation Victorians might have felt the first time they rode on a train, listened to a disembodied voice on the telephone, or first viewed 'moving pictures'.

Jacobs' adaptation of this iconic imagery from cinema's infancy releases the spectral energy that infused turn of the century motion picture cameras and projectors, and the attendant supernatural beliefs subsumed in the footage they produced. What was buried under the emulsion of the forgotten/repressed history of filmic representation is brought into the light. Instructional ghouls, vision-inducing angels, and nefarious imps stick their fingers into our grey matter's psychological recesses, wreaking havoc on any comforting grasp of 'reality'.

A 'Nervous System' performance releases a pantheon of monsters from the collective unconscious, as Jacobs, like a postmodern Virgil, leads the audience through an inferno of transubstantiations: the womb, the ocean, ghastly apparitions, demons and angels, lunar landscapes, cosmic eggs, interplanetary space, atomic bombs, the inner machinations of mind itself.

As viewers, our incessant desire to resolve into order is continually confounded as we whirl into seemingly three-dimensional spaces. An image begins to take shape and almost stabilises into a coherent figurative illusion before suddenly breaking into abstract basic visual elements again. In these performances, we enter a disturbing perceptual landscape of continual temporal and spatial displacement. The screen seems to move, rotating as it draws us deeper and deeper into impossible spatial depths until motion itself becomes a living mysterious entity. Tom Gunning beautifully illustrates the sublime horror of this perceptual disequilibrium:

> Jacobs ... calls into question the coherence of our position as viewers and masters of vision. The effect is both exhilarating and frightening. In becoming aware of our role in making the moving image we also realize the power the apparatus has over us. I have never watched a NERVOUS SYSTEM performance without the vertiginous sensation that I was teetering out of control on the brink of some primal threshold. (Gunning, 1989)

In this way the viewer enacts his own Jekyll and Hyde experience. The perceptual capabilities of one's own body, upon which often rests a secure understanding of the self in the world, falter and become alien and monstrous. A Jacobs performance creates a cinematic sensorium in which the viewer experiences sublime horrors of perception. His performances vividly illuminate the seemingly stable delineations of life as immaterial, incomprehensible, and endlessly transforming. Rather than representing perceptual disequilibrium, Jacobs *induces* it in the viewer. In 'primitive' cultures the shaman, the witchdoctor, the magician entered and led others into such altered perceptual states, for the sake of enlightenment or healing; similarly, Jacobs' disorientating effects are essential to his aim of inspiring 'wakefulness, consciousness' in the viewer (Jacobs, 1999).

A Jacobs performance explodes sanitised, standardised cinema by igniting the horrors of the fallible imperfect body; his performative methods present film almost as a living organism , bringing the viewer into contact with the horrors of the nervous system itself, and how its modes of perception can be frighteningly unstable. Indeed, the questions raised in experiencing a Jacobs performance 'can literally be questions of physical imbalance' (Gunning, 1989). Without the usual filters of narrative, dialogue, and characters, images engage the human nervous system with raw immediacy. The pulsing, strobing light directly impacts the viewer's autonomic responses. In the process, the viewer merges with Jacobs' projection apparatus, together forming a kind of cinematic sensory body, an electro-sensory network of pulsating signals. Jacobs' 'Nervous System' performances display a profound awareness of the mind and body's inscrutable matrix. They plug us directly into the infinitely mutable consciousness, allowing a more immediate understanding of how physical-neural apprehension is so intimately linked to emotional and perceptual states.

Jacobs' is a cinema of disequilibrium that explores, explodes and reconfigures the mind's perceptual habits. In these ways, Jacobs' aims invoke Antonin Artaud's radical call for a 'body without organs' (Artaud, 1988: 570–1), a desire to bypass oppressive humanist regimes of 'organic' order that define the body in terms of its mechanically repetitive functions. In their cinematic engagement with the nervous system, Jacobs' 'Nervous System' and 'Nervous Magic Lantern' performances recall Artaud's desire to destroy the body's dependence on its organs until it becomes 'nothing but a fine Nerve Meter' (Artaud, 1988: 79–87). In many ways, Artaud's ideas about cinema anticipate Jacobs' methods. Artaud's rage against the organic and perceptual confines of the body parallels his rage against the narrative confines of cinema. He desired a 'raw cinema' (Artaud, 1988: 150), a film 'with purely visual situations whose drama would come from a shock designed for the eyes' (152). Both Jacobs' and Artaud's aims demand a physical immediacy between image and viewer that would make passive spectatorship impossible. Artaud calls for – and Jacobs creates – an experiential cinema of nervous encounter with the image's purely visual elements, inducing new emotional, physiological, and mental states. In his *Sorcery and the Cinema*, Artaud declares 'order' and 'clarity' to be the 'enemies' of cinema. For Artaud, 'The cinema is essentially the revealer of a whole occult life with which it puts us into direct contact. But we must know how to divine [it] ... To use [cinema] to tell stories ... is to deny its best resources, to go against its most profound goal' (Artaud, 1988: 49) urges filmmakers to channel cinema's magical powers to transform the sensorial landscape, rather than waste it in the service of narrative and representation. For Artaud and Jacobs, when cinema is liberated from these shackles of narrative and representation, it can be used to delve into the drama that exists within matter itself, and in the mind's experience of it. One can easily make the leap from Artaud's words in 1927 to the experience of a Jacobs performance in 2005:

> [There] is ... a kind of physical intoxication which the rotation of the images communicates directly to the brain. The mind is thrilled irrespective of any representation. This visual power in the images searches out in the depths of the mind possibilities as yet unused. (Artaud, 1988: 45)

Similarly, Jacobs strives to really offer the audience a complex way of thinking, a real

> mental ... imaginative exercise ... But an exercise – I hate to use the word, I won't say 'soul' and I won't say 'spirit' – but that can really put our deepest psychological existence through stuff. It can be a powerful exercise ... the mind is not complete yet ... the higher function of art for me is its contribution to the making of mind. (Jacobs, 1999)

Monstrous projections: Jacobs' 'Nervous Magic Lantern' performances

Jacobs' 'Nervous Magic Lantern' apparatus is similar to his 'Nervous System' performances, but it pares the cinematic experience down to even more primitive elements. The 'Nervous Magic Lantern' utilises a single projection device, with almost no moving parts other than a few small fans, a shutter and a busy projectionist. Jacobs creates the spellbinding imagery of his 'Nervous Magic Lantern' performance without a shutter or sprocket wheels and without film. Instead, he manipulates objects through the beam of his projection apparatus. Importantly, Jacobs is not entirely forthcoming about the elements of his 'Nervous Magic Lantern'; like a true stage magician, he doesn't give away all of his secrets.

Jacobs' 'Nervous Magic Lantern' piece, *Mountaineer Spinning* (2005), elicits a nearly indescribable journey into the depths of the perceptual psyche. The only somewhat discernible figurative image is that of a woman's face and upper torso, which suggests that perhaps Jacobs is manipulating an old photograph or postcard through his 'Nervous Magic Lantern'. The woman's face appears in a strobic rhythm of light, a kind of cosmic electric shock treatment that gently pulses her into life, once again evoking the Frankenstein motif. Jacobs' formal machinations create a confoundingly abstract cascade of images, without the comforts of narrative or context, from which the viewers' limpid consciousness ascertains relationships between shapes and spatial elements that seem to be communicating in a language that we cannot understand.

In a slowly enveloping churn of abstraction, the woman's image initially serves as a kind of anchor and reference point. However as everything pulses, morphs and shifts around her, she too dissolves, slowly disappearing into the surrounding miasma. Audiences are drawn into a cavernous landscape, only to find that the woman's image has slowly, almost imperceptibly, re-emerged, subtly (re)establishing a temporary figurative order. This mechanical distortion seems to hint at the psyche's perpetual desire to assign meaning and assert an intractable 'self' over the chaotic terrain of perception. Similarly, the film's title, *Mountaineer Spinning*, evokes the clarity of a mountaineer taking in an unobstructed view of the world below, only to be consumed, once again, by vertigo.

Jacobs' *Mountaineer Spinning* displays several of his characteristic techniques; for example, a mutating image stabilises somewhat – but just as the viewer is almost allowed to get into a comfortable perceptual spot, the entire image frame disconcertingly shifts. We are always kept on precarious perceptual ground. With no attempt to create an illusion of realistic space, Jacobs throws the viewer into an utterly unfamiliar universe. Another signature Jacobs technique is to create the sensation of being led into the depths of the screen, while simultaneously feeling like one is not really getting anywhere. A delirium of metaphors and associations resonate throughout the film's abstract terrain. A recurring motif of rooms and caverns hosts the strangely ominous presence of what might be a bed. What may or may not be the grating of a heating system looks strangely skeletal. Jacobs leads viewers through a secret history of rooms and furniture, into the hidden life of matter.

These manipulations contest the very act of perception. As a result, it is likely that two audience members watching the same Jacobs performance will have radically different experiences.

Without words, characters, or plotline, Jacobs' abstract images nevertheless evoke deep psychological epiphanies. Lacking context, dialogue or narrative, Jacobs' subtle formal manipulations create a spectacularly suspenseful, beautifully haunting and frighteningly disturbing encounter with the nature of the human psyche. Such performances facilitate extended sojourns into the intimate and infinite realms of our own perceptual and psychic landscapes, and beyond. Watching a Jacobs performance, one often feels that one is encountering not only historical time, but cosmic time. One feels a shift from one's individual consciousness to a meta-consciousness. Spectators drift away from a reliance upon the ego as a rational controller of the universe and into great realms of unknowing.

For Jacobs, nothing dispels the 'crazy-making' mysteriousness of how the film image 'taunts us' with its 'seeming presence'; the fundamental 'magic act' of his filmmaking is the utterly confounding possibility of 'making things apparently more real, as we confront their essential existence as imaginary beings' (Jacobs, 2004). Because Jacobs' works hover at the enigmatic boundary between the material and the immaterial, it can be difficult to exorcise the supernatural shades that cling to his material excavations. Indeed, while Jacobs' work produces effects that many describe in mystical metaphysical terms, his art does not align with the cinemagic that so much of the avant-garde has embraced. Consequently, describing Jacobs' cinema as a kind of ritualising of film is problematic and dangerous.

Harry Houdini was another magical contemporary of Crowley, Méliès, Freud, and the birth of the motion picture. Jacobs, however, shares his vehement scorn of Spiritualism as well as his approach to magic. In fact, Jacobs saw himself working within the tradition of directors like Méliès, whose early technical manipulations tricked audiences into literally seeing the impossible. Jacobs leads his audiences through film's flickering surface and into the heart of the matter – the magic is there *in the matter*, and *in its manipulation*. Again we return to Artaud: 'The human skin of things, the epidermis of reality: this is the primary raw material of cinema. Cinema exalts matter and reveals it to us in its profound spirituality' (Artaud, 1988: 49).

Jacobs describes his filmmaking as if portraying a mortal battle and he recalls Houdini as he struggles to free himself, and the viewer, from perceptual confines. He approaches this need to transform consciousness and to challenge the ritualisation of cinema with a revolutionary fervour. In this vein, Jacobs' work can be illuminated by the ideas of Walter Benjamin, who anticipates Jacobs' methods when describing the unique abilities of the movie camera and projector:

> With the close-up, space expands ... The enlargement of a snapshot ... reveals entirely new structural formations of the subject ... slow motion not only presents familiar qualities of movement but reveals in them entirely unknown ones. (Benjamin, 1968: 236–7)

Benjamin's ideas about the occult and the extraordinary characteristics of cinema share a striking kinship with those of Jacobs. Benjamin illustrates how the magic of film is rooted in materiality by comparing painting to cinema. The painter is like a magician (or supernatural healer), and painting and magic are similarly infused with aura and cult status. A filmmaker, on the other hand, is like a surgeon. The surgeon looks at the patient as material, and mechanically cuts into him – and similarly, the cameraman 'penetrates deeply into (reality's) web' (Benjamin, 1968: 233). In this way the filmmaker, like the surgeon, destroys aura and the ritual dimension of artwork- and this has tremendous revolutionary potential.

Benjamin was attracted to the 'exploration of occult ... phantasmagoric gifts and phenomena' (Benjamin, 1986: 177–92); however, he approached them as a materialist, arguing that infusing the magic of film with sacred and supernatural attributes is reactionary (Benjamin, 1986: 232–3).

Benjamin's ideas here perfectly illustrate Jacobs' approach to cinema and magic:

> we penetrate the mystery only to the degree that we recognize it in the everyday world, by virtue of a dialectical optic that perceives the everyday as impenetrable, the impenetrable as everyday. (Benjamin, 1986: 216.)

In adapting film's occult-laden legacy, Jacobs locates the spellbinding mysteries of the 'everyday' within the body's nervous system and the projector's mechanisms, and summons forth cinema's spectres from the ineffable splendour of the here and now.

The Gorgon: adapting classical myth as Gothic romance

I. Q. Hunter

According to its director, Terence Fisher, *The Gorgon* (1964) was not a horror film at all, but a romantic fairy tale and 'frustrated love story' (Ringel, 1975a: 24). Although the film is set in Hammer's usual stylised middle Europe, the Gorgon herself derives not from Gothic literature, like Dracula and Frankenstein's monster, but from classical mythology – unfamiliar imaginative territory for the British studio. Relocating an ancient monster within the paraphernalia of Victorian Gothic, the film was Hammer's most striking experiment in free adaptation before the frankly bizarre transnational genre-fusion of *The Legend of the 7 Golden Vampires* (1974).

The Gorgon was Fisher's first Hammer film since *The Phantom of the Opera* (1962) and his only film about a woman. Significantly, it marked an attempt to invent a new monster at a time when, as the Dracula and Frankenstein films trailed off, Hammer sought to diversify its range for a wider international audience. In the same year as *The Gorgon* the studio ventured into fantasy with *She*, also centred on an imperious and terrifying woman, and in 1966 it began a series of prehistoric exotica with *One Million Years BC*. These films, like *The Mummy* (1959) and its sequels, strayed from Hammer's usual nominally Christian framework into what might be described as archetypal drama, 'the poetry', in Fisher's words, 'of the fantastic, rather than horror' (quoted in Ringel, 1975b: 13). *She* and *The Gorgon* stage encounters with Jungian *anima* figures, while the prehistoric films, extrapolating wildly from Darwinian evolution, offer schematic visions of human origins, reinterpreting stereotypes of the pin-up as archetypes of healthy sex and primitive vitality. Far removed from the banal landscape of 1960s consumerism, these films improvise myths of lost worlds of magic, desire and irrationality, in which women are celebrated as symbols of primordial beauty and terror. Whereas the Dracula films pathologise sex as the repressed erupting into bourgeois normality, *She* and the prehistoric films are nostalgic visions of virile energy, in a period when, as Peter Hutchings notes, Britain was sunk in the unheroic aftermath of war (Hutchings 1993a, 2002). *The Gorgon*, however, has an altogether more uncomfortable and pessimistic tone, more akin to classical tragedy than to the horror genre.

The Gorgon is set in 1910 in the German village of Vandorf, overlooked by Castle Borski, which has been plagued by a series of murders. When his son Bruno dies under mysterious circumstances, Professor Paul Heitz (Michael Goodliffe) sets out to discover the truth. Heitz confronts Dr Namaroff (Peter Cushing), who runs a hospital-asylum with Carla (Barbara Shelley), with whom he is secretly in love. Namaroff rejects Heitz's theory that the killings are the work of a Gorgon whose gaze turns those who see it to stone; frustrated, Heitz contacts Professor Meister (Christopher Lee), but before he arrives Heitz is lured to the castle and turned to stone. Meister discovers that Carla is the Gorgon. He and Namaroff confront her at the castle, where the Gorgon kills Namaroff but Meister, guiding his sword by the Gorgon's reflection in a mirror, beheads her.

The Gorgon was based on a synopsis submitted to Hammer in 1963 by J. Llewellyn Devine; the screenplay was written by John Gilling and rewritten, to Gilling's dismay, by Anthony Hinds (Murphy, 1995: 9). The film doesn't really work as horror, for the Gorgon herself is not so much an active predatory villain as a figure in an allegorical tableau. Unlike Dracula, the reverse coloniser from the East, the Gorgon has no imperialist ambitions but merely waits patiently for victims to stumble into her lair. Detached from the values of Gothic, she is a signifier of inexplicable Otherness, independently malignant and, unusually for Hammer, a female outside male control. As a thriller the film is hampered not only by its passive monster, whose silent appearances in green make-up and a wig of rubber serpents are more humorous than horrifying, but also by its lack of suspense. The plot's chief mystery is given away in the film's title and its major surprise, that it is Carla who is possessed by the Gorgon, is not only a foregone conclusion (Carla is the only major female character) but a cliché in the werewolf film of which this is a variation.

Considered as a love story, *The Gorgon* is remarkably dark and unhappy. Love between men and women is either impossible or, like Namaroff's love of Carla, unrequited and repressed. As Jonathan Rigby remarks, 'The fraught emotional triangle between Namaroff, Carla and Paul is so joyless it makes petrification seem like an attractive alternative to the agonies of love' (Rigby, 2000: 106). The fiercest affections are felt between the male characters, especially fathers and sons (there is an unmistakable homosocial subtext to this tale of men uniting to defeat an overpowerful woman). Women are objects either of fear, over-romanticisation or distant aesthetic contemplation; for both Bruno, the artist, and Namaroff, the surgeon, they are to be desired and studied rather than treated as equals. The film's atmosphere is suitably grim and foreboding with murky day-for-night photography and a colour scheme of drab greens and browns. In short, *The Gorgon* is a closeted drama of thwarted emotions, played out in a handful of symbolically conceived sets: the cottage, strewn with Bruno's drawings of Sascha, in which men seek to penetrate the mystery of the Gorgon; Namaroff's asylum, a place of pain and death; and the ruined castle, in which all intruders perish. This *Kammerspiel*-like setup was enforced by economies of production: 'the castle is a stock glass shot from *The Evil of Frankenstein* (1964), exteriors are self-evidently *interiors*, and the action is typically restricted to interchanges between sundry village habitats and the weird castle on the hill' (Meikle, 1996: 178). Claustrophobia and a sense of fate are further reinforced by the film's repetitive structure. As Wheeler Winston Dixon explains, 'Fisher frames the film's central narrative with a smaller one, compressing the structural cycle of the work into a 10-minutes "rehearsal"' (Dixon, 1991: 419). So in the first act, a man is killed and another arrives to investigate; this is recapitulated and elaborated on in the second act, in which two men investigate the reasons for another's death. The murders are ritualised, with each attack by the Gorgon preceded by three shots edited as rigorously as the opening sequence of *Un chien Andalou* (1928): a cross in a little shrine on a tree, then an image of the full moon and finally the castle silhouetted on the hill. This air of predestination and stasis follows through the film's master trope of gorgonisation, the freezing of lives and emotions. The film's love affairs are thwarted; the young leads die; nothing in the end changes. Even the monster herself, being a roaming spirit, may live again and return to possess somebody new.

The Gorgon reverses the subtexts of *Dracula* (1958). *Dracula* is usually seen as transgressing the conformities of the Macmillan era before the vampire's flamboyant threat to the sexual status quo is repressed by anxious bourgeois patriarchy. Dracula is a curiously modern figure, despite his aristocratic lineage and ancient curse, who prefigures 1960s sexual liberation as surely as the virile consumerism of James Bond. With Dracula the pre-bourgeois past returns to unleash violent passions and debauch the oppressed young. *The Gorgon*, by contrast, is a film without much sexual energy. The monster turns her victims to stone rather than into a brood of ravenous libertines, and romance is frustrated by the enforced blockage of emotional release. One should not, however, underestimate the complexity of the film, whose subtexts are more elusive than *Dracula*'s and which is full of tantalising details and unexplained events. Why does the Gorgon turn up in this little German town in 1910? Why does she possess Carla? What is the link between her and the Castle Borski? And, most puzzlingly, why is the Gorgon called Megera rather than, say, Medusa or one of the other Gorgons of myth? The film refuses to explain itself, not so much from slipshod screenwriting, but from a desire to maintain a certain fruitful incoherence and to encourage symbolic and psychological interpretations.

Indeed, one of the film's pleasures is that it is mysterious and poetic in its severe and allusive imagery, and in its uncompromising statement of men's fear of and desire for women: what Harry Ringel called a 'thorough demystification of the Romantic Ideal' (Ringel, 1975b: 13). On the other hand, if one is persuaded by the countless varieties of Freudian criticism still dominant in horror film criticism, *The Gorgon* is almost *too* readable. The Gorgon herself cries out for Freudian analysis, which has been supplied in previous readings of the film. The Gorgon in Freudian terms embodies fears of castration and impotence. Her gaze is both arousing (it hardens men into bodily erection) and literally petrifying. Wreathed in snakes, she is, in Lacanian/Kristevan terms, the phallic mother, both desired and feared. As such the Gorgon, in the film, can be seen not so much as a character as a convenient manifestation of an archetype of the male unconscious. Peter Hutchings gives an historicising interpretation along these lines, arguing that the film is transitional for Hammer (Hutchings, 1993a: 82–6). According to him Hammer's Gorgon is not simply a demonised woman, a standard issue object of terror in a misogynistic genre, but a symbol of female independence, which the film understands self-reflexively to be a projection of male fears: 'she is what [the men] want Carla to become, the female as object, as an extension of their own being' (85). Hutchings notes the frequent images of mirrors in the film, which emphasise visually that the Gorgon is linked to the psychology of the male characters: 'the Gorgon is given us as a "male" problem, arising as it does from a man looking at himself' (85). Although the Gorgon is ultimately killed, Hutchings argues that the film represents a defeat for the men – the usual Hammer patriarchs, even the masterful Meister, are much weaker than in previous films – and is therefore expressive of both Hammer's recognition of the claims of female subjectivity and its waning confidence in the restoration of male authority. Elsewhere, Hutchings takes a different, more ahistorical approach, offering a conventional interpretation of the Gorgon as an archaic mother figure. '[T]he Gorgon, the all-powerful figure who waits beyond the desirable woman and is inseparable from her, functions as an image of the archaic, pre-Oedipal mother, before whom all men are rendered helpless infants' (Hutchings, 1993b: 89). Like the entry on the film in the *Aurum Encyclopedia of Horror*, Hutchings, in both interpretations, confirms Barbara Creed's reading of the Medusa as a grand transhistorical symbol of terrible matriarchy.[1] Creed doesn't mention *The Gorgon*, but one can sees how her interpretation might apply to it. In a film bereft of mothers – and indeed of wives – and overpopulated by father figures, the Gorgon stands, simply and alarmingly, in the mothers' place. She is the mother of all mothers, a Gorgon in the popular sense of the term, who denotes the revenge of the repressed matriarch, outraged at male mistreatment of the female characters. Bruno, for example, is unfeeling towards Sascha, who complains, 'I think you're the most selfish man I've ever met'. To news of her pregnancy he coldly replies that 'I want your father to know that I'm not going to evade my responsibilities'. Carla meanwhile is imprisoned by Namaroff's desire, while a mad woman in the asylum ends up dissected by his scalpel. Men use women to their own ends to pursue research, whether scientific like Namaroff or aesthetic like Bruno, and the Gorgon explains why: she is the symbol of the archaic, phallic and castrating power men disavow in oppressing women; the great mother whose memory they cannot face directly.

There is in fact, even if we stick doggedly within a Freudian–Lacanian context, an embarrassment of potential readings. Is the Gorgon a representation of female genitals (menstruating or not), a throwback to the primal scene, the phallic mother or something else – something perhaps frightening on its own account rather than representing a fear no one ever knew they had? It is impossible to tell. If psychoanalysis works well with horror films, it's partly of course because the genre matured in its shadow and quickly took on board popularised versions of its 'discoveries'. *Cat People* (1942) was all too knowing about its subtexts of frigidity and repression (Newman, 1999: 32–6). And by the late 1950s Hammer was certainly aware of the latent as well as the manifest content of its Gothic raw material. But it is also partly because in inventing his private mythology Freud fell back on the imagery of Gothic, reinventing the self as a haunted castle, troubled by the return of ghosts from the past which need to be confronted and exorcised. Indeed in Freud, as in *The Gorgon*, motifs from Gothic intermingle confusingly with those of classical mythology (Edmundson, 1997: 34–5).

Let's start, therefore, with the film's innovative and free-wheeling adaptation of mythology. In Greek mythology, the Gorgons were three sisters, Medusa, Sthenno and Euryale. Medusa, the only one of the three who was mortal, was loved by Poseidon and killed by Perseus, who beheaded her while she slept by watching the reflection of her image in his shield. The Gorgons were sisters of the Graiae, old hags from birth and symbols of the terror of old age. Descriptions of the Gorgons vary. In some versions Medusa was originally beautiful but is turned into a monster when she vies in beauty with Athene, but in most representations the Gorgons have serpent hair, boars' tusks and can transform those who see them to stone. As a symbol – consciously rather than unconsciously wrought – Medusa is thereby adaptable to many purposes.[2] Mario Praz saw the Medusa as one of the key early statements of the Romantic and later the Symbolist and Decadent conception of the beauty of horror, in other words, the *femme fatale* (Praz, 1951: 45). The monster in the film is, however, complicated by a range of generic as well as classical allusions, just as the film itself is enriched by its collision of Gothic and myth. For example, *The Gorgon* reworks the imagery of the werewolf film, though without the implication of lupine transmission. In this it bears comparison with *Cat People*, both Jacques Tourneur's original and Paul Schrader's 1982 remake, which unlocked some of its source's subtexts. Both versions of *Cat People* specifically feminise the werewolf film, with heroines inhabited by mythic archetypes that enabled them to escape from the domestic oppressions of men. Carla is possessed by the Gorgon during bouts of amnesia at the full moon, which reminds us again that the Gorgon has been read not only as a mother figure but as a 'cursed' menstruating mother.[3] Women, by this reading, are especially in need of control at times of menstrual power, when they are in synch with primal forces outside the narrow understanding of male reason. The Gorgon, like the cat woman in both versions of the story, bodies forth the archetypal power that men both revere and fear in women, in particular their closeness to Nature, which men can neither compete with nor fully comprehend.

Hammer's Gorgon lacks the more elaborate characteristics of the mythic creature: there are no boar's tusks, for instance. An old woman in a snake-wig, she comes across as a close relation of Bette Davis in *Whatever Happened to Baby Jane?* (1962), a demonised symbol of old age in a period of rampant nymphophilia. It is a little ungallant to describe Prudence Hyman, the actress who plays her, simply as old, but she is certainly more mature than Barbara Shelley. The original concept was to have Shelley as both Carla and the Gorgon, but to preserve what was left of the film's mystery Hyman ended up in the role. Although it was unusual for Hammer to have a female monster, the studio had begun in the early 1960s to emphasise the 'glamorous' attractions of its films, though its female leads were more often iconic objects of erotic fascination than dramatically complex characters. Their significance to the films and interest to the audience could be summed up in a still photograph: Ursula Andress in *She*, fresh from *Dr No* (1962), the very image of untouchable blonde disdain; Raquel Welch, hypnotic and preternaturally gorgeous in

One Million Years BC – these are pre-modernist visions of Beauty and the Eternal Woman, luminous figures from Leighton and Alma-Tadema updated in the idiom of the centrefold. Karim, the voluptuous disciple of Kali in Fisher's *The Stranglers of Bombay* (1959), anticipates Carla's duality of beauty and terror. Luxuriating in the ritual torture of men like an Indian Mme Defarge, she is a cartoonish assemblage of erotic signifiers: a mountainous cleavage, passive and silent, overseeing the spectacle of male death. But even as Hammer began its series of glamour films, with their *Playboy* aesthetic and imported Amazonian beauties, so it introduced the ageing woman as source of horror. Robin Wood argues that late 1960s American horror films tended to demonise the young, perhaps as a conservative response to the revolt of the younger generation (Wood, 1986: 76). In British horror films, however, the old are more often monstrous symbols of the return of the repressive.[4] On the one hand, there are Bette Davis's malevolent matriarchs in Hammer's *The Nanny* (1965) and *The Anniversary* (1968); on the other, echoing the duality of the Gorgon, there are *She* and *Countess Dracula* (1971), in which the two Hammer stereotypes, nubile youth and wizened crone, are combined in a single female character. Ayesha's timeless beauty perishes in the cleansing fire and she devolves to apishly wrinkled old age; the Countess is transformed in an instant from smooth-skinned sex-goddess to desiccated granny. There is a straightforward gerontophobic equation in these films: beauty is youth, old age is terror and punishment: Hammer's women switch from sex object to death's head without ever passing through middle age. (It is worth noting that the Gorgon herself is linked to the imagery of ageing: her victims go grey, lose mobility and, you might say, become their own memorial statue.)

Oddly, as I mentioned before, the Gorgon is not named Medusa: the film is very precise about this. Instead she is Megera, who in classical legend was not a Gorgon at all. Megera ('grudging'), in Virgil, was one of the Furies or Erinyes along with Alecto and Tisiphone; collectively they were sometimes known as the Eumenides or 'kindly ones'. In naming the Gorgon Megera, the film's academics may have got their facts muddled. Megera never announces her name and the men may, therefore, with rationalising male arrogance, be simply fitting her into a system of their own convenience: it would be appropriate, in a film in which men so confidently misunderstand women, that they should lumber the Other with the wrong name. Or perhaps the filmmakers fumbled their references and didn't have a classical dictionary to hand. In any case their aversion is understandable to labelling the Gorgon so bluntly as Medusa: the allusion was perhaps too specific for what was meant to be an innovative monster, whose purpose is to connote the realm of classical mythology without simply being transplanted from it.

In cross-referencing the Gorgon to other female monsters the film makes her out to be some sort of grand coalition of male terrors, a comprehensive designation of Otherness – not only Gorgon, but also Fury, werewolf, siren, and exotic invader from the East. But, more important, the connotations of Megera are viable in the film in their own right if we choose to pursue them. The Furies, sometimes represented as winged or with snakes about them, personified retribution. They carried out revenge against those who betrayed the family by, for example, matricide and, according to some sources, also ensured revenge against those who escaped justice. In Aeschylus's *Eumenides*, for example, the third play of the *Oresteia*, they pursue Orestes who murdered his mother Clytemnestra. As such, they are agents of natural justice and conscience, whose ravages enforce the supernatural order that is above human law. Although the Gorgon's murders seem unmotivated within the plot (she simply kills whomever she sees), her being a Fury at least suggests that some scheme of poetic justice is being secured. This overdetermines the film's theme of resistance to male oppression, the Gorgon being not only an all-purpose proverbial symbol of masculine fears but also an active principle of righteous revenge. It would also explain why she kills women as well as men, which on the face of it undermines the assumption that the Gorgon must be understood strictly in relation to the male characters. After all, why should Sascha, victim of Bruno's reckless impregnation, be singled out for murder? If we place Carla at the centre of the film and see the Gorgon as *her* return of the repressed, then the film comes sharply into focus. Killing the pregnant Sascha is explicable as revenge for the fecundity denied Carla by her imprisonment by Namaroff, who controls her, as he does the hysterical mad women in his asylum, with his superior knowledge of female illness. Throughout, as Dixon remarks, Namaroff does not so much treat his female patients as use them to further his own research. Like Frankenstein his cold male rationality, as he slices women open on the autopsy table, enables him to disavow his yearning for power and erotic fulfilment:

> The citizens of Vandorf have little more status than that of a laboratory animal in a double-blind experiment; if they are allowed to live without interference, it is only the will of Namaroff that allows them to do so. The police are content to follow his instructions. (Dixon, 1991: 427)

By this reading the Gorgon emerges from ancient myth to possess Carla in order to enact revenge against the symbols of her entrapment. As Rigby notes, 'Both [Namaroff and Paul] objectify Carla in their different ways. Namaroff tries to keep her under house arrest ... while Paul, whose view of her is entirely romanticised, refuses to believe the truth about her condition until it is far too late' (Rigby, 2000: 106).

The Gorgon, then, rather than a projection of the male sexual unconscious, is an image of a woman's power to devastate normality (psychoanalytically, this is more Jung than Freud). Her ancient knowledge is liable, like the panther in *Cat People*, to burst forth and challenge not only masculine reason and science but a 'societal structure so firmly grounded on social and sexual repression' which defines and controls her (Dixon, 1991: 432). The Gorgon is rather like the Sumerian demon who possesses Sigourney Weaver's character in *Ghostbusters* (1984), or like Catwoman in *Batman Returns* (1992) and Alex Forest with her frizzy Medusa hairdo in *Fatal Attraction* (1987): woman as the unreasonable Other, full of inexpressible asocial violence. The grounding opposition here between male reason and female irrationality is of course a dreadful cliché, even if it can be reinterpreted and mystified in certain feminist discourses to the advantage of 'natural' and intuitive woman.[5] But the film makes imaginative and revisionist use of this cliché rather as Hammer's imperialist films, such as *The Abominable Snowman* (1957), *The Stranglers of Bombay* and *The Legend of the 7 Golden Vampires*, employ otherwise racist commonplaces about the purity and naive primitivism of other cultures in order to criticise the violence, secularism and hypocrisy of the West.[6] The trope of woman as transcendent Other is a means of countering the male-identified world of science and rationality with an image of something – *anything* – irreducible to everyday common-sense.

This imagery of mythic female power is focused in the depiction of Castle Borski. Although essentially a male space, redolent of ancient aristocratic privilege, it is now dominated by a woman who looms over the village. She claims precedence not only because classical myth chronologically precedes Gothic, but because Myth (that is, Woman) comes before, and is repressed by, Science (that is, Man). The exile of an older order of male power (bloodline aristocracy, on whose behalf Dracula revenges himself on the bourgeois family) enables an even older order to take up residence. The Gorgon is a fragment of myth, weirdly at odds with both modernity and its Gothic Other, shoring the film against the meaninglessness of the present. The castle is split-level, as we see when Paul enters. Above, there is a throne in which Carla sits; like Ayesha in *She* and Margaret in *Blood from the Mummy's Tomb* (1971) she is the embodiment of some ancient power. Below, with Paul on the ground floor, there is a broken statue of a male torso lacking its arms and head. In (the inevitable) Freudian terms the statue can be construed as 'castrated' at the heart of this deserted shrine to male power and lineage. The torso sets the imagination racing in two directions. First, since it looks like classical statuary, or some mid-Victorian imitation of it, the torso corresponds to the Gorgon: both inappropriately revive the classical in a Gothic setting. Second, it figuratively anticipates transformation of the Gorgon's victims into useless statuary: the Gorgon is a kind of artist who turns her victims into unwilling works of art. The imagery of men as objectified works of art reverses that of the first scene of the film, in which Bruno draws Sascha's torso (she is turned away from him, as if he were avoiding her eyes) so that she is the focus of the aestheticising male gaze. Throughout the film women are viewed by men via some sort of distanced mediation – mirrors, art, the scientific gaze of Namaroff's dissecting mind.

In the 1960s Hammer moved away from reworking Romantic Gothic and turned more towards fantasy and self-contained myths; its interests became archetypal, as it were. Always frank about their erotic component, the films became more adept at arranging little allegories about gender relations in trouble and transition (as in the extraordinary *Slave Girls* (1967), a sadomasochistic piece about a modern man suddenly thrown into a primeval world of phallus-worshipping beauties). Bizarre tales like *The Lost Continent* (1968) were not only theatrically rich but shot through with anxieties about class, Otherness and sex, from which historical concerns their alternative worlds were temporary relief. On the crudest level, this involved a worried engagement with the 'Permissive Society', which rendered women both more available and more fearsome in their sexual demands, threatening not only men but the family and society itself. But it wasn't only about sex. *The Gorgon* and the prehistoric movies evoked an older, archaic world of myth and spiritual meaning. Hammer's oft-noted nostalgia for the Victorian past was not, in fact, entirely conservative. The films were elegies for lost enchantment as much as for the end of Empire, patriarchal confidence and bourgeois hegemony. (Since *The Gorgon* takes place in Germany in 1910, it is poised on the verge of the First World War, which demolished all the old certainties. The Suez crisis, for Britain at least, demolished the few that were left. That the film is set in Germany and involves a quasi-vivisectionist doctor suggests some of allegory, too, of the coming terrors of the twentieth century, with the Gorgon a metaphor for the horrors Nazi Germany would repeatedly unleash.)[7] They lamented a world discarded by modernity: a world of gods, taboos, magic and mythology of which horror films (and indeed psychoanalysis) are an accidental echo.

So rather than see the Gorgon as caught up in a strict allegory of gender relations, we can understand her as a symbol of all that is exiled by secular and scientific modernity. Feminists, it is true and indeed appropriate, might gloss her with reference to the Kristevan Symbolic and point to the film's association of women with madness. The insane woman in the asylum, like Sascha's pregnancy and Carla's monthly spells of amnesia, identifies women with worlds of meaning beyond male rationality and control. But you could also see the Gorgon as standing for art itself, the aesthetic realm which, in the absence of God, confers meaning on life but which modernity has demystified and banished along with myth, religion and the promise of transcendence from historical contingency. As an aside, one notes that critical interpretation, the hermeneutics of suspicion underpinned by theories like psychoanalysis, embodies the disenchanting work of modernity. Like Perseus' shield, it is a mirror in which art can be safely viewed before it is summarily dispatched.

In *The Gorgon*, as in so many Hammer films, a forgetful deracinated modernity encounters a richer mythic past. *Moon Zero Two* (1969), for instance, Hammer's last science fiction film, predicts that the future will be boring, unheroic and scarcely worth visiting; the modern world is a dull place and meaning depends on reviving myth, recapturing old fantasies, not being too knowing.[8] For the Symbolists, back in the nineteenth century, the yearning for transcendence was an escape from history, certainly from women to some extent, and especially from the trivial world of consumerist boredom.[9] For Hammer in the 1960s, as consumerism secured its hold, the fantasy genre expressed, for those who cared to identify with it, resistance to the secularism, disenchantment and triviality of the age.

Marion Crane dies twice[1]

Murray Pomerance

Interdit a ceux qui n'ont pas encore vu Psycho.
Douchet (1960: 7)

'Gender identity' in film differs in style and consequence from its model in everyday life, if only because our everyday gender careers constitute what Vivian Sobchack might call 'embodied narratives' (Sobchack, 1995: 280). While lived gender has medical, political, linguistic, emotional, and navigational facets, filmed gender is constituted as a set of signals *about* rather than instantiations *of*, and is therefore an index: of motive, alignment, history, probability, and piety (Burke, 1969; Goffman, 1976). Screened gender, an attribute of and code for experience-as-represented, may come to function in the everyday world indexically, referentially, played out or recounted as what Goffman (1974) would call a 'keying'. Though screened gender may metaphorise and point, it has less to do – in its structure – with the nature and social organisation of gender in everyday life than with the history and conventions for exploiting and depicting gender, more generally, pictorially, and more precisely, filmically.

That representational art is not an unframed window upon the world, and that our ability to learn about life by studying pictures depends upon our knowledge of the techniques and strategies of representation used by an artist, was proposed by Gombrich. The pictorial arts, he argued (1960), rely upon informed *schemata* of depiction. The technique of representation continually evolves, through what Gombrich referred to as a process of 'schema and correction' (quoted in Miller, 1983: 218–21). Works of art are manifested through modifications to the conventions and principles by means of which it has been agreed upon by artists to depict things and by viewers to see things depicted. In film, it has been suggested (Carey, 1974), the conventions according to which certain narrative elements are both placed and developed through history are themselves negotiated with viewing audiences; so that the history of conventions for representation is accessible as a history of such deals.

Remaking film

In that they give further play and schematic modification to the representational conventions established earlier in the medium; and in that their elements can best be understood as making reference to those conventions rather than to the modelling world, all films are 'remakes'. But a fascinating limiting case can be found in those infrequent, narratively bounded, and stylistically resplendent works that *openly claim* to be remakes of earlier films. Douglas Sirk's 1959 reconstruction of John M. Stahl's 1934 *Imitation of Life* exemplifies. In the officially declared *remake,* taken as genre itself (one that turns the lens most directly upon the filmic process), we see, without the masking purport of 'originality', transformations and transpositions, borrowings and developments, reiterations and poeises – evidences, in short, for a theory of historical change as posited by a filmmaker by means of the accentuating idiosyncrasies of his representational style: 'See what I have done to update this old story and make it relevant for today's audience!' As a way of picturing gender, the remake assumes, negotiates, and plays upon new interpretations of understandings and recognitions presumably placed in the locus of the audience's attention and involvement.

What is significant in an explicit remake is not that it stands objectively to report some renovated aspect of the social world, but that viewers can be expected to believe it does by the sheath of progressivity within which it presents itself. Such nostalgic, but also purposive, viewers can be addressed by filmmakers as though they have a live present memory for 'historical' conditions that may have been depicted once through a helplessly immediate, unselfconscious process of representational fidelity in the past version, yet are now superceded by notable forthcomings as obscure to earlier prediction as they are lambent to current hindsight. How quaint and old-fashioned, then, do Janet Leigh and

John Gavin seem early in the twenty-first century making out only *half-naked* at the beginning of *Psycho* (1960). Gus Van Sant's 1998 retelling of Alfred Hitchcock's film is not seen as a mere ineffectual mechanical repetition of Hitchcock's complex narrative, then, but as evidence of inevitable historical development in mores and sexual etiquette and of the passage of time; it possesses and worries a progressive subtext, situating itself in turn-of-the-century filmmaking as a nostalgic reflection and a 'presence' and causing the earlier thematic statement – even, in this case, one filmed by an acknowledged master of the medium – to recede in meaning into an 'antiquity' that can be set nostalgically in an outmoded 'past'. 'People in the 1960s were so obsessed about sex, so dramatic,' moan undergraduates now. 'We take it for granted.' How modishly hot, even provocative, then, must Anne Heche and Viggo Mortensen seem (the latter stark naked, gazing out the window), and especially because Leigh and Gavin were there so 'prudishly' before them.

Without here attempting to dichotomise the cultural and economic differences of present and past societies, it can be useful to examine the two *Psycho*s in some detail regarding the presentation of gender as itself a commodity whose value is grounded in social currencies; for with each film, however bizarrely expressive or putatively representational it is of the social context in which it was filmed, gender as a fact and the gender programme as a myth were ultimately readable to the audience. While I do not here wish to entertain the claim that our social treatment of gender at the end of the twentieth century indicated a step in a particular direction, nevertheless I hope to show that at least in respect of certain key scenes in this one film – remade in 1998 with an attempt to replicate dialogue, scenic construction and even shots – the social codings of the past are in some ways illegible in the light of present expectation.

Gender play

Waylaid exegetically by Hitchcock's titling practices, many critics have treated *Psycho*, a film in which what popular thought configures as psychosis plays a major role, as a film *about* mentality – or at least psychological derangement – and have sought throughout the exposition for symptoms of psychological trouble or justifications for the assuring, even nourishing, application of psychiatry which is its finale (see Douchet, 1999). That the film takes its gross narrative form and its name from Robert Bloch's novel (1959), which is in fact told from a set of interior positions all indicating one degree or another of emotional and psychological discomfort, does not diminish the fact that Hitchcock chose books like *Psycho* not on the basis of their own fictional qualities but because they were ready-built narrative frameworks that would support his own subtler and philosophically denser designs (Truffaut, 1985: 268). Hitchcock certainly had philosophical designs, even though his most recent biographer insists he was 'never philosophical' (McGilligan, 2003: 560). Notwithstanding the psychiatrically-tainted observations of Harvey Roy Greenberg – '[*Psycho*] represents the extremity of Hitchcock's black vision of human vulnerability and corruptibility' (Greenberg, 1993: 118) – or of other psychologically-influenced critics he cites, generally to the effect that mentality is the central motive in *Psycho*, Hitchcock's film can be seen as a construct, employing psychological and emotional language merely as a means of audience engagement while its design explores two fascinating and related – but not implicitly psychological – issues: the structure of gender, and the shape of narrative unfolding.

All the dramatic action in *Psycho* is gender-focused: the theft, the trysting, the killing, the housekeeping, the flight. In the introduction Sam and Marion are served up in a state of half-nudity as, after a lunch hour's petting in a Phoenix hotel room, they dress themselves in garments, statuses, and moral arguments. The topic of their discussion is marriage, that fusion of gender and political economy. Marion has been reserving herself sexually for an idealised future, though Sam's hopes have been threatened by the impoverishing pressures of a divorce. In prim white underwear, her hair severely cropped and her lips tidily painted to demarcate her demand that Sam make an 'honest woman' of her, Marion is personified by Janet Leigh as the paragon of Betty Friedan's 'feminine mystique' (1959), eager, because powerless, to succumb to the dictate of a male-controlled society that she subordinate her sexual hunger to conjugal pieties. Soon afterward, in the real estate office where she works, blatant evidence of male power and control of women is offered by the millionaire Cassidy (Frank Albertson), who for $40,000, and apparently on the spur of the moment, is buying a house for his 'little girl', who has never known a day of pain in her life. Handed to Marion's boss Lowery (Vaughn Taylor) over Scotch and locker room banter in the back office, this male money is the treasure entrusted to her safekeeping and that she decides to divert to produce that 'decent' marital bliss. Since it is still in underwear (serious and black), that Marion fashions her plan to leave town with the propulsive male element – the MacGuffin – of this tale, the rectangular wad of bills, it is in sexual availability that she takes action.

Escaping northward, Marion encounters dominating men: a nosey highway patrolman (Mort Mills) and a manipulative used-car salesman (John Anderson), both of whom use gendered aggressiveness to increase her self-consciousness about her social position as a woman. Chafing in vulnerability and powerlessness, then, and shaken by a sudden rainstorm, she is quite prepared, even desperate, for the hospitable friendship of a young man with a distinct lack of brashness and a reassuringly hesitant, stammering manner. Norman Bates in Anthony Perkins's performance is not only a mother's boy, but a boy who seems in some ways like a mother. His shyness of posture; his fascination with the dexterous hobby of taxidermy; his learned speech and wounded tongue; the extreme measure of his nursely devotion to the sick old matriarch in the 'castle' on the hill; the dainty domestication of his cooking – all suggest he is a very different kind of man than Marion has met before, or than most of the other men in this story who reflect dominating, heterosexist masculinity (Corber, 1993; Cohan and Hark, 1993).

In Norman's little parlour adjacent to the motel office, where he and Marion spin a conversation about being 'in our private traps', as she nibbles the delicate chicken sandwich he has made her, we detect his genteel identification with her femininity in his confiding tone and fastidious, though stuttering, diction. Though he refers to birds, words like 'clamped', 'scratch', and 'claw' and the notion of being 'born in' a trap all suggest the debilitating confinement by ascription that fell to women in late 1950s Western society – where a woman's future is marriage to an eligible man; where brutalising patrolmen can provoke female drivers even as they seek to ensure their safety; it is women, not just people, who are trapped. So it is women, not just people, Norman invokes in his attempt at confidence. Behind a framed picture in this somber little room, he has poked a peephole and can watch Marion, later, preparing for her shower – a withdrawn, timidly preadolescent, inexperienced male. Spying, he feels for his target a sense of wonderment and associative curiosity, not the latent aggression of Michael Powell's *Peeping Tom* (1960).

The slaughtering of Marion Crane – Rothman suggests enthusiastically that the famous shower scene is 'the most celebrated sequence in all of Hitchcock's work' (Rothman, 1982: 292); Sterritt more precisely that it constitutes 'the most celebrated montage of Hitchcock's career' (Sterritt, 1993: 108) – is a gender study, not simple violence; a choreography of unprotected female modesty, the victim twisting and vocalising, pointlessly covering her ventrum with splaying fingers against the swift, inescapable knife. It is femininity, not thievery, addressed and undressed by this (unmistakably male) blade slashing through the shower (prefigured earlier by the wiper blade slashing across Marion's windscreen). Gender play features, too, in the legend of Norman's mother and the 'man from the east' who married her and died by her side, and in the presumptuousness of Arbogast (Martin Balsam), a man on the trail of not only crime but *female crime*. Here is a second questionable male, Norman's echo – too verbal, too cerebral, too intuitive – whose interrogation of Norman is a flaccid echo of the brutalising capitalist male bonding of Lowery and Cassidy. And the gender of motherhood – Norman's mother's replete closet, her dressing table; her modalities of voice; her symphony of motives; indeed, her very *perduration* as a character, given the nature of her history – is a central and unifying riddle, fusing essence and appearance, intent and claim, sincerity and performance.

As a clue to that riddle, let us examine Norman's illuminating statement about having been born in a private trap yet not minding it anymore. Chided by Marion that he should mind, he makes bold to explicate that in fact he does, but *says* he doesn't. His character is an open travesty, constructed artfully of sayings and silences – all coverings. His masculinity is worn upon a sleeve, slid into and drawn out of a jacket pocket. In the broadest sense, this sartorial view of gender – that it is dramaturgic, situational, performed – suggests that it does not inhere in biological fact, but resides in social application, an idea commonplace enough now but unspoken in these terms in 1959 (Oakley, 1972).

Norman and Marion's 'gender trap' is built of regulations and preferences, legal treatments, shaped condescension and probable outcomes, *layers* permitting that we might appear, and thus socially 'be'. As what we can see covers what we cannot, we may suspect that under the soft masculinity of Norman Bates there lurks an essence that is hard. And the form of Marion's victimisation becomes a peel (under running water), an attempt to disclose (wash off) the being inside her. In the climactic vision of *Psycho* – in the fruit cellar – we see in one swift intoxicating shot not only the innermost nature of Norman's mother but most importantly the layers of integument and intelligibility that have covered it. Interestingly, Van Sant vitiates the shock of this moment, placing a busy aviary in the background and then having Mrs Bates, in her throne, swivel oh so slowly into view for Lila Crane. We have so much time to estimate her essence (the shot becomes an anatomy lesson) that only a spider crawling out of her maw can revive in us the shudders produced in 1960.

Hitchcock shows that gender in the late 1950s was an affair of coverings and portrayals. Norman's peephole, by means of which he performs a purely gendered relation to Marion, is an apparatus of gender, a pathway for what Mulvey could call the empowered male gaze (Mulvey, 1975: 6–18) but what can also be seen as an associating fixation of vision. Similarly, Mrs Bates's closet, Bates's careful performance of language, the shower curtain, the swamp, the newspaper secreting the money that Marion has taken, are all appurtenances of gender dedicated to the central role of covering as an organising feature of social display. All are intimations of what is beyond themselves; wrappings of what is wrapped. One could add the coverlet on Mrs Bates's bed; Marion's hands in the shower; the highway patrolman's sunglasses; Marion's claim to migraine; Arbogast's deflective style of questioning. These elements shape the engenderings put in play in this film, principally by offering to viewers hints as to the nature of a hidden and inner, presumably truthful, personal world.

Perhaps most central of all gender teases is architectural structure, the setting of sexual and financial interplay designed to be held off from the public eye. Jean Douchet begins his critique (1960: 7) with filmic architecture in view, proclaiming, 'This article is forbidden to those who have not yet seen *Psycho* … It is impossible to study this film without revealing its secret' but then proceeds to actual edifices, suggesting the opening scene is a play on our desire to penetrate the sorts of boundaries to perception offered by the Phoenix hotel. The hotel is thus another gender façade, as is the Bates Motel, a façade for the gender play that takes place in its rooms. Norman's office is a façade for his parlour; his parlour is a façade for Marion's room; her room is a façade for her bathroom, the bathroom a façade for the shower stall, the stall a façade for what lies beyond the drain. Gender is face; and sex is the end of gender.

Colouring Marion

But what has happened to all of this pudeur and pretence by 1998, at a time when 'women's liberation', 'gender equality', 'male domination', and 'female modesty' are treated as slogans of a vanished, even antiquated, past by a Hollywood power structure squeamish to portray social conflict and eager to claim, on women's behalf, political progress in order to ease its own sense of obligation? I want to suggest that Van Sant's film extracts, exteriorises, and diffuses gender onto the surface of consciousness, making of it less a romantic secret to be penetrated through shadowy hints and cloaks of anxious ambiguity and more a uniform topography of social fact, presence, utility, and kinesis. If it was earlier a catafalque and chrysalis for desire, it is now a banality, like weather. The rainstorm through which Marion (Anne Heche) drives to the motel, once pathetic fallacy, is now nothing more than a realistic setting (the wiper blade is no longer lit to be slashing). There is realism, too, as Marion packs to take flight in underwear that is money green – the film is in full colour – bringing to the surface of awareness and attention a stash that was earlier a guilty secret. And the behaviours that constitute Van Sant's gender stylings, as we shall see, call up the real more than the imagined, as though we have celebrated the death of imagination; they would have been unreadable in the context of the gender assumptions made by Hitchcock's generation.

But in order to effect these stylings, which I shall discuss, Van Sant had to overcome some difficulties. He had cast in the female lead a talented, yet hardly famous, young actress – no contemporary reflection of the Janet Leigh who had already, by the time she contracted with Hitchcock, shot *Little Women* (1949), *The Forsyte Saga* (1949), *Angels in the Outfield* (1951), *It's a Big Country* (1951), *The Naked Spur* (1953), *Houdini* (1953), *Prince Valiant* (1954), *Living It Up* (1954), *Pete Kelly's Blues* (1955), *My Sister Eileen* (1955), *Safari* (1956), and the resonant *Touch of Evil* (1958). Because Leigh had a huge name at the box office, Hitchcock knew his viewers would be stupefied and confused to see her killed off in the first third of the film, and contracted arrangements with distributors, here for the first time in the history of modern film distribution, to forbid audiences entrance to the cinema after the screenings had commenced. However, for a contemporary audience, most of whom would be familiar with at least the publicity blurb of the story of *Psycho*, and many of whom would have no particular associations with the name of Anne Heche (who had had only a major role in *Donnie Brasco* (1997)), the shock (to our engagement) of the shower killing would be reduced. A technical address to this problem through colour cinematography is made by Van Sant as an attempt to re-elevate the shower scene, since at least the aura of legend and publicity surrounding the Hitchcock film for a contemporary audience required that this scene be powerful.

Shooting in colour in the white bathroom provided for blatant splashes of red blood. While the tonal contrast between the blood and the tiles and bathtub is not greater here than it was in the black and white original, there is added an intense *colour contrast*, in which the frenzied and intimate emotional associations with the redness of the blood are pronounced within the screen space. Blood shot in black and white appears very dark grey, and it falls to the viewer to imagine the redness implicit in – that is, *beneath* – the grey. The imagistic tones in the original *Psycho*, then, comprise another construction, another mask to cover some deeper, more direct and more passionate substance. In the Van Sant *Psycho*, this deeper and dirtier layer of meaning is surfaced and openly articulated, cleaned up, in a process analogous to the 'erasure of nineteenth-century squalor' Anthony Vidler attributes to modernist architecture (Vidler, 1992: 63). So, paradoxically, the shower scene is less ambiguous, less erotic, less troubling, yet more newsworthy because less covert and more reported/reportable. In the original, Norman's voice is out of control, and therefore acoustically emphatic, when he stumbles into the motel room and discovers what is in the bath: 'Mother! Oh God! Mother! Blood! Blood!' But that mantra, trilogising life-giving fluid, deity, and maternal presence, is now reduced to a photo caption.

According to the scriptwriter Joseph Stefano (quoted in Lucas, 1999), Hitchcock produced a startling shot only to withdraw it from the final cut to ensure that the film would not be denied a rating. Gus Van Sant was at liberty not only to reproduce this shot but to leave it in his final cut. From high above, just as Marion tears away the shower curtain in her final living gesture, we see her body fall across the lip of the bathtub, the head dropping to the floor and the legs splaying apart so that the dark perineal area is visible under the pouring water. Certainly, if it is true that Hitchcock made this shot, it offers up the Leigh-Crane that had been withheld, the prize that had been promised to Loomis and that was never to be delivered; just as for Van Sant it presents the Heche-Crane Loomis has had many times over, what we may have been eager enough to share with him (his is the flesh to which we are given access most in the film), the public truth, the known topography. It may be worth noting, however, that the shot we do actually find in the earlier film leaves Leigh positioned facing along the length of the bathtub – when she falls (but we won't see it) she will not quite fall over the lip; whereas Van Sant's requires Heche to fall across the width. Since Leigh's orientation in the bathtub does not precisely match Heche's, if Van Sant duplicated a Hitchcock shot precisely (and there is little but publicity to suggest he did) the Hitchcock shot he duplicated – and that was cut – would not have been a longer version of the one we see but a second shot taken on-set, probably at the same time. If Hitchcock doubled this shot, it was an act untypical in his working style. But either way, it is clear that Hitchcock was operating with a keen sense of what social propriety would deem it honourable and respectable to show. Not simply was less gendered reality to be seen onscreen in 1960 than may be seen today; but the sense of propriety and impropriety, of revelation and hiding, was denser and more palpable in the social world where cinemas, film-going, and spectatorship existed.

Colour activates a system of openness, flatness, and anti-ocularcentrism (Jay, 1993) in the 1998 *Psycho*, then, producing all objects and all space equally for the eye and therefore eliminating the visual allure and organisation to be found in the Hitchcock. Similarly overt and matter-of-fact in Van Sant's film – that is, satisfying to a new appetite without prurience and hungry for 'reality' – and indeed even promiscuous, is Heche-Crane herself, whose tawny bra and underpants melt into her flesh in the opening hotel sequence and are metamorphosed as green as leprechauns as she prepares to skip town; whose lover (Viggo Mortensen) displays in her presence a casual and full male nudity with which she is blasé, thereby implicating her sexual experience and capacity; whose gestures and expressions utterly lack the moral containment and painful repression of Leigh-Crane. The formula of Heche-Crane's sexual knowledge reduces Loomis from motive to accomplice. And Marion, for her part, becomes capacitated in her relation with the patrolman; controlling in her relation with her boss; canny and agile in her banter with the millionaire Cassidy (the puissant Chad Everett); savvy in her relation with the used-car salesman (James LeGros). 'You can do anything you have a mind to. Being a woman, you will,' he smirks. In 1960 we knew he was being superior and coy, really speaking about himself. Now we know he is telling the blunt truth.

Bates and Bates

If the contemporisation of *Psycho* has taken the female protagonist off the knifepoint adjustment to a world of perduring and extenuating disempowerment and resuscitated her in a flat topography where desire, capacity, effort, achievement, and expression are both everywhere and at a minimum, if it has brought her pensivity and anxiety to a multicoloured – that is, conflict-free – surface where skin is indistinguishable from underwear and the fabrics from which her dresses are cut are like the landscapes through which she drives, its transformation of male engenderedness is similarly radical and exteriorising, and a pretext for at least two startling developments. Against the performance of Vince Vaughn, that of Anthony Perkins now stands out in the nudity of its denial and the starkness of its fear. In his gaunt face, the darting avian eyes, often photographed in high-key lighting which emphasised patches of darkness from which they could glow, are both a signal and a mystery, indicative of a frenzy in residence utterly beyond our vision. Vaughn, on the other hand, has a full-frame athletic body and a fleshy face with pouting, expressive lips. His facial expression is self-sufficient and projective, implying its target but not its source, an open and incontestable marker of male aggression and achievement orientation; it is a teleological face, a purposive face, appropriate for the demands of our multinational economy, where the $40,000 fortune Marion Crane took in 1960 is become a puff in the wind, and a house for a little girl who's never known a day of pain costs ten times as much, profit and success being valourised as critical at every instant, regardless of the banality of the frame of reference in which they are achieved. Vaughn-Bates's mother is only a projection worn by a violent and ambitious man; while Perkins-Bates was a mask worn, and ultimately eaten, by a violent and hungry mother.

The inability of Vaughn-Bates to restrain himself from projective expression toward a situated end is conveyed by Van Sant in an astonishing modification of the peephole scene. Perkins-Bates was shown in a medium-close shot profile as he peered through the hole into Marion's room. We saw what he saw: Marion undressing. As she performed the final gestures we jumped to a macro-close shot of his glowing, mystified, impotent eye swollen to occupy (be trapped by) the entire screen. This shot is witty, Rothman shows: 'While we were viewing this eye, it was viewing ... a view of which we were deprived' (Rothman, 1982: 289). Vaughn-Bates's eye is shown in a duplicate macro-close shot but the medium shot is extended as he peers through the wall to allow him to look down, reach below the frame edge, presumably withdraw his penis in shadow, and masturbate to the display that is unavailable to us. Where Hitchcock used the image of seeing to hide the object of sight – reflecting the devotion to the lens implicit in his filmmaking technique: while the lens sees the director does not see what it sees – Van Sant shows Bates's orgasm as signal of the public look and the open, thus unimaginable, new male who performs it. Vaughn-Bates secretes his male power; Perkins-Bates made a secret of it. And the peephole itself, that earlier reflection of the shady world of gay clubs and porn theatres, has now become a central site of contemporary sexual – and social – life. We are watching orgasm by surveillance. From a society in which male sexuality was desire invested and denied, converted into kinesis, violence, wit, posture or charm – and in which such desire unavoidably configured a dominable other – we have moved into public, and independent, male expression, the 'other' traced only as a visible aphrodisiac. Domination is doubled, since the figure of Marion is only a passive and unresponding stimulant; and since Bates's self-absorption and self-pleasuring utterly evaporate her – and us – from social interaction. Domination now implies definition and control, not rights to exploration by (even violently) probing boundaries. At the edge of the swamp, waiting to see whether Marion's car will *go in*, Vaughn-Bates is not standing in eerie trepidation as Perkins-Bates was. Instead he smirks with knowledge of his own technical capacity to produce the event (like Van Sant, who learned from Hitchcock that it could be done), willing the vehicle down in a demonic inversion of the ceremony of enlightenment in *The Empire Strikes Back* (1980), where Luke Skywalker raises his X-Wing from the swamps of Dagobah.

Concluding packages

Hitchcock's *Psycho* was altogether a film about packaging, the essential process in the maintenance and outplaying of gender identity at a time of Cold War internationally and civil war between the genders at home (Leibman, 1995; Marling, 1994). Indeed, the film is a package of packages, and the Bates who does mind about being born in a trap (package) but says he doesn't is therefore a model for it, an entrapment by suits and trappings. With $40,000 illicitly packaged in her vehicle (it is presumed to be licitly packaged at her home, waiting to be packaged in a bank account), Marion finds a concealed (packaged) back road (in a concealing rainstorm) and thence the obscure Bates Motel. She repackages the cash in the *Los Angeles Times* (itself a packaging of accounts) then packages herself in a final(ising) shower. Dead, Marion is packaged in the shower curtain, this package itself being packaged in the boot of the car along with the money packaged in the newspaper. The car is packaged in the swamp. Then the entire case of Marion Crane, packaged in the consciousness of Milton Arbogast, is repackaged when he is killed and packaged in his car in the swamp. The swamping is ostensibly done by Mrs Bates herself, packaged inside her son Norman for long years until she emerges (was the monster of *Alien* (1979) a homage?), packaging him and everything he has done inside a perfect silence – the ultimate package.

Forty years later, however, entropy and publicity have triumphed. Gender is now configured in a pansexual – or at least panerotic – universe where the potentials of performance, staging, camouflage, concealment, and anxiety are no longer keynotes. Gender identities are only rationales on the basis of which to take specific action toward specific success, roads to boredom and tranquillity at once. Dying a second death, Marion Crane is not packaged in guilt or gender, but is only and pathetically a passer-by in the wrong place at the wrong time. The chilling 'psycho' has become a mere psycho, certifiable, to be sure, but not so strange. For him, gender and brutality are facts of contemporary life, not moral mysteries.

In the context of his claims to having achieved a precise shot-by-shot remake, Van Sant's treatment of Norman Bates's scopophiliac moment is itself something of a theory of *Psycho*, not only part of its revision. Vaughn-Norman's response to Marion undressing in her motel room is genital auto-erotism, but Perkins-Norman's response was a fixated gaze. For Vaughn-Norman, an intense gaze leads the way to masturbation. For Perkins-Norman, the moment's impulse is embedded in, and entirely absorbed by, the act of the gaze. Van Sant's Vaughn-Norman, however, is, if we take Van Sant seriously, to be taken as a re-embodiment of Hitchcock's Perkins-Norman, indeed a precise re-embodiment. Van Sant is thus speculating that in his peeping, Hitchcock's Norman was committing masturbation in his way. But this idea, that the spectacle develops for, services the ends of, and stimulates male genital pleasure is, I think, contradictory to Hitchcock's original meaning, not a restatement of it. For Hitchcock, just as for Perkins-Norman, the fixated gaze is not produced or experienced in the name of ultimate sexual pleasure and release – thus, for power or for knowledge or for mastery of position. It is the philosophical fulcrum of our experience of vulnerability and desire, our need to connect and the impossibility of our connection. Thus, the experience we have, and that Hitchcock produces for us, of Perkins-Norman's peeping transcends sexuality and dominance altogether.

Mrs Bates had been buried, we learn from a sheriff's gossipy wife, in a dress that was *periwinkle blue*. As we watch *Psycho* in black and white, this is a profound, entrancing, almost debilitating vision of desire and unattainability, one that perfectly embodies Norman's visionary debility and romantic wound. In colour, however, it is a perfunctory datum. Periwinkle blue, persimmon pink, any colour – every colour – will do. In such a sensible consumerist world as Van Sant depicts, the radical tale of camouflage and revelation is itself suspect, pure cheese. So now, as we are regaled by the attending psychiatrist with a history of Norman's possession, even consumption, by his dominating mother, we come in this post-Freudian post-erotic post-theatrical era *not to believe him at all*. Another empty theory pompous to claim truth. He may not be Norman, to be sure, but this killer is surely not his own mother. At worst the diagnosis is a scriptwriter's failure, closure, and dead end, a pathetic masculinism incanting to redeem itself. At best it illuminates a fabulous – and theatrical – scam. Instead of suffering a *frisson* of mixed terror and delight we are suspended in readiness for the next banality as we step homeward to watch the evening news.

Part IV

Displacements and border crossings: horror cinema and transcultural adaptation

Adapting legends: urban legends and their adaptation in horror cinema[1]

Mikel J. Koven

Urban legends, those apocryphal stories told in university dormitories and around campfires about hook-handed psycho-killers and boyfriends discovered hanging above the parked cars, are a form of oral literature. I have previously explored how many urban legends were adapted into several well-known 'slasher' films in the late 1970s and early 1980s (Koven, 2003). In this study, I will take a step backwards, and explore the adaptive processes these largely formless narratives (Georges, 1971: 18) have undergone to be made into mainstream cinematic horror narratives. I will expand on Paul Smith's typology (1999) by considering some of the structural issues of the urban legend film – that is, films based primarily or largely on orally circulated belief narratives. Much of my previous work in the area of folklore and film has focused primarily on an individual legend, or cycle of legends, and how they are manifested in popular cinema and television (see Koven, 1999; 2000; 2003). That work presents how these films operate as cultural discourse: how popular cinema reflects and transmits popular belief traditions, specifically in the case of legend and film. I am forgoing that level of analysis here in order to define some of the more textual dimensions to the urban legend horror film in an effort to expand on what Smith began.

Two 1990s films generated much debate amongst legend scholars, for obvious reasons: *Urban Legend* (Jamie Banks: 1998) and *Candyman* (Bernard Rose: 1992). Both films utilise urban legend materials as a central aspect of their narrative.[2] Elsewhere, I have discussed *Candyman* from a folkloristic perspective by drawing upon the literature surrounding ostension (Koven, 1999). Overall, however, a useful methodology for the analysis of legends in popular cinema has been slow to develop.

An obvious starting point would be a consideration of the narrative structure of those films either based on or utilising urban legends. Although Paul Smith and Sandy Hobbs's work (1990) is useful, they do not distinguish between films which *include* individual legend motifs and those films which are *based* on urban legends. Of the 29 films they survey, 17 (59 per cent) are based fully on legends, while 12 (41 per cent) use legend motifs within their narrative. Later, Smith will further break this category down, dividing his 'Group C: Fiction [films]' into five sub-categories: 'Asides', 'Embedded Narratives', 'Sub-plots', 'Multiple Plots' and 'Complete Plots' (Smith, 1999: 140–5). This aspect of his typology is largely based on how important the legend is to the overall narrative; but it is problematic, as it is not sufficiently descriptive of *how* the legend is being used in popular cinema. As it stands, Smith's typology becomes increasingly unsatisfactory with regard to his first three sub-categories: 'asides', 'embedded narratives', and 'sub-plots'. At first the distinction is quite clear: namely, 'sub-plots' are where '[urban] legends are used as an integral part of the film's sub-plot' (Smith, 1999: 141), whereas 'asides' and 'embedded narratives' 'usually ... do not contribute to furthering the overall plot of the film' (Smith, 1999: 140). There is some confusion regarding the difference between what Smith identifies as 'embedded narratives' and 'asides'. The former is relatively clear; as the author notes, 'I have used this term to cover those scenarios where a character in a film relates a ... legend – much as someone would in ordinary conversation' (Smith, 1999: 141). In this sense, Smith is referring to legend texts that are *embedded* into the narrative's dialogue. However, Smith is less clear about 'asides': 'these are sometimes *textual*, but can also be *visual*' (Smith, 1999: 140). What remains unclear is if Smith identifies a *textual* legend reference (that is a non-substantive aspect of the narrative), when is it an aside and not an embedded narrative?

While the 'embedded narratives' sub-category is useful, Smith's distinction between 'asides' and 'sub-plots' is too ambiguous. As noted above, 41 per cent of the films Smith and Hobbs cite use legend motifs within their diegesis: that is, within the filmic narrative, urban legends are either told or demonstrated, but are not necessarily substantive to the overall film-story. Some of their examples (significantly, none of them horror films), like *Bliss* (Ray Lawrence: 1985) which features a circus elephant sitting on the protagonist's car after mistaking it for its stool in performance (Smith and Hobbs, 1990: 141), or *Superman III* (Richard Lester: 1983) where 'a computer operator rounds down the odd cents in customers' accounts and transfers the "loose change" to his own account' (Smith and Hobbs, 1990: 142), use a kind of ostensive demonstration of legend texts to 'flesh-out' their filmic narratives. Other examples the authors cite include feature films wherein diegetic characters relate orally the legend texts: for example, in *Night Moves* (Arthur Penn: 1975) the 'Alligators in the Sewers' legend is *told to* private detective Harry Moseby (Gene Hackman) (Smith and Hobbs, 1990: 142).

Within Smith's typology, *Superman III* would be an 'aside', *Night Moves* would be an 'embedded narrative', while *Bliss* would be a 'sub-plot'. All three examples embed their legend texts within an overall narrative structure but the difference in legend *performance* – that is, whether the legend is told or ostensibly demonstrated – is rarely taken into consideration. We should, therefore, within the larger narrative category of Smith's 'Group C' films, distinguish between *ostensive* and *dialogic* legend motifs: those legends represented (as action) and presented (as dialogue).

The vast majority of films Smith and Hobbs identify as using urban legend motifs *within their diegesis* use ostensive motifs – that is, rather than present the legend narrative orally, these films represent the legend *in situ*. Whether we are dealing with a representation of 'The Driver's Revenge' in *Smokey and the Bandit* (Hal Needham: 1977) (Smith and Hobbs, 1990: 142) or 'The Pet in the Microwave' motif in *Gremlins* (Joe Dante: 1984) (Smith and Hobbs. 1990: 145), these urban legends appear incidentally in the film *as action*, not orally.

The other kind of incidental legend manifestation in film *is* orally presented – characters tell the urban legend to others in what I call *dialogic* motifs. More often than not, these occur in fictional contexts with great verisimilitude to actual legend transmission: they take place in casual conversation or in sessions around a campfire. For example, in *Meatballs* (Ivan Reitman:

1979), Tripper (Bill Murray) tells his junior counsellors 'The Hook' legend around a campfire. He concludes his narrative by noting that 'some say he's still around here. And I say . . . they're *right*!' This final line is punctuated with Tripper revealing a hook for his hand, successfully scaring the other counsellors. By playing with the conventions of legend storytelling, and bringing the action to the here-and-now, this sequence in *Meatballs* demonstrates the slippage between dialogic and ostensive legend telling: what began as an oral presentation of the narrative (complete with appropriate context) becomes playful representation for the diegetic characters in the mock hook Tripper reveals at the end. This example demonstrates that these categories should not be seen as essentialist, but often feature slippage between the two. This sequence also demonstrates some further generic slippage: *Meatballs* is a comedy, not a horror film. In both legend telling and its cinematic equivalent, the slippage between comedy and horror, like that between dialogic and ostensive legend telling, is often mutually dependent.

Therefore, any film which is not directly based on an urban legend text, but uses legendary materials within its diegesis (either as a substantive or non-substantive aspect of its narrative) can be considered *embedded narrative*. However, within this sub-category of *embedded narratives* we must also distinguish between *ostensive* and *dialogic* embedded narratives.

Single-strand narratives

When it comes to films which are based on urban legends, Smith identifies two categories: 'multiple plot' and 'complete plot' films (Smith, 1999: 144–5). I have identified four main narrative strategies that filmmakers avail themselves to within Smith's 'complete plot' category: *extended*, *resultant*, *structuring* and *fusion* narratives.

Those films that begin with a legend text, and then extend the filmic narrative to explore the repercussions of the incident for the remainder of the film I have called *extended narratives*. In *When a Stranger Calls* (Fred Walton: 1979), the first twenty minutes of the film is a 'basic dramatization' (Smith and Hobbs, 1990: 139) of 'The Babysitter and the Man Upstairs' legend. This is extended to explore the effects of this incident seven years later.

The babysitter, Jill (Carol Kane), has now married and has a family of her own, but 'the Man Upstairs', Curt Duncan (Tony Beckley) is released from prison and desires to finish what he started with Jill. While the first 20 minutes of the film is a tense realisation of the legend, in the attempt to extend this narrative for another 70 minutes, too much deviation from the original urban legend occurs. There are two possible reasons why the extended narrative fails: one is that by extending the narrative to 'seven years later', Jill is no longer a point of identification for the mostly adolescent audience. By becoming a housewife and mother, the character is too distant for the audience to relate to experientially. The other violation of the legend's cultural logic is the film's focus on the experiences of the newly-released Duncan. Again, the young audience cannot identify with the experiences of the killer. 'Francois Truffaut claims that we identify with a character not when we look *with* the character, but when the character looks *at us*' (Bordwell and Thompson, 1986: 197, emphasis added). We therefore do not identify with Curt Duncan when he is watching Jill babysit, but when Jill returns our gaze on-screen, we relate to her fear and predicament. By moving the narrative away from that point of identification, either by progressing Jill's life beyond the audiences' level of experience, or by focusing on the killer's story, that early identification is violated. While *When a Stranger Calls* could be considered an *embedded narrative*, since only the first section of the film is concerned with representing the legend itself, the legend acts as a leitmotif throughout the entire film, particularly in Duncan's taunting phone calls with their chilling catch-phrase asking if Jill has 'checked the children'.

A slightly more successful demonstration of this narrative strategy is the film *Dead Man's Curve* (Dan Rosen: 1998). Despite not being strictly speaking a horror film, it is a sufficiently dark thriller. *Dead Man's Curve* begins with a voice-over telling us the legend of 'The Suicide Rule' – if your roommate commits suicide, you get an automatic Grade Point Average of 4.0 for that semester (a *dialogic embedded narrative*). Chris (Michael Vartan) is in his final semester and his grades are falling. His roommate, Tim (Matthew Lillard), convinces him to utilise 'The Suicide Rule' and together they plan to bump off their third roommate, Rand (Randall Batinkoff). This film extends its narrative to explore the effects this plan has on the students, and develops into a dark 'who-killed-who' thriller. But, unlike *When a Stranger Calls*, *Dead Man's Curve* maintains its points of identification throughout, so the plot twists and reversals in the movie, although not based in legendry, still hold the audience's attention, interest and identification.

Another strategy filmmakers employ gives us the lead-up to a legend story: *resultant narratives*. For example, in *The Harvest* (David Marconi: 1993), Charlie Pope (Miguel Ferrer), a writer working on a 'true-crime'-type film script, is suffering from both writer's block and pressure from his producers to keep the script exciting. Pope goes down to Mexico, where the original murder occurred, and begins his own investigations. While down there doing his research, Pope meets a woman in a bar, gets drunk, and while walking with her on a beach is knocked out by unknown assailants. Regaining consciousness, Pope discovers he is inside the 'Organ Theft' legend. Thinking the woman was a decoy to lure him to the organ thieves, he tracks her down and together they become involved in trying to stop an international black-market organ trade. In *resultant narratives* we get the behind-the-scenes story, about the lead-up to the familiar legend. The actual legend acts almost as a punch-line to the film. Ideally under this narrative strategy, we have identified with our protagonist(s), and so are more receptive to the horror of what happens to them once the legend-aspects are revealed.

Another *resultant narrative* is *I Know What You Did Last Summer* (Jim Gillespie: 1997). Based on the 'young-adult' novel of the same name, the overall story involves a pact between four newly-graduated high school students who accidentally kill someone during a drunk-driving incident. They are sworn to secrecy, but a psycho killer hunts them down, leaving the enigmatic message 'I know what you did last summer.' The killer – dressed in oilskins and carrying a longshoreman's hook – suggests the urban legend of 'The Hook'. Before the accident, Julie (Jennifer Love Hewitt), Helen (Sarah Michelle Gellar), Barry (Ryan Phillippe) and Ray (Freddie Prinze Jr) sit around a campfire telling the 'Hook' legend. Here the storytelling context is represented along with the presentation of the legend itself (again an example of a *dialogic embedded narrative*). But there is disagreement among the characters over how the actual story runs – the 'Hook' story gets confused with variants of 'The

Boyfriend's Death'. The conclusion of the sequence, Ray's comments that although 'folklore', these stories are based somehow in truth, sets up the urban legend matrix: the hook-*carrying* killer that will stalk Julie and her friends the following year becomes the hook-*handed* killer in the oral tradition. In an intriguing hypothesis, *I Know What You Did Last Summer* acts as *precognitive resultant narrative* – the film is primarily about the lead-in to the 'Hook' story (*resultant narrative*), but this *resultant narrative* structure is set up a year previous to the film's main action. Interestingly, Lois Duncan's original novel is a straightforward murder mystery which omits this urban legend aspect (added into the film by screenwriter Kevin Williamson).

A third narrative strategy uses the urban legend as a *structuring outline* and develops its diegesis from within. In the black comedy *Dead Man on Campus* (Alan Cohn: 1998), Josh Miller (Tom Everett Scott) is a scholarship student who needs to maintain a high grade point average in order to keep his funding. Unfortunately, he ends up rooming with wild-man Cooper Fredrickson (Mark-Paul Gosselaar). Introduced to sex, drugs and rock and roll, Josh watches his marks plummet. Enter again the urban legend of 'The Suicide Rule'. Josh and Scott scheme to find the most psychologically unbalanced roommate they can and push him over the edge. As Scott says within the movie, 'They're probably going to commit suicide anyway. Why not have their death actually benefit someone.' With that outline, *Dead Man on Campus* takes the legend and structures an *Animal House*-type black comedy as these two students try to find the perfect roommate for their purposes. On the level of audience identification, the pressures of academic achievement and the seemingly *ad hoc* administration of university dormitories – of being forced to get along with complete strangers in a living situation – get reflected in the 'Suicide Rule' legend and in films like *Dead Man's Curve* and *Dead Man on Campus*. In particular, the latter film, as a 'gross-out' comedy, puts a different emphasis on the legend – we still have similar college-aged fears going on, but by laughing at them, the wish-fulfilment quality comes to the fore: to live as irresponsibly as possible without any reprisals in terms of grades or expulsion. But, the profound impact of adolescent suicide is dealt with by not putting those characters established as points of identification (here Scott and Coop) in positions of mortal danger (unlike in *Dead Man's Curve*). The boys' potential victims are established as 'spectacles': Cliff (Lochlyn Munro), the alcoholic and psychotic jock; Buckley (Randy Pearlstein) the paranoid conspiracy theorist; and Matt (Corey Page), the faux-British musical nihilist. The one 'real' suicide attempt within the diegesis, the boys' genuinely neurotic neighbour Pickle (Aeryk Egan), is treated with sensitivity and respect.

Finally, *fusion narratives* are filmic narratives which fuse two mutually exclusive urban legends together. In *Alligator* (Lewis Teague: 1980), the film starts off as the 'Alligators in the Sewers' legend, but in order to explain how the alligators in question became mutated – in addition to light deprivation and changes in food – this filmic narrative also introduces another legend narrative about pets abducted for medical experimentation. Specifically, for this film's diegesis, these pets are genetically experimented upon, and the resulting carcasses are thrown into the sewers where the flushed alligator feeds. Eventually this movie becomes a *Jaws*-like, man versus animal movie – but what keeps it from being an *extended narrative* is the 'Alligator in the Sewers' legend fused with the legend about 'Pet Abductions for Medical Experiments'.

Multiple-strand narratives

Urban legends are characteristically short: that is, unlike fairy tales, legends often take less time to tell and feature less complicated plots. The variety of 'single-strand' filmic narrative strategies demonstrates some of the ways in which filmmakers have attempted to expand, or extend, legend narratives. However, regardless of narrative technique, most legends cannot sustain a full-length movie. Other narrative techniques are required to transform legends into film: in particular, using several legend texts in the same movie – or what I call, 'multiple-strand' narratives.

Urban Legend is the most obvious example of *multiple fusion narratives* – films that fuse together a number of legend texts (either represented through ostension or dialogue). In the movie, undergraduate student Natalie (Alicia Witt) is terrorised by a psycho killer using urban legends as *modus operendi* – that is, the film uses *ostensive embedded narratives* as a murder device in a horror film.

But beyond that aspect of *Urban Legend*, the film also features some more benign forms of *ostensive embedded narratives*. For example, Natalie and her friend Brenda (Rebecca Gayhart) attempt a variation on the 'Bloody Mary' ritual at the now boarded-up entrance to Stanley Hall, the site of a student massacre twenty-five years earlier. Likewise, we see Professor Wexler (Robert Englund) tell the story about Mikey from the Life brand cereal commercial having died from consuming Pop Rocks with Coke to demonstrate the 'fallaciousness' of these stories to his folklore class. Both of these examples, while a form of ostensive legend representation, are benign in the sense that no one is actually hurt.

Urban legends are also presented in the movie as more serious *ostensive embedded narratives*: the whole premise of the film is that a killer is enacting these legends 'for real'. The movie begins with Michelle Mancini (Natasha Gregson Wagner) being killed in a re-enactment of the legend of 'The Killer in the Backseat'. Damon Brooks (Joshua Jackson) is killed using the scenario of 'The Boyfriend's Death', and Natalie's roommate, Tosh (Danielle Harris), is murdered in a representation of the 'Aren't You Glad You Didn't Turn On the Light' story. Sasha (Tara Reid), the campus 'shock-jock' radio personality, is murdered on-air, and while perhaps not based on a specific legend itself, echoes the stories about 'snuff' movies, or deaths recorded on-air. Even Natalie is nearly a victim of ostension as the killer attempts to steal one of her kidneys.

Professor Wexler is murdered off-camera, but his body is discovered in the boot of a car by the smell of his decomposing corpse. Is this an intentional echo of the 'Death Car' legend? And although Parker (Michael Rosenbaum) is actually killed by the forced ingestion of drain cleaner (to my knowledge not a legend), this murder is preceded by his dog maliciously exploded in a microwave. The killer's motive, is also based on an urban legend: Brenda's fiancé was killed in a car accident resulting from Natalie and Michelle enacting the 'Car-Lights Initiation' legend, and she is now avenging her own boyfriend's death. In all of these examples, ostension is used, diegetically, to murder people – Brenda is taking the legends and making them real.

There is a more complex level of ostension operating in *Urban Legend* at the level of the filmmakers' self-reflexivity: from a semiotic perspective, and ostension is primarily semiotic, the actors in the film are left at the level of signifier to their other, extra-textual identities. For example, Joshua Jackson is primarily known for his role in the television series *Dawson's Creek*, created by Kevin Williamson, who also wrote the legend-based film *I Know What You Did Last Summer* and *Scream*. This self-awareness is textually indicated in the film, as Damon is attempting to make out with Natalie and puts on the radio. When Paula Cole's 'I Don't Want to Wait', the theme tune to *Dawson's Creek* starts playing, Damon turns it off with disgust. This level of ostension appeals to the *Dawson's Creek* audience, those cinema goers whose experience of horror movies begins with *Scream* (Wes Craven: 1996). But furthermore, Danielle Harris ('Tosh') is known primarily as the star of both *Halloween 4* (Dwight Little: 1988) and *Halloween 5* (Dominique Othenin-Girard: 1989), at least within the horror fan community – i. e. another audience likely to see *Urban Legend*, and who are likely to know about *Halloween 4 & 5*. If this example is a tad esoteric, Robert Englund ('Prof Wexler') is quite a celebrity within this fan community as the man who also played Freddie Kruger in the *Nightmare on Elm Street* movies. So, while the casting of Harris and Kruger appeal potentially to one kind of fan audience for this particular film (the horror audience), the casting of Jackson and the 'in-joke' about the Paula Cole song appeals to another kind of fan audience (the teen audience). If, as Linda Dégh seems to indicate, ostension can run the gamut from murdering one's university colleagues, like Brenda does in legend-like scenarios, to the wearing of legend-referent Halloween costumes (Dégh, 1995: 241), then, as I argued elsewhere (Koven, 1999), *cinematic* ostension, as the game played by movie audiences participating in a film, can also run a similar gamut which includes the recognition of this self-reflexive game of semiotic referencing.

Yet beyond these explicitly ostensive methods of representing legends, *Urban Legend* also features incidents of *dialogic embedded narratives*. In particular, two characters are the focus of these legend tellings. Sasha, as a regular section of her seemingly endless radio-show, has her listeners phone in. It is these listeners who relate the legend texts. Interestingly, these stories, although they are presented to us as *dialogic embedded narratives,* within the diegetic world of *Urban Legend,* are off-screen *ostensive embedded narratives*: her callers have actually replaced a roommate's birth-control pills with baby aspirin, been the 'promiscuous cheerleader', or phoned in whilst stuck in a new sexual position.

The other focus for *dialogic embedded narratives* within the film is the character Parker, who relates the 'University Cover-up of Campus Murder', the 'Spider Eggs in Bubble Yum', the 'Richard Gere and the Gerbil', and the 'Babysitter and the Man Upstairs' stories. In all of these cases, Parker tells these stories with great pleasure, both debunking the belief in them and just relishing a good and grisly tale. The positioning of Parker as debunker also parallels him with Professor Wexler, who not only retells the 'Babysitter and the Man Upstairs' story as part of his folklore lecture, but is equally concerned with debunking 'wrong beliefs'.

Clearly, the film is intended to appeal to college students as it reflects their experiences and social fears. However, *Urban Legend* seems to have two social anxiety themes, both of which reflect that experiential dimension of college life: one is the fear of strangers at university, of feeling alone and not knowing anyone, even your would-be killer. The other one is more implicit. Brenda's motivation for killing her classmates is a direct consequence of her fiancé's death resulting from Natalie and Michelle's playing around with the 'Car-Lights Initiation' legend. The film seems to be warning young people, the movie and genre's chief demographic, that even seemingly benign forms of ostension, of just playing around *without* murderous intent, can be deadly.

Candyman is another film which fuses a number of legends into a similar construct. We hear about 'The Hippy Babysitter' who cooks the child and puts the chicken to bed, as well as the 'Alligators in the Sewers' story (*dialogic embedded narratives*). We are offered visually images intended to echo with the 'Razor Blades found in Halloween Candy', the 'Child Emasculated in the Public Washroom', and even the historical legend of 'Gelert', where the blood from a faithful dog is mistaken for the blood of a baby (*ostensive embedded narratives*). Candyman's (Tony Todd) body is also a small compendium of legend texts: he has a hook for a hand ('Hook-Handed Killer'), his body is a beehive (an echo of the stories about 'Killer Bees'), and is summoned by the 'Bloody Mary' ritual (all of which can also be considered *ostensive embedded narratives*).

Another narrative strategy filmmakers sometimes avail themselves to in conveying a variety of urban legend texts is the *anthology film*. Anthology films are films that rather than try to fuse a number of narratives together, anthologise them, usually with some kind of framing device. This technique recognises the short-story quality of urban legends, and rather than expanding or extending the narratives, treats each story as distinct. For example, Smith and Hobbs identify the first story in *Nightmares* (Joseph Sargent: 1983), 'Terror in Topanga', as 'The Killer in the Backseat' legend (Smith and Hobbs, 1990: 142). Examples like Sargent's film only use urban legends for single sections of their anthology.

However there is at least one anthology film that draws heavily on urban legendry: *Campfire Tales* (Matt Cooper, Martin Kunert, David Semel: 1997). *Campfire Tales* is noteworthy in part for its narrative structure: not only does it follow the basic anthology structure – four teens are stranded in the woods after a car accident, they build a campfire and tell the legends which are then represented dramatically – but this framing narrative is prefaced and epilogued by another legendary representation.

The movie opens in monochrome, even before the opening credits sequence, with a three and a half minute representation of 'The Hook'. The time period seems to be the late 1950s/early 1960s, reflecting the time period when this story was first recognised as circulating. The climax of the story, where our hero, Eddie (James Marsden) discovers the dismembered hook hanging from Jenny's (Amy Smart) side of the car is punctuated musically by a *Psycho*-like chord of strings as the camera pans up the car door revealing the hook stuck in the doorjamb. This shot is followed by two quick successive close-ups moving ever tighter on the hook itself, before cutting to black for the opening credits sequence where we hear our framing narrative characters, Cliff (Jay R. Ferguson), Eric (Christopher Masterson), Alex (Kim Murphy), and Lauren (Christine Taylor) debate the 'probability' of that story's veracity, creating verisimilitude with ethnographically documented legend-telling sessions (Oring, 1986: 125).

Returning from a rock concert, the four teen storytellers are involved in a car-accident on a deserted stretch of road. While waiting for assistance, they build a campfire and tell scary stories. These narratives are then dramatised for the cinematic audience (*dialogic* becoming *ostensive embedded narrative*). The first of these narratives, titled 'The Honeymoon', is, for the most part, a werewolf story. Rick (Ron Livingston) and Valerie (Jennifer MacDonald) are driving west for their honeymoon. They run out of gas on a deserted stretch of highway, but are warned to stay in their vehicle until sunup by a spooky local (Hawthorne James). They are told that something is hunting them in the darkness and that they will be relatively safe inside. Rick dismisses this warning and heads out to find a gas station on his own, leaving Valerie to fend for herself in the trailer. Although werewolves are 'legendary' in the broadest sense of the word, they do not often appear in *urban* legends, which seem to favour more human monsters.

However, the climax of this short narrative brings 'The Honeymoon' back into urban legendry. The werewolves eviscerate Rick on his search for gas, and the monsters then attack the caravan. Valerie successfully holds off the monster assault until morning, when she is awakened by a hesitant knock on the camper door. A police officer tells her to step out of the vehicle and not to look back – a verbal signifier which cues us to the urban legend represented – 'The Boyfriend's Death'. Here is perhaps the best example of what I referred to above as a *resultant narrative*: we experience the flow of the filmic narrative, assuming it to be one thing, or at least taking us in one direction (here, as a werewolf story) only to reveal its legend at the end of the sequence.

The second narrative told/dramatised is what I referred to above as a *fusion narrative*. Titled, by the screenwriters, 'People Can Lick Too', this sequence ends in that particular legend (that is, the sequence is also a *resultant narrative*). However, in order to get to the legendary dénouement of the story, we begin with a variant of the legend Barbara Mikkelson calls 'Shannon's Friend'[3] – here a 12-year-old girl gives out personal information to her online 'friend', who she believes to be another child, but who is actually an internet predator, thereby fusing two different urban legends much in the same way as did *Alligator*.

The third story presented in the film, titled 'The Locket', is a romantic ghost story about a young motorcyclist (Glenn Quinn) who, having engine trouble, stops at an isolated house inhabited only by a beautiful but mute young woman (Jacinda Barrett). In the dead of night, they experience the paranormal reoccurrence of a horrendous murder. Although ghost stories are themselves legends, and there are many urban legends *about* ghosts, 'The Locket' does not have a direct correlation with the oral tradition. It is, however, possibly a Mexican-American variant on 'The Vanishing Hitchhiker' legend, whereby instead of meeting the spectre on the road hitchhiking, the human and the ghost meet at a party or a ball (Glazer, 2002).

Likewise, although not a specific contemporary legend, but using a broader definition of legendry as 'belief narrative', the framing narrative about the four campfire story-telling teens concludes with the revelation that the four are dead after the car accident. The characters from the narratives they have been telling are actually the people around the crash site. The film's end credits begin to roll, but after the director, screenwriter and cast credits for each of the segments, we are given a single tracking shot, pulling away from the accident scene along the line of backed up traffic. The final car we see is an old Thunderbird, and out of the car's widow, resting on the window frame, is a prosthetic hook, as the colour drains from the shot returning to the monochrome cinematography we began the film with.

Conclusions

Smith's revised typology, while a useful beginning, is clearly in need of further development. His typology of 'Group C: Fiction' can be developed as suggested above. This current development can be summarised thus:

I. Embedded Narratives
- Dialogic
- Ostensive

II. Single-strand Narratives
- Extended Narratives
- Resultant Narratives
- Structuring Narratives
- Fusion Narratives

III. Multi-strand Narratives
- Fusion Narratives – often embedding both dialogic and ostensive narratives
- Anthologies – which may use any of the techniques of single-strand or embedded narratives

That being said, this revised typology does not cover the entirety of Smith's schema: his 'Group C' has two previous 'Groups' to contend with – 'Non-fiction' (like ethnographic films, news and documentaries) (Smith, 1999: 138–9) and a combination category of 'Non-fiction/Fiction' films (legends used in education, as propaganda, etc.) (Smith, 1999: 146–52). I am merely dealing with the adaptation of these legends in the (predominantly) horror fiction film.

And yet, within the relatively large discourse of horror movie adaptations, urban legends appear relatively infrequently. This surprises me as, firstly, these orally circulated stories are copyright free and therefore horror film producers do not have to pay any rights for the stories; and secondly, urban legends are good, gross, frightening, and suspenseful stories. The folk have been grossing each other out for centuries; horror movie producers should pay attention to that.

Fulcanelli as a vampiric Frankenstein and Jesus as his vampiric monster: the Frankenstein and Dracula myths in Guillermo del Toro's *Cronos*

Brad O'Brien

Fulcanelli, an early twentieth-century alchemist, describes his art as 'a spiritualistic chemistry, for it allows us to catch a glimpse of God through the darkness of substance' (Fulcanelli, 1999: 49). Unlike chemists, who limit their studies to the composition, structure, properties and interactions of matter, alchemists search for the animating, or spiritual, forces that bring about these interactions. Alchemists thus combine science with the supernatural. They direct their research toward what Fulcanelli calls 'the unknown animator, agent of so many marvels' (49).

In the opening scene of Guillermo del Toro's *Cronos* (1993), a fictional representation of Fulcanelli has discovered the secrets of the unknown animator. This Fulcanelli, who, in 1526, fled to Veracruz, Mexico to escape the Inquisition, has harvested God's animating force in order to create the 'Cronos device'. It works by piercing its user's skin with its insect-like legs and 'stinger', filtering the user's blood through some kind of life-giving insect contained inside the device and then pumping it back into his or her body. While the user gains eternal life, he or she must now drink human blood in order to survive. The device extends Fulcanelli's life by 400 years, but he eventually dies during an earthquake when a shard of metal pierces his heart. Del Toro thus portrays Fulcanelli as an alchemist-turned-vampire.

Because *Cronos* contains very few conventions of the modern vampire film, and parodies most of the ones it does contain, critics have praised its uniqueness. In her review of the film in the

New York Times, Janet Maslin calls it 'a very stylish and sophisticated Mexican variation on some age-old themes' that proves 'the vampire film is resoundingly undead' (Maslin, 1994: 16); Jonathan Romney, who reviewed *Cronos* for *New Statesman and Society,* refers to it as 'a vampire film with a difference' (Romney, 1994: 34); and for Ramiro Cristobal, who discusses *Cronos* in a *World Press Review* article entitled 'A Latin Mini-Renaissance', del Toro's film 'is an unusual story about vampires' (Cristobal, 1994: 50). In more academic essays, John Kraniauskas views *Cronos* as 'the story of a reluctant vampire' (Kraniauskas, 1998: 143), and Shohini Chauhuri (1997) examines it as a vampire narrative containing alien invasion themes.

But these critics ignore an interesting layer that del Toro adds to his film with the character Fulcanelli. They mention his creation of the Cronos device, but they make little or nothing of the fact that although Fulcanelli is a vampire, first he is a mad scientist playing God, a postmodern version of Prometheus, a late twentieth-century take on Frankenstein. *Cronos* is, therefore, just as much an atypical Frankenstein film as it is an atypical vampire film. Del Toro has combined the myths of Dracula and Frankenstein in order to form his own creation myth.

According to David Skal, who refers to Dracula and Frankenstein's monster as 'the dark twins', both characters are such familiar cultural icons that 'each conjures the other by contrast':

> Dracula is suave, sinister, supernaturally masterful, an aristocratic wraith slipping through a keyhole as a mist, transforming himself from man to bat to wolf and back again, with never a hair out of place. The Frankenstein creature, by contrast, is relentlessly downscale, a proletarian clod. Like a parody of the scientific method, he moves slowly, deliberately, one heavy step at a time. Dracula flaps ahead effortlessly, shape-shifting at will. The vampire's manner is seamless. Frankenstein's monster shows all his seams, literally. Taken together, the monsters constitute an overwhelming gestalt, representing the intuitive right brain and the logical left, shadow and substance, superstition and science – the oddest of odd couples. (Skal, 2001: 81)

While these 'dark twins' have their origins in Mary Shelley's *Frankenstein* and Bram Stoker's *Dracula*, Skal refers not to the original representations of these characters, but to the images they have evolved into largely as a result of the 1931 film version of each novel. Skal points out that in Stoker's novel, 'Dracula spends little time on social niceties and is physically repellant, a cadaverous old man who grows younger as he drinks blood but who never becomes attractive' (Skal, 2001: 83). However, in Tod Browning's film of the novel, Bela Lugosi plays a suave aristocrat with whom Lucy Westenra becomes completely enthralled the minute she meets him. As in the novel, Lugosi's Dracula hypnotises Lucy in a way that has more to do with his supernatural powers than with his appearance, but the 'girl talk' that Lucy and Mina Seward have while preparing for bed the night they meet Dracula at the opera suggests she has a conscious attraction to him as well. Throughout the film, Dracula is an aristocratic gentleman who blends in well with his new countrymen. While Frankenstein's monster is quickly recognisable as not-quite-human in both Shelley's novel and the various film adaptations of this novel, the 'proletarian clod' to whom Skal refers is clearly the monster that Boris Karloff plays in James Whale's film *Frankenstein*. It is difficult to imagine a monster who 'moves slowly, deliberately, one heavy step at a time' effortlessly scaling the steep mountains of Switzerland as the much more agile monster does in Shelley's novel.

Although the images of the main characters have changed as the myths of Frankenstein and Dracula have evolved, these myths' similar themes have remained relatively intact. In the novels that originally popularised the myths, Skal finds that 'the narratives . . . contain nearly as many similarities as polarities' (83). The most notable similarities are that

> both stories hinge on novel forms of self-replication (Frankenstein creates his own doppelganger by piecing together tissue from graveyards and slaughterhouses; Dracula reproduces his kind by a mystical blood transfusion) . . . both . . . are cautionary daydreams about failed attempts to overcome death, the scientist by rational enterprise, the vampire by irrational curse. (Skal, 2001: 83).

The myths of Dracula and Frankenstein thus involve very similar themes that revolve around very different characters. For Skal, these characters are 'two sides of a coin' (84). The coin is the theme of creation: on one side is an awkward, sympathetic creature created by science; on the other is a masterful, sinister creature with a supernatural origin.

Cronos, which can also be read as a 'cautionary daydream about failed attempts to overcome death', synthesises the myths of Frankenstein and Dracula in such a way that the dark twins become one. Del Toro's film, therefore, takes the evolution of these myths one step further. Rather than containing an image of one dark twin that conjures the other by contrast, or an image of each character, as in films like *House of Dracula* (1945) and *House of Frankenstein* (1944), *Cronos* presents us with the scientific, vampiric Fulcanelli and his vampiric monster, Jesus. Each dark twin lives inside each of these characters, and Fulcanelli and Jesus must reconcile the twins' opposing elements.

As I have already suggested, Fulcanelli is both a Frankenstein-figure and a Dracula-figure because he uses his scientific knowledge to prolong his own life, but in order to sustain this life, he must drink human blood. Fulcanelli the alchemist, therefore, creates two monsters: the vampire Fulcanelli and the vampire Jesus Gris. Because Fulcanelli is in the film for only about five minutes, we know very little about how he deals with his condition. However, because he lives as a vampire for 400 years, it is safe to assume that his studies in alchemy help him understand this condition and prepare him to deal with it.

His creation Jesus Gris, who unwittingly, and somewhat unwillingly, becomes a vampire, does not understand his new condition and is not prepared to deal with it. Fulcanelli does not abandon his creature in the way Victor Frankenstein abandons his, but Jesus, the newborn vampire, does lack parental guidance. The absent father, or the creator's abandonment of his creature, is an element of the Frankenstein myth that has remained important from the beginning. In Shelley's novel, Victor Frankenstein tells us, 'Unable to endure the aspect of the being I had created, I rushed out of the room' (Shelley, 1998 [1818]: 39). Victor thus abandons his creation when he is only minutes old. Left on his own to deal with the new experience of being alive, the Creature must learn not only to provide water, food and shelter for himself, but also to understand the various impressions he receives from his five senses. Later in the novel, when he and Victor finally meet face to face, the Creature describes this confusion to Victor: 'A strange multiplicity of sensations seized me, and I saw, felt, heard, and smelt, at the same time; and it was, indeed, a long time before I learned to distinguish between the operations of my various senses' (79–80). He refers to himself as a 'poor, helpless, miserable wretch' and says, 'I knew, and could distinguish, nothing; but feeling pain invade me on all sides, I sat down and wept' (80).

The vampire Jesus Gris has similar experiences during the first night of his new life. After accidentally using the Cronos device, Jesus, understandably, feels helpless and confused while dealing with the changes this device causes to happen to his body. On the night after he is 'stung' by the device, Jesus opens the refrigerator, removes a jug of water and takes a long drink from it. But when he replaces the jug and attempts to close the refrigerator, his eyes are drawn to a very bloody piece of raw meat. He stares at this bloody meat for several seconds, fighting the urge to eat it. His new vampiric-body craves it while his mind resists this craving.

After closing the refrigerator door, Jesus walks upstairs and removes a shoebox containing the Cronos device from its hiding place under a bed. He then walks halfway down the stairs, places the device in his hand and, addressing the device as if it were a god, says a short prayer to it: 'Please, please, please. Be very careful with my soul, please.' This prayer helps illustrate Jesus's fear and confusion. He knows the Cronos device has done more than simply pierce his skin, that it has awakened forbidden desires within him, but he does not understand these desires, and he fears the device is affecting his body and his soul. He realises it has power over him, and thus views it as some sort of god. Unable to resist its power, he gives in to the urge to use the Cronos device again.

While waiting for the device to appease his new desires, Jesus stares at the ceiling and says a prayer to his Christian god, but the Cronos device cuts this prayer short when it pierces Jesus's skin and he collapses on the stairs in pain. When the device begins to filter his blood through the life-giving insect it contains, this pain turns to pleasure, which quickly turns to shame when Jesus looks up and sees his mute, five-year-old granddaughter watching him. Jesus is thus overwhelmed with nervous confusion on his first night as a vampire. He seeks salvation from two different gods, but the dark one grants it more quickly, so Jesus obeys this god more readily. He obeys it not only in the presence of his granddaughter, but also within view of a brightly lit Christmas tree.

The next morning, Jesus's anxiety seems to have passed. He shaves his moustache, and when his wife, Mercedes, tells him he looks much younger, he replies, 'Exactly, that's why I did it. That's how I feel.' At this point in the film, Jesus resembles Stoker's Dracula, who, after he has gorged himself on blood, looks 'as if his youth had been half renewed' (Stoker, 1997: 53). Within Jesus's first 24 hours as a vampire, del Toro thus reveals that he embodies both Frankenstein's monster and Dracula.

Although Jesus seems at ease with his condition in the morning of his first full day as a vampire, in the afternoon of this day, we learn that he is not. When he returns home after his first meeting with Dieter de la Guardia, Jesus craves the power the Cronos device gives him, but when he attempts to retrieve it from its hiding place, the shoebox is empty. With a look of anger on his face, he says, 'Aurora, my God.' He seems angry at his granddaughter for taking the device, angry at himself for allowing her to see him use it the night before and for leaving it where she could find it, but also angry because he cannot have his fix right when he wants it.

He rushes upstairs to Aurora's playroom in a storage room on the roof of the house. When he enters the room, he says, 'Aurora? I know you've got it.' He then digs through her toy box looking for the device. When he sees her feet under a curtain she is hiding behind, his anger subsides. He sits down and explains that he does not understand what's happening to him, but it is best if they stick together. Aurora steps out of her hiding place, gives him the Cronos device, which she has hidden in her teddy bear, and then hugs him.

Jesus wants to retrieve the device immediately because he craves the power it gives him, but he does not want to frighten Aurora, and he wants to preserve their close relationship. Like Frankenstein's monster, he wants to be understood and accepted. Jesus has a good relationship with Mercedes, but he keeps this new aspect of himself hidden from her. It is too late to hide it from Aurora, so he talks to her about it. At this point in the film, and at this point in Jesus's development as a vampire, his need for human companionship overrides his desire for the pleasure he gains from the Cronos device. Jesus successfully reconciles the opposing elements of the dark twins that now live inside him.

But the darker of the dark twins takes over when the vampire Jesus smells human blood for the first time. He is enjoying a New Year's Eve party with his wife and granddaughter, seemingly as human as one can be, when he stands up from his seat next to his wife and forgets about everything else except the blood dripping from a man's nose on the other side of the room. He excuses himself from the table, follows the man into the restroom, and when he has the restroom to himself, lies on his belly and licks up a puddle of blood that has dripped from the man's nose onto the floor. Jesus thus experiences his first taste of human blood. He now craves human blood rather than just the effect of the Cronos device, and this new craving is much more difficult to resist.

At the point in the film when Jesus is most like Dracula, he is also most like Frankenstein's monster, which makes it easy for us to see the twins' opposing sides having their way with Jesus. When Angel de la Guardia puts him in a car and then pushes it over a cliff, Jesus dies a natural death but continues living as a vampire. The man Jesus Gris, who had been dying ever since Jesus first used the Cronos device, is now dead. Like the popular image of Karloff as Frankenstein's monster, the undead Jesus has grey skin and staples in his head, and he walks with a limp, moving 'slowly, deliberately, one heavy step at a time' (Skal, 2001: 81). He wears a cape, like Count Dracula, and because the sunlight burns his skin, he sleeps during the day in Aurora's toy box, which functions as his coffin.

The Frankenstein monster that lives inside Jesus also manifests itself in Jesus's need to understand his condition. In Shelley's novel, Victor's creature tells him that he wondered, 'Who was I? What was I? Whence did I come? What was my destination?' (Shelley, 1998 [1818]: 104). Victor's 'papers', which the Creature finds in a pocket of a shirt he has taken from Victor's apartment, provide some of these answers. He tells Victor:

> Every thing is related in them which bears reference to my accursed origin; the whole detail of that series of disgusting circumstances which produced it is set in view; the minutest description of my odious and loathsome person is given, in language which painted your own horror, and rendered mine ineffaceable. I sickened as I read. 'Hateful day when I received life!' I exclaimed in agony. (105)

Jesus's questions are answered in a similar way, and he has a similar reaction to these answers. Because his creator, Fulcanelli, has been dead for decades, the closest thing he has to a father is Dieter de la Guardia. Dieter, who is dying of cancer and hopes to extend his life with the Cronos device, owns Fulcanelli's notebook, which explains how he built the device, how it works and how to use it. Dieter, therefore, has the knowledge to gain eternal life, but he lacks the technology to apply this knowledge, the Cronos device. Jesus is in an opposite position; he possesses the technology, and although he knows how to use it, he does not understand how it works or what it has done to him. He confronts Dieter and demands answers about his birth and his undeath.

From Dieter, he learns that although his skin is rotting, new marble white skin is growing underneath. He then whispers, 'What's happening to me?'

> DIETER: You've been reborn.
> JESUS: What's this? Why the new skin? And don't answer in riddles!
> DIETER: You talk about insects, alchemists, artefacts, but what is it that I need?
> JESUS: Blood.
> DIETER: Human?
> JESUS: Of course. You can't gain eternity with a cow or a pig.
> DIETER: I can destroy the artifact, pulverize it.
> JESUS: As you wish. If the device goes, you go.
> DIETER: But, we can share eternity.
> JESUS: What do I care about eternity? I don't want to be eternal, I just want to get out of this!

Dieter explains that he can help him, and then stabs him in the stomach, but before he can pierce his heart, Aurora, who has followed Jesus to the de la Guardia factory, hits Dieter on the head with his own cane. When Jesus sees a puddle of Dieter's blood on the floor, he bites his neck and drinks deeply from it.

We thus see the darker of the dark twins take over. When he finally learns what he has become, Jesus is horrified; he rejects his new condition and seems determined to take his own life. But when he gets a scent of human blood, in full-on neck-biting vampire fashion, he takes steps to sustain the very life that moments earlier he'd resolved to end.

However, when Jesus realises just how much the monster he has become endangers Aurora, his determination to end his life returns. After he fights and kills Angel de la Guardia, who attacks Jesus when he finds him in his uncle's room, Jesus has lost a lot of blood. He approaches Aurora, places his hands on her shoulders, and slowly moves toward her neck. She submits and mutters, 'Grandpa,' – the only word she speaks in the entire film – but Jesus stops himself, stands up and smashes the Cronos device with a rock. He thus destroys himself, ending the Fulcanelli bloodline and making sure other monsters like him will not exist in the future.

The film's climactic battle is, therefore, not the one between Jesus and the de la Guardias, but the one between the dark twins. Throughout the film, they exchange blows and then back off, but when Jesus becomes undead, and his appearance betrays the presence of each twin living inside him, they seem at ease with each other. However, when Jesus confronts Dieter and learns what he has truly become, the Frankenstein monster living inside Jesus, the part of him that wants to continue living as a human in this new undead state, resolves to destroy itself and its twin, rather than drink human blood to survive. But the Dracula side of Jesus's new personality wants to abandon what humanity it has left, and embrace its new life as a bloodsucker. Aurora's only spoken word, 'Grandpa', gives the Frankenstein monster the strength to defeat its twin.

By combining the myths of Dracula and Frankenstein in *Cronos*, del Toro turns his adaptation of their stories into a mythic, psychological struggle between two sides of the vampire Jesus's personality. For Skal, 'the dark twins have rarely enjoyed the power they have today', and he refers to their relationship as a 'long and codependent dance' (Skal, 2001: 351). Del Toro sets them free to continue this dance inside Jesus's head, and the positive critical response to *Cronos* suggests that by doing so, he has added to the twins' power, even if critics give the darker one all the credit.

Gothic horrors, family secrets and the patriarchal imperative: the early horror films of Mario Bava

Reynold Humphries

This study will analyse four films written and directed by Mario Bava between 1960 and 1966: *La Maschera del demonio* (aka *Black Sunday*, 1960), *La Frusta e il Corpo* (aka *Night is the Phantom* and *The Whip and the Body*, 1963), *Operazione Paura* (aka *Curse of the Dead* and *Kill, Baby . . . Kill!*, 1966) and *Sei donne per l'assassino* (aka *Blood and Black Lace*, 1964).[1] The first three titles belong to what I shall, for argument's sake, call 'the supernatural horror film', the latter to the Italian genre of the *giallo*.

The first point worth noting is that the three examples of 'supernatural horror' are all 'period pieces', set in the nineteenth century, whereas *Sei donne per l'assassino* is set in the contemporary period. Apart from the thematic and aesthetic concerns the four films share, this manifest break between two different time periods is the major factor in the choice of these films as the focus of my study. The principal thematic concern of the films is what I shall call 'the martyrised body of the woman'. The witch in *La Maschera del demonio* is branded prior to having a spiked mask hammered onto her face. The heroine of *La Frusta e il Corpo* is savagely whipped by the hero. In *Operazione Paura* a young girl is exorcised, first by being whipped by the local witch, then by having barbed wire tied tightly round her body; and the film opens with a woman apparently committing suicide by hurling herself onto the spikes of a railing. The victims of the killer in *Sei donne per l'assassino* are beaten up, strangled, stabbed, drowned or burned to death. The cruel and calculating nature of these acts of violence against the female body has much to tell us about the persistence of certain social structures people naively assume to have disappeared generations ago. Not only shall we see that this is not the case, but that these structures are arguably more intense today than in the nineteenth century, albeit more covert.

There is a specific scene within *La Maschera del demonio* which encapsulates perfectly the issues at stake here. It occurs towards the beginning of the film and introduces us to the descendants of the aristocratic family of the witch and her elder brother who condemned her to death two centuries before. A shot shows us a young woman playing the piano. A movement of the camera frames her from behind so that she remains in the foreground; in the middle distance is a young man cleaning a rifle and, on the wall in the background, a portrait too far away to identify. We are obviously in the salon of a castle or mansion belonging to a wealthy family. The camera then moves away from the young woman and tracks past the young man towards an armchair placed before an open fire. It continues its movement until it is placed in front of the armchair in which is seated an elderly man. Bava thus presents us with the reverse of the shot described above: now the elderly man is in the foreground and the young woman in the background, with the young man still in the middle distance. At one point the man in the armchair and the portrait share the frame to the exclusion of the other characters and we see the portrait is of a tall man of noble bearing.

The three characters are the Princess whose body the witch, duly brought back from the dead, intends to possess, her elder brother and their father. The portrait is of one Igor Javutich, executed in a like fashion at the same time as the witch and accused of being the 'Devil's servant' with whom she had had sexual relations. The witch's brother refers to this as a 'forbidden love', a crucial notion introducing the hierarchy within the family and the power wielded by the elder brother who has total control over his sister, especially in the domain of sex. The head of a household is automatically a male whose sole concern is to ensure the female members marry the 'right' man, in this case the man chosen by the brother. If we return at this juncture to the first shot described, then we can grasp its narrative and symbolic function. The young woman is foregrounded as it is around her that the action turns because of her kinship and resemblance to the witch, whereas the spatial structure of the shot is, in reverse, the image of the real social situation. Hence the fact that the second shot seems to be its mirror image. That the young man with the rifle (the brother) remains in the middle distance in relation to his sister (shot one) and his father (shot two) shows that things have not changed an iota since the good old days of witch-hunting: the father is in control if alive, the brother takes his place as patriarch after his death. This is taken up in different ways in *La Frusta e il Corpo* and *Operazione Paura*.

The presence of the portrait complicates issues somewhat but its spatial and symbolic functions are not difficult to ascertain. In shot one its function is both narrative and symbolic, indicating both that it has a role to play in the narrative and that, in some way to be clarified later, it 'dominates' the scene as it is constructed by the camera and the use of space and depth. In shot two, however, things are less clear. During the tracking movement of the camera the portrait now physically dominates the man in the armchair who is visibly frightened. With shot two inaugurating the mirror image of shot one, we are faced with the hierarchy within the family and, now that the portrait is no longer present on the screen, with the influence exerted over the generations by the past, the curse made by the witch against her brother (who clearly takes it very seriously, as do the other men present at the execution).

The father's anxiety stems from the feeling that his family – and, implicitly, his function as patriarch – is doomed to extinction. This, in turn, has turned him into an hysteric, symbolised by his infirmity. Unconsciously, he feels he is not the man he ought to be: noble, upright and courageous. Instead, he is precisely the opposite. It is now the 'Devil's servant' Javutich who is represented in the portrait as all that the Prince and head of the family should be. Within the ideology of patriarchy, where the male is supposed to behave in a certain 'virile' fashion, to do otherwise is to be 'feminised'. Hence my argument that the Prince is an hysteric: he is asking himself the question 'Am I a man or a woman?'. We shall see presently that both *Operazione Paura* and *La Frusta e il Corpo* are more elaborate investigations into the social and psychological implications of these two shots and of the way *La Maschera des demonio* articulates them with the treatment of the witch and her symbolic relationship to her elder brother. She has transgressed the place assigned to her by patriarchy and its male representatives and must pay the penalty. In other words: the woman either 'adapts' or is punished, the act of adaptation being synonymous with a submission both social and sexual. The sister, denounced by her own brother as a witch, identified with this social position and returns as a monster. In the other films, what is 'monstrous' is the society that has begotten such perversions of values.

What is implicit in Bava's first movie as a director is explicit in *La Frusta e il Corpo*. When Kurt Menliff returns after many years to his family mansion, conversations between him and his father, his father and younger brother after Kurt's murder, then between the brother and Katia, the woman he loves, show both the role of family ties and the power invested in the father. Not only has he disinherited Kurt because the latter has brought shame on the family – he seduced the daughter of a servant and the girl committed suicide – but he refuses to change his mind on Kurt's return, having already obliged his other son Cristiano to marry Nevenka. That Cristiano submitted to the command to marry Nevenka, despite his love for Katia, has poisoned the lives of all three (both Nevenka and Cristiano are in love with someone else, Katia is miserable because her love must go unrequited), showing that the little matter of being disinherited means exile and a loss of social standing. What is implicit here, however, will become explicit in the context of *Sei donne per l'assassino*: the role of money. Since he is directing a 'period piece', Bava chooses to concentrate on questions of honour, the family, patriarchy and the selfishness of a power that goes without saying as everyone accepts it. *La Frusta e il Corpo* extends the notion of submission to take in the male members of the family, but the concomitant notion of adapting for the woman remains intact: now two women are unhappy. We shall return to the special case of Nevenka later, after considering *Operazione Paura*.

Dr Eswai is summoned to a village by the police to perform an autopsy on the body of a woman who committed suicide by throwing herself onto a spiked railing. Everything is done by the villagers to prevent the autopsy and to drive the doctor away, the villagers believing that any attempt to get at the truth will only mean further unnatural deaths. Truth and knowledge are central to the film and are seemingly set up in opposition to ignorance and superstition, with Eswai finding himself frustrated at every turn by the villagers. Things are far less cut and dried, however. To start with, Eswai is also prey to a particular form of ignorance called 'prejudice'. When a certain Monica Shuftan is sent by the Police Commissioner to help him perform the autopsy, Eswai is displeased: as she's a woman, she cannot be of any use. She points out, with quiet dignity, that she is a science student at the university, which shuts the good doctor up. Simply but subtly Bava shows that a rational approach to life can hide reactionary and repressive values: for the doctor, a woman's role is not so much socially determined as biologically pre-ordained and does not include the search for knowledge, a male preserve. The Burgermeister shares the fears of the villagers, although manifestly both better educated and from a different social class. In both cases the film shows that beliefs are more powerful than knowledge, even when the latter is the apparent aim of the men involved. If we take 'beliefs' as a synonym for 'ideological values', then *Operazione Paura* will have much to reveal.

When the truth is revealed, the film does indeed take on the appearance of 'supernatural horror'. Those who die have been forced to kill themselves by the evil spirit of little Melissa Graps who has returned to punish the villagers for being indirectly responsible for her death. Superficially, the film completely endorses the script's version of events. We learn that Ruth, the village exorcist, has been helping Melissa's mother, the Baroness Graps, to get her revenge on the villagers through the dead Melissa. The ghost is therefore only too 'real'. However, Eswai also falls victim to Melissa, although this takes the form of hallucinations only: he does not die. There is a crucial difference between Eswai's encounter with the little girl and that of Nadine, the girl exorcised by Ruth. We see Nadine's look of horror offscreen, then we glimpse Melissa through her gaze, whereas we see Eswai facing Melissa in a corridor of the villa. There is *no* subjective point-of-view shot introduced in the case of the doctor. Either Melissa exists or both spectators and Eswai are hallucinating.

It is striking to note that children in particular are the victims, a fact that should make us sit up and take notice, given what we have seen of the representation of family values and patriarchy in the other Bava. Let us take the case of Nadine, the adolescent daughter of the innkeeper and his wife. She tries to talk to Eswai but dare not, because of her parents. The way the family is represented makes it clear that for her to address a strange man is tantamount to seeking to escape from her condition as servant (we see her cleaning up the inn at one point). Nadine, consciously or not, wants to leave ignorance and superstition behind her, a crime for which she is speedily punished. Believing herself to be Melissa's next victim – she remains very much subjected to superstition and its attendant fears – she is promptly exorcised by Ruth. The way Bava films the sequence – and the sequence where Eswai discovers Nadine in bed, the barbed wire cutting into her flesh – is openly erotic. One woman in a position of power and (for the villagers) knowledge scourging the body of an adolescent smacks very much of a woman anxious to keep a certain form of power in her hands (and those of Baroness Graps) and making sure that Nadine adapts by submitting ('body and soul', as it were) to her situation, inferior and subordinate both socially and sexually. Nadine's desire for knowledge is of a sexual nature, but the adolescent is unaware of her subjective status. Thus the parents are accomplices in their daughter's degradation, passing on to her the ignorance and superstition which they have raised into a fetish without which they cannot function. Ideological values are the imaginary way people relate to their real social situation and status.

Eswai's hallucinations follow a most extraordinary sequence where the doctor pursues a man he takes for an intruder. When he catches up with him, the man turns round: it is Eswai. The doctor is faced with an image of himself, inasmuch as this encounter heralds the beginning of the character's hallucinations. This leads us seriously to question Eswai's claims to rationality which, as we pointed out above, code him unconsciously to consider any woman to be his inferior. This subject position is masculine in nature, but it finds a revealing parallel in the attitudes of Baroness Graps. She too is identified with a particular position of power, that which grants her the right of life and death over the villagers, the right of the feudal baron over his serfs. She also exploits Melissa and Monica who, it transpires, is Melissa's younger sister.[2] The Baroness is therefore occupying a *masculine* position socially and it is significant that no mention is made of her husband whom she thus replaces. At the same time her status as a woman tends to forbid such a function. I would argue that, if the Baroness is mad, it is not because she uses the spirit of her dead daughter to get her revenge. This reverses cause and effect. Rather she is mad because she has been forced to identify with a masculine position to which she cannot adapt: that belonging rightly to her late husband who is absent from the film. The Baroness can be termed a 'bad mother', as if she had abandoned this 'natural' role for an unnatural one: that of playing the role of 'Baron Graps'. Her madness is thus the madness of schizophrenia, brought on by being constrained to adapt to a social role that is also proscribed. An obligation enters into conflict with a prohibition.

The film does not completely face up to the radical implications of this question of social roles and responsibility, preferring to have Ruth and the Baroness – the two 'usurpers', as it were – kill one another, which tends to displace social pressures and psychological repression onto individual cases. The fact that Eswai and Monica go off together at the end accords the former the phallic rights that have been obviously wanting. The insistence on 'supernatural horror' has been made at the expense of a certain coherency in the representation of women. Such disavowal is dispelled in *La Frusta e il Corpo* which, I shall argue, is not supernatural at all but an exceptionally subtle representation of female desire through the character of Nevenka. Her masochism – she enjoys being whipped by Kurt – will lead to the interpretation that Bava is a sexist who considers that women like to suffer and be humiliated. However, desire is far more complicated than that, sadism and masochism do exist and the question is: how is Nevenka's particular form of *jouissance* represented? For whatever interpretation we give to the scenes where Kurt whips her, the simple fact remains that she *enjoys it*. First, however, we must analyse the ways Bava films these scenes.

The key scene for grasping the possible implications of Nevenka's morbid libido takes place on a beach where she encounters Kurt who has just returned. Nevenka is alone, sitting brooding by the water's edge, clearly disturbed by this unexpected and problematic presence in the family home. Bava insists on her pensive mood, going to the extent of intercutting a shot of the sea from her point of view (which the audience shares) to stress the fact that her mind is 'elsewhere'.[3] Nevenka doodles in the sand with her horse whip, then suddenly starts. Cut to a shot of a boot standing on the whip. Bava then moves his camera slowly up the body till it reaches the face: it is Kurt. I would argue that, as from this moment, the entire scene can be interpreted as a pure *fantasy* on Nevenka's part. And that the other whipping scenes, as we shall show, partake of the same unconscious logic. It is noteworthy that, when the two former lovers kiss on the beach, it is Nevenka who shows the stronger passion, after which she turns away, visibly shocked and disgusted with herself, then turns and strikes Kurt across the face with the whip. There then follows the first case of flogging, which she manifestly appreciates. If the Lacanian notion of *jouissance* – going as far as possible in the pursuit of a drive, even to the point of extreme pain – co-exists here with *jouissance* in the sense of 'orgasm', I wish to stress in particular the way in which Bava shows the co-presence of sexuality (the way Nevenka kisses Kurt) and *guilt*. Herein lies the meaning of Nevenka's ulterior behaviour.

Following Kurt's murder, Nevenka has nightmares of him returning to haunt and flog her, nightmares which she claims are real. However, the argument she uses – the muddy footsteps left by Kurt – turn out to be non-existent, so it is not until Cristiano finds such traces himself that he takes her claims seriously. However, it transpires that Nevenka has killed Kurt, gone mad and walked the corridors and crypt of the castle dressed up as her dead lover (an interesting sexual reversal of *Psycho*). Whenever Kurt does 'return' to Nevenka in her bedroom, the encounter – or confrontation: she claims to hate him – ends with her being whipped. Here, however, everything points to her telling the truth: Cristiano, like the spectators, notices the weals on her back. Self-flagellation, however, is not unknown – especially in case of religious fervour there co-exists a persistent erotic drive and the guilt that this triggers off. As religion, family values and the rigid hierarchy of patriarchy underpin the entire film, it is hardly an exaggeration to claim that such masochism is inherent to Nevenka's character. The question is: why?

An answer lies in the way Bava films one of Kurt's apparitions: first a disembodied hand appears out of the dark to terrorise Nevenka, then Kurt appears and taunts and finally flogs her. The hand, interestingly, is the signifier of the co-presence of violence and tenderness: first tearing her nightdress, then caressing her hair. Lust and guilt, violence and tenderness, love and hate, all add up to one thing: desire and punishment, where the punishment is for a desire that is considered a crime. It is also unconsciously recognised as such by Nevenka. By desiring, even lusting after, Kurt, Nevenka has committed two abominable crimes: she has committed adultery (in her unconscious this *desire* becomes a *reality*); and she gives precedence to the rights of Kurt – rights both phallic and social as he is the elder son – over against the will of the father, the film's unbending patriarch. It must be pointed out here that the scene on the beach ended with the couple making love; as a fantasy is unconscious, Nevenka has repressed this act – or desire – and now pays for it by being flogged. Her guilt returns to punish her in a way that affords her pleasure, a perverse form of compensation.

In which case, the appearance of the hand is a perfect instance of forclusion where what is rejected in the Symbolic returns in the Real in the form of a hallucination. By insisting on her woman's rights, by flouting convention on all levels – religious, social, sexual and partiarchal – Nevenka has behaved as if she had the phallus, thus rejecting the notion of castration. The disembodied hand is the signifier of a purely repressive patriarchy, its hallucinatory and Angst-ridden dimension a dire warning to Nevenka of the consequences for a woman who refuses to adopt the way men see the world and to adapt accordingly. Rather a woman unhappy like Katia than sexually defiant like Nevenka. Thus the whipping is the condensation of an unconscious need to be punished for sexual 'transgression' and of the male need to control the female body by any means necessary; hence the extreme violence shown by Kurt (surely standing in for his father). By enjoying her suffering, Nevenka is in reality identifying with a sadistic masculine position, her masochism an essential component of a typical male fantasy of the ideal, submissive woman. Sexual pleasure for a woman means emancipation, a scandalous contradiction.

What, then, of *Sei donne per l'assassino* which takes place in the contemporary world, apparently light years away from the repressive climate of the nineteenth century? I shall argue that repression here is more intense, because it can and does hide behind a discourse of equality and freedom of choice that masks the true situation. Class and economics are massively present, but in a radically different way: there are no servants, just models treated badly by their employer, Cristina, whose House of High Fashion is the setting for the film. Moreover, the models are well paid but must take orders unquestioningly. Feudalism may have moved on to capitalism but the forms of exploitation have not changed: those with the economic power dictate to and control those who depend on them. The film is in fact an extended investigation into exploitation and how those who must sell their labour are turned into just so many commodities and thus objectified.

The articulation of the opening credits sequence and the early scenes of *Sei donne per l'assassino* creates a particular world that imposes this reading. The credits introduce to the spectators the various actors and actresses by presenting them on screen in the presence of dummies. This at once presents the theme and setting of the film – the world of *haute couture* – and the political subtext, the Marxist implications of which are obvious. Cameron Mitchell, Eva Bartok and the others stand rigidly and seem just as inanimate as the dummies; indeed, they seem to be models themselves, wax figures dressed up like human beings, with the features of the various players added. This is taken up in a scene near the opening where Bava's camera tracks through adjoining rooms in the House of High Fashion, where both inanimate and human female models are 'on display'. I use the formula advisedly as there are moments when the women are as still as the actors and actresses in the credits sequence, so still in fact that it is difficult to tell the ontological status of the model we have before us on the screen. This is exploited by Bava later when one of the female victims is pursued around her boyfriend's antique shop. Suddenly a hand enters the frame from the right and it takes us a moment of readjustment to realise that it belongs to a dummy and not to the killer. Animate and inanimate either merge or change places, creating a sense of the uncanny.

In this dialectic of animate/inanimate, *Sei donne per l'assassino* represents the commodification of women or, rather, of women's bodies. For what is a fashion show? A place where wealthy buyers go to see clothes, raised to the level of so many fetishes. The human models are merely bodies used to show the clothes off to the best advantage. Models may move around, but their immobility in the scene described above relegates them rather to the status of the dummies that display clothing in shop windows and which co-exist with the stars in the credits sequence.

The six women of the film's title all work for Cristina and are ultimately so many chattels. Woe betide them if they try to rise above their station! It is on this theme that the film turns, the first victim being dispatched as she was indulging in a bit of blackmail in an attempt to supplement her income. By so doing she was refusing the exploitation of the female body for profit and tried to get her share in the only way open to her. A criminal way, to be sure, but less so than the traffic in drugs with which Cristina and her partner (in both the sexual and economic senses) increase their already high standard of living. As there is no honour among thieves, the lover tries to kill Cristina, but she returns to get her revenge when his plan fails and they die together, with her draped over his body. This image refers back to the killing of the second victim in the antique shop. The killer drags the body into a corner and, for some curious reason, covers it with a suit of armour.

Rather than see this as an (unconvincing) attempt to hide the body, I would interpret it as the logic of the text which returns in the shot of Cristina covering the body of her lover. The two shots are an ironic comment on the ways in which, in a society based on commodity fetishism where objects (such as clothes) are more important than people, the relations between objects uncannily take on the status of the relations between people, duly reduced to objects themselves: for the killer, the woman is just a 'suit of clothes' akin to a suit of armour. This parallel can tell us something about the relation between Cristina and her lover, particularly about Cristina herself. For in *Sei donne per l'assassino* it is no longer a case of criticising patriarchy as a system based solely on male power and privilege. Cristina in no way yields to the central male character when it comes to getting the most economically out of patriarchy. As such she has a masculine function in the film, which suits her perfectly as it enables her to exploit other women and live in luxury. That she should replace her lover as killer at one point to throw the police off the scent (the lover is in custody) only goes to show that, in killing one of the six women, she is identifying with male sadism as a libidinal factor shown by the film to be part and parcel of the profit motive. Unlike the female characters in the other films discussed here, she therefore adapts willingly to the demands of patriarchy whose economic dimension is now highlighted to become the object of the film's highly politicised discourse.[4]

'In the church of the poison mind': adapting the metaphor of psychopathology to look back at the mad, monstrous 80s

Ruth Goldberg

> There are no hard distinctions between what is real and what is unreal, nor between what is true and what is false. A thing is not necessarily either true or false; it can be both true and false.
>
> Harold Pinter

> Love is hard to find/In the church of the poison mind.
>
> Culture Club

This chapter examines *American Psycho* (2000) and *Donnie Darko* (2001), two films that look back at aspects of the American experience in the 1980s. These titles represent only two out of a larger series of recent 'Monstrous 80s' films, including *Capturing the Friedmans* (2003) and *Monster* (2003), which I have written about elsewhere. Each of these films adopts the framework and language of psychopathology in contextualising its monstrous protagonist. The apocalyptic tenor of the films suggests an emerging national metaphor, as if the cultural pathology which was latent in the 1980s is finally becoming manifest in our retrospective understanding of history.

Monstrous 80s films take up a belated exploration of how we arrived at the current crisis of violence and apathy in America. Cult film *Donnie Darko*, in particular, explicitly addresses the idea of literally going back in time to figure out 'where we went wrong'. The retrospective analysis of US history through film and the overarching metaphors of psychopathology and prophecy that characterise this cycle of movies will be explored as constituting an adaptive interpretive process in the horror genre.

Monstrous transformations

The horror film has long concerned itself with monstrous transformations. The indeterminate and unpredictably shifting 'in between' states of changing and becoming are inevitably the locus of our greatest fears. We are constant, as viewers, in our overwhelming fear of disruption. The particular details of these transformational states, moreover, are often 'read' closely for insight into what they can tell us about evolving, culturally specific definitions of horror.

In looking at the history of the horror film in the US, scholars note that major trends often reflect metaphoric treatment of era-specific fears, which may account for the powerful resonance of certain films upon their initial release. While the fear of disruption, as already stated, remains constant throughout the history of the horror film, the 'face' of horror changes over time, patterned in distinct cycles. Each of these notable trends or cycles within the genre marks a point of adaptation in our attitudes regarding monstrosity.

Most relevant to the current inquiry is the cycle that Barry Grant has dubbed the 'yuppie horror film', a sub-genre defined by the disruption of bourgeois values – a dark twist on the 'American Dream'. The yuppie horror film gives us a vision of the 'horror movie as economic nightmare' in which the protagonist must face the idea of losing all the material wealth and status they have accumulated, in an unsettling inversion of the social order (Grant, 1998: 283).

Grant's article chronicles the development of this sub-genre and also includes an incisive look at Bret Easton Ellis's infamously violent novel *American Psycho* (1991), one of the defining cultural artefacts of its time. This chapter will build on Grant's foundational work, turning first to the screen adaptation of *American Psycho* directed by Mary Harron, and continuing with an exploration of the direct relationship *American Psycho* has to later retrospective Monstrous 80s films like *Donnie Darko* and *Monster.*

In the previously cited example of the yuppie horror film, the on-screen monsters reveal our cultural fears in a classically dualistic way, through the dramatic schisms between heroes and villains. In looking at *American Psycho*, *Donnie Darko*, and the other Monstrous 80s films that would follow, the generic adaptation which becomes evident is that the classical dualities are blurred as *American culture itself* is revealed to be the source of all the horror that ensues; and the 1980s, the Reagan years, are belatedly re-examined as a pivotal moment in an ongoing apocalyptic process.

> Apocalyptic visions have long been the privileged domain of mystics and madmen … Janus-like, the apocalyptic vision gazes behind and beyond the present moment, binding in an eternal future perfect cataclysmic conclusions and beginnings – the Harrowing of Hell and eternity in a grain of sand. (James, 1988: 1)

As horror film scholars are fond of reciting, the word 'monster' comes from the French and Latin words meaning 'to show' and 'to warn'. Monsters come to show us something about ourselves; to warn us (inevitably too late) about some fatal imbalance in our lives. By embodying our fears and flaws and desires and imbuing them with terrible force and agency, monsters dare us to face our own inner darkness made manifest.

It is significant that many of the public's favourite onscreen 'monsters' have been characters suffering from mental illness (Norman Bates, Hannibal Lecter and Jack Torrance, to name but a few). The terrifying process of watching a human being descend into madness is, after all, a trope that has haunted the horror film since its earliest beginnings. Psychosis, the ultimate shifting ground of consciousness, is one of several monstrous transformations with which we can all identify, and which we all fear, because anyone might be vulnerable to madness given the right circumstances. Watching mental illness on the screen is almost inevitably cathartic, albeit in the most unsettling possible way. The central question of this article, then, is why do Monstrous 80s films develop their incisive cultural/historical critique in such a way that the truth comes spilling out of the mouths of madmen? What have the monsters come to show us this time?

In taking up the mantle of disseminating prophetic, apocalyptic visions, the mentally ill protagonists of the films under examination position themselves in a lineage of 'damaged' prophets and martyred heroes throughout history. As Joseph Goldberg explains:

> Yet mythology and literature have again and again portrayed the 'damaged' human being as God's fool, speaking truth among liars, as the one-eyed Odin who plucks out his other eye in exchange for drinking the waters of wisdom; as society's scapegoat, as the sacrificial lamb, the 'despised and rejected of men' who is in fact the Messiah. From Lear's Fool to Prince Myshkin and beyond, the person adjudged crazy, maimed or unacceptable is often seen as exercising a more lucid vision, having access to a deeper wisdom, or being purer of heart than the world that judges him. (Goldberg, 1967: 42)

The classical hero/villain divide is confounded in Monstrous 80s films, because the heroes in these films are unstable, unreliable narrators, often with deeply flawed or violent personalities. In forcing us to identify with disturbed protagonists as *even they* react in horror to the larger pathology of American culture, the films also force us to position *ourselves* in relation to the American cultural landscape, as if it were an additional character in these films, another monster on the loose.

It is interesting to note that in both *Donnie Darko* and *American Psycho* this positioning happens in relation to historical footage of the Iran/Contra affair, a cultural memory which has been almost entirely suppressed in terms of popular consciousness, but which resurfaces in the two films to drive home a cynically political teaching. The purposeful references to the scandalous and surreal political situation unfolding in the background give these otherwise lightweight films their edge – suggesting that perhaps these misfit protagonists are direct products of the crazy times in which they live.

'Let's hear it for the boy': *American Psycho* and American politics

American Psycho is, by turns, hilariously funny, surreal, ironic, dark and grisly. The film tells the story of Patrick Bateman (Christian Bale), a 27-year-old soulless yuppie misanthrope obsessed with status and appearance. The film unfolds as a black comedy, set against the backdrop of 1980s Manhattan, with Bateman alternately preaching about the genius of Huey Lewis and the News and hacking people to bits. As Stephen Holden elaborates:

> As this character metamorphoses from preening, wolfish yuppie to chain-saw wielding maniac to whimpering crybaby, Mr. Bale makes us feel the underlying connections between these multiple personalities. One minute Mr. Bale's Patrick is a cowering corporate geek and self-described empty shell, the next an arrogant, name-dropping smoothie, the next a hysterical wimp unable to distinguish reality from fantasy. (Holden, 2000)

Much has been made of the idea that the film refuses to 'fix its meanings', as Brecht might say. It leaves us wondering whether the events we have witnessed are 'true'. Of course, at both the level of metaphor and in the experience of the spectator, everything we see on screen is true and real (in that we watch it happen and it constitutes our experience of the drama), and on this experiential level Bateman gets away with his many crimes, just as he 'gets away with' the injustices of inheriting his upper class status, not doing any work in a highly paid corporate executive job, and living an outrageously opulent lifestyle, even though he deserves none of it.

Monstrous 80s films are more ironic than immediately frightening, and like the yuppie horror films that came before, they are often funny. It is only through the process of analysis and in realising that the films bear the burden of real social insight that they become terrifying. *American Psycho*'s funniest moments are also its cruelest and most surreal, as Bateman, through his obsessional rantings about needing to be fashionable, to be seen, and to indulge his every destructive impulse, creates an unnervingly accurate portrait of the narcissistic 'me generation'.

Bateman reveals the stressful 'survival of the fittest' quality of having to be in vogue – the neurotic competitive fear that one might easily make a wrong move and suffer a painful change of status. He breaks into a sweat at the idea that a colleague has a business card that is flashier than his own or may have a more expensive apartment; and is beside himself at the possibility of getting an inferior table at a popular restaurant.

Crouching in a dark alley, he stabs a homeless man. His reasoning? 'I have nothing in common with you.' Bateman also tortures, humiliates and dismembers the women he sleeps with and then, in public, gives politically correct speeches that are so wildly incongruous with his pathological actions that now, in retrospect, they seem almost prophetic in their ability to evoke what many have come to recognise as the voice of the true American 'serial killers' in our midst: the ruling class.

> BATEMAN: (with a creepy grin on his face) We have to end Apartheid, for one. And slow down the nuclear arms race, stop terrorism and world hunger. We have to provide food and shelter for the homeless; and oppose racial discrimination and promote civil rights, while also promoting equal rights for women. We have to encourage a return to traditional moral values. Most importantly, we have to promote general social concern and less materialism …

Bateman shows us through his murderous actions exactly what the hegemony in American culture would indicate for the future – a violent backlash against the poor and against women, waged by elite assassins capable of paying eloquent lip service to the need for progress. The 60s are over, dude. Cold-blooded killers are running the show.

As already noted, many horror films from other eras reflect repressed American cultural fears of forces or groups that might disrupt the status quo (the poor, communism, emancipated women, etc.). In this way, horror films are consistently reactionary in terms of their internal politics and serve to reinforce normative values and ideas. It is important to note that *American Psycho* represents a different twist on these particular ideas. In *American Psycho*, the fears which were latent or metaphoric in earlier films are exposed in a manifest way, as Bateman clearly voices his revulsion for humanity and indicates what the natural results of his value system might look like.

Bateman's killing sprees are punctuated by his obnoxious and hilarious sermons about 1980s pop culture and creepy interior monologues in which he recognises his own pathology:

> I have all the characteristics of a human being – flesh, blood, skin, hair – but not a single clear, identifiable emotion except for greed and disgust. Something horrible is happening inside me and I don't know why. My nightly bloodlust has overflowed into my days. I feel lethal, on the verge of frenzy. I think my mask of sanity is about to slip.

Bateman's sense of reality is later called into question when, towards the end of the film, he confesses his guilt to a lawyer, and his confession is greeted with absolute denial. Bateman is flatly informed that he has *not* committed any crimes; has not killed anyone at all. He must be joking. At this point the movie has gone to great lengths to set up its point: its not that nobody knows the truth about the monsters running amok – it's that nobody actually cares. You can tell people the truth, but no one wants to hear it. Meanwhile, just in case the point wasn't clear enough, the repressed Iran/Contra Scandal suddenly rises to the surface of the film's consciousness. The following occurs right after the lawyer insists that Bateman has imagined all the murders:

> Bateman returns back to his friends' table, in a daze. They are all looking at the television, where Ronald Reagan is giving a speech about Iran Contra. They are halfheartedly arguing about whether or not he's lying.
> BRYCE: How can he lie like that? How can he pull that shit?
> How can he be so fucking, I don't know, cool about it?
> VAN PATTEN: Some guys are just born cool, I guess.
> Bateman laughs at this. Bryce shoots him a look ...
> BRYCE (waving at the image of Reagan on television): Oh, brother.
> Look – he presents himself as this harmless old codger. But inside ...
> but inside ...
> BATEMAN (V. O.): *But inside doesn't matter ...*
> As the film ends the camera moves CLOSE on Bateman. He is leaning back in his leather armchair, drinking a double Scotch, his eyes blank.
> The camera reveals a sign on the wall behind him:
> 'THIS IS NOT AN EXIT.'
> BATEMAN (V. O.): There are no more barriers to cross. All I have in common with the uncontrollable and the insane, the vicious and the evil, all the mayhem I have caused and my utter indifference toward it, I have now surpassed ... My pain is constant and sharp and I do not hope for a better world for anyone. I fact I want my pain to be inflicted on others. I want no one to escape. But even after admitting this, there is no catharsis. My punishment continues to elude me and I gain no deeper knowledge of myself. No new knowledge can be extracted from my telling. This confession has meant nothing.

In both *Donnie Darko* and *American Psycho*, the cultural details and the overtly referenced drama of US involvement in Latin America and the Iran/Contra scandal emerge as substantial reminders of the real horror behind these dark, funny films. For as outrageous as the two films may be, they pale in comparison to the surreality of the actual moment in our political history to which they refer.

'Facts are stupid things.' (Ronald Reagan)

In many ways, the US involvement in Latin American during the 1980s, and the example of Nicaragua in particular, is an especially potent memory to stir up right now, given the many similarities of that affair to currents in US foreign policy and the intervention in Iraq at the time of this writing. It is as if we are trapped in a recurring national dream – a dream about governmental deceit, betrayal, war crimes, apathy and denial. And, as any analyst will tell you, a dream only recurs when the dreamer repeatedly fails to understand the message that the dream is trying to bring to light. Conversely, as long as the dreamer fails to understand the meaning encoded in the dreamwork, the dream will continue to recur.

In his recent acceptance speech upon receiving the Nobel Prize for literature, Harold Pinter invoked the memory of the Iran/Contra affair 'as a potent example of America's view of its role in the world, both then and now.' Pinter made his case at length in order to drive home a point about the current US presence in Iraq, bringing attention to a series of lies which were initially fed to the public in order to rally support for the invasion, and the historical precedent for deceiving the American public in precisely this way, as exemplified by the Iran/Contra scandal in the 1980s.

Pinter described being present at a meeting at the US embassy in London in the late 1980s, when the United States Congress was about to decide whether to give more money to the Contras in their campaign against the state of Nicaragua. The most important member of the pro-Nicaragua delegation was Father John Metcalf, who said to Representative Raymond Seitz:

> Sir, I am in charge of a parish in the north of Nicaragua. My parishioners built a school, a health centre, a cultural centre. We have lived in peace. A few months ago a Contra force attacked the parish. They destroyed everything: the school, the health centre, the cultural centre. They raped nurses and teachers, slaughtered

> doctors, in the most brutal manner. They behaved like savages. Please demand that the US government withdraw its support from this shocking terrorist activity. '
>
> Raymond Seitz ... listened, paused and then spoke with some gravity. 'Father,' he said, 'let me tell you something. In war, innocent people always suffer.' There was a frozen silence. We stared at him. He did not flinch ... Finally somebody said: 'But in this case "innocent people" were the victims of a gruesome atrocity subsidised by your government, one among many. If Congress allows the Contras more money further atrocities of this kind will take place. Is this not the case? Is your government not therefore guilty of supporting acts of murder and destruction upon the citizens of a sovereign state?' Seitz was imperturbable. 'I don't agree that the facts as presented support your assertions,' he said.

Pinter's point was that at various moments, either no one realised what was happening, or no one cared. Ronald Reagan quickly regained his popularity, after all, in spite of his overt complicity in the scandal. Bush won the next election by a landslide, and now the affair has been largely forgotten. This is precisely where the Monstrous 80s films pick up the thread of cultural memory. It would be a mistake, or at least a serious oversight, to dismiss films like *American Psycho* and *Donnie Darko* because of their pop culture status and juvenile, sarcastic take on the Reagan years. They may not have the 'street cred' of Harold Pinter's speech, but they resonate on the same note – in showing us how much the present resembles the past.

Looking at our history in terms of these metaphors of monstrosity and psychopathology forces us to examine certain aspects of the present. There are indications that our reality has come to resemble Brett Easton Ellis's violent prophetic vision in increasingly disturbing ways. Characterised and defined by the utter lack of empathy which is unique to psychopaths, Ellis's Patrick Bateman rampages unnoticed and undeterred across the American landscape, leaving a bloody trail behind him. In order to show how the idea of 'loss of empathy' in *American Psycho* figures into the complex metaphors of mental illness, prophecy and political memory that converge in later retrospective works about the 1980s, it will be necessary to first talk a little about *Donnie Darko*.

'The killing moon/will come too soon.' (Echo and the Bunnymen)

Like *American Psycho*, *Donnie Darko* looks back at the Monstrous 80s, but from a very different perspective. The film serves both as a kind of spiritual 'response' to *American Psycho* and also as a broader commentary on the escalating crisis of violence and alienation in American youth culture that led directly to the Columbine High School Massacre in 1999, among many other incidents. In looking at *Donnie Darko*'s take on the nightmare that is high school, it is critical to track the relationship the film has with a second genre: the youth film. For it is in creating a tense dialogue between the genre of horror and the John Hughes-ian high school fantasies of the 1980s that *Donnie Darko* forms its unique contribution to film history.

The youth films that were popular during the 1980s may have represented the most facile incarnation of absurdist comedy, but they were also strangely comforting in their fantastic view of American youth culture. They posited that somewhere in America there were high schools full of teens whose greatest worry was finding a prom date (*Pretty In Pink*), having a crush (*Sixteen Candles*), borrowing their parents' Ferraris (*Ferris Bueller's Day Off*) or mild peer pressure (*The Breakfast Club*); when, in fact, many American teens had much heavier era-specific issues to deal with: watching friends and parents die of AIDS, and grappling with heroin and cocaine addictions chief among them – even though we were supposed to 'just say no'. In contrast to the new 'shop 'til you drop' credit card ethos and mythologising the super rich (Donald Trump, Ivan Boesky), unemployment was at a high, and many people suffered the effects of the economic recession.

Teenagers (and the films made about them) serve as a kind of national repository of sarcasm. Their function is to snarlingly respond to these discrepancies between the way things are and the way they're supposed to be. True to form, *Donnie Darko* reveals these heavy ironies which are implicit in maintaining the façade of normalcy; and, like the 'Suburban Surreal' 1980s classics *Blue Velvet* (1986), *Parents* (1989) and *Heathers* (1989), *Donnie Darko* focuses on exposing the 'dark underbelly' of high school and suburban life (Romney 2002: para 3).

The story of the film's success has become legend. It bombed at the box office and then rose from the dead on DVD to become one of the most popular cult movies of all time. The film has attracted an almost religious following, with hundreds of web sites, listservs and fan clubs dedicated to unravelling its intricate meanings. Some critics defended it from the very beginning, Amy Taubin among them:

> My personal Sundance favorite, *Donnie Darko* is set in 1988 and, like Todd Haynes's *Safe*, is informed by the toxic combination of Reaganite politics and New Age philosophy. The mercurial Jake Gyllenhaal stars as the borderline-schizophrenic teenage hero whose delusions revolve around a malevolent monster rabbit named Frank (shades of *Blue Velvet*). Opening with the line 'I'm voting for Dukakis,' *Donnie Darko* is a sci-fi time-warp narrative – it also could be read as a deathbed fantasy of rescue and redemption – that eerily mirrors our current Bushwhacked back-to-the-future scenario ... Leavening despair with manic humor, *Donnie Darko* draws on the sacred texts of Spielberg and Zemeckis, but is both darker and more openly fragile than any of those films. It's also a heartbreaking portrait of the kind of suicidal adolescent who internalizes the institutionalized violence that most of us take for granted. (Taubin, 2001)

In looking at how the film develops and contextualises the metaphors of psychosis and apocalyptic prophecy within its historico-political moment, several scenes from the first quarter of the film are most instructive. After the initial dinner table stand-off over whether or not Donnie's teenage sister will vote for Dukakis to upset her conservative parents, Eddie Darko, the Republican *pater familias*, is left alone watching the presidential race on television. It is worth noting that *Donnie Darko* begins shortly after *American Psycho* ends: in 1988, during the last month of the Bush/Dukakis presidential race, with the specter of Irangate lurking in the shadows:

> DARKO HOUSE, LIVING ROOM
> MICHAEL DUKAKIS (on television): I want to be a president of the United States who makes sure that we never again do business with a drug-running Panamanian dictator.
> EDDIE DARKO is sitting in a chair watching television.
> MICHAEL DUKAKIS (on television): That we never again ...
> EDDIE DARKO: Dukakis ...
> MICHAEL DUKAKIS (on television): ... funnel aid to the Contras through convicted drug dealers.

EDDIE DARKO: Son of a bitch.
GEORGE BUSH (on television): Panama is a friendly country. I went down and talked to the President of Panama ...
EDDIE DARKO: Tell him George!
GEORGE BUSH (on television): ... about cleaning up their money laundering. And Mr. Noriega was there ...
Grandfather clock begins to strike midnight.
GEORGE BUSH (on television): ... but there was no evidence at that time. When the evidence was there, we indicted him.

It is right then that Donnie, lying in bed, has his first hallucination of the giant rabbit named Frank. The first words Frank says to him are particularly important, and represent the overall message of the film, accounting for its powerful appeal to young people.

FRANK: Wake up.

It is only because Frank then lures him out of the house that Donnie is not present shortly afterwards, when a jet engine from the future falls through a rip in time and crashes into Donnie's bedroom, triggering a sequence of events which, Frank tells him, will bring the world to an end in 28 days. As Ed Caesar elaborates, the plot gets trickier from that moment forward:

> Donnie falls in love with a classmate, Gretchen, discovers time travel and does terrible, destructive things ... Donnie is convinced he needs to save his family and Gretchen from being killed, but to do so he realizes that he must go back in time to be killed himself by the falling jet engine.
>
> Simple, right? Time travel is always tricky, but throw in oversize fantasy rabbits and the Dukakis presidential bid and the head starts to spin. This, needless to say, is hardly the kind of film Hollywood producers dream up over a power lunch. No three-act structure, no happy ending, no multigenerational appeal – this little gem wouldn't have made it past the prawn cocktail. (Caesar, 2005)

The film effectively evokes the apocalyptic preoccupations of the 1980s, and also uses them as a kind of metaphorical framework to examine how much of a difference one's actions can make, even if fate is predetermined. The question became important during the Reagan years, while the country was being governed by a president who believed that the end of days was imminent and who wondered aloud whether we were the generation that would see Armageddon (Boyer, 2001: 142).

It was a time when Gallup polls showed that evangelicalism was the dominant religious force in America, with a public that overwhelmingly believed that they would face God on judgement day, and thus saw Armageddon as a necessary step in bringing about the world to come (Boyer, 2001 :3). With Reagan in the White House, biblical prophecies about the world being predetermined to end 'by fire' took on new urgency, as a great many people wondered whether this would influence the president's decision to enter into a nuclear war. As Reagan himself once remarked sombrely:

> That's a sign that the day of Armageddon isn't far off . . . Everything is falling into place. It can't be long now. Ezekial says that fire and brimstone will be rained upon the enemies of God's people. That must mean that they'll be destroyed by nuclear weapons. (Quoted in Boyer, 2001: 142)

'And as things fell apart, nobody paid much attention.' (The Talking Heads)

And into this 'end of days' scenario comes Donnie – the sacrificial lamb; a mad visionary prophet raving about the end of the world, 'the despised and rejected among men who turns out to be the messiah' (Caesar, 2005: para 4–5). This contemporary film is extraordinary in its ability to retrospectively invoke the apocalyptic preoccupations of the 1980s while also clearly evoking and addressing the Columbine shootings and the current crisis in American youth culture which was still a kind of open cultural wound at the time of the film's release. The metaphor of 'time travel' in the film, moreover, and the frequent references to going 'back to the future' to restore order, allow this association to become urgent and imperative.

The film suggests that this is what high school in the suburbs really looks like: the holier-than-thou self-help writer turns out to be a paedophile; the only decent teacher gets fired for being controversial; the other kids are cruel, empty, in pain; a disturbed, violent teen may be sent to counselling, but the therapist is incompetent, etc. What the Columbine shootings revealed was that for teenagers who had been awake to the pervasive cruelty ingrained in the American high school experience, the shootings did not come as a total shock. They knew that eventually someone would be driven mad by the contradictions that young people find almost too painful to bear. Likewise, in *Donnie Darko*, when there is an attack on the local high school, the parents are the only ones who see it as mysterious. The kids, on the other hand, understand perfectly well how someone could want to sink an axe into the school mascot's head, and are just happy to get a day off from going to class.

In this cinematic portrait of youthful alienation, the children are divided up between predators and prey, having seemingly lost all empathy for one another. If the words 'loss of empathy', (used earlier to describe Patrick Bateman's psychopathology in *American Psycho*) resonate here, it may be because the media hammered the phrase into our collective consciousness following the Columbine massacre. Luvox, the SSRI that Columbine shooter Eric Harris took for his depression, is reported to potentially cause a 'loss of empathy' along with other violent and grandiose destructive tendencies associated with drug-induced mania. Harris's diagnosis, then, became a broader diagnosis of cultural pathology, as the Columbine shootings brought to light just how grave and volatile the situation had become on a national level.

All of these violent and grandiose symptoms (except, notably, 'loss of empathy') are also Donnie's symptoms. He is a contradictory, divided character – sleepwalking though much of the movie, and capable of both great destruction and total self-sacrifice. He is also the only real voice of humanity in the film, being overwhelmingly aware of the painful nature of existence, and taking it upon himself to save the world. In creating a mentally ill protagonist who suffers, if anything, from being *too* awake and *too* empathetic, the film is unabashedly prescriptive: go back to the future and open your hearts. Change the course of events. Maybe it's not too late.

Donnie becomes a kind of superhero who takes us back to the future and, in effect, saves a generation of children by martyring himself, as he elaborates in the poem that he reads aloud in class:

> A storm is coming, Frank says / A storm that will swallow the children / And I will deliver them from the kingdom of pain / I will deliver the children back to their doorsteps / And send the monsters back to the underground / I'll send them back to a place

> where no-one else can see them / Except for me / Because I am Donnie Darko.

Even though the action of the film takes place in the 1980s, how can we avoid hearing echoes of Columbine in those words? It is important to remember that this film has captured the imagination of a generation of young people who didn't live through the 1980s, but who nonetheless feel deeply understood and comforted by the narrative. Cult films are often uneven works, and part of their appeal may be that they leave themselves wide open to interpretation. Like *El Topo* (1970) and other cult films that made a strong impact on a generation of viewers, *Donnie Darko* makes little sense at the level of linear narrative, but resonates deeply with religious and spiritual overtones, in a time when American teens are still trying to come to terms with a painful set of events.

As Ed Caesar muses:

> So if the movie is not really going anywhere, how can it be about anything? We look for clues in the mini-narratives that permeate the picture, but what we find are huge, iconic events or images – arson attacks, the classroom rebellion, Frank. All these things look serene and beautiful in Kelly's blue-infused filmic universe, but there is endless room for interpretation of what, if anything, they signify.
>
> Where do we look for clues as to the identity of Frank the rabbit? . . . He's awash with different possibilities, but ultimately bereft of significance in any greater filmic or narrative strategy – the product of a teenager's warped imagination, and now a totem of this film's ability to invade the imagination without requiring a closed explanation. The same could be said of the falling jet engine. (Caesar, 2005)

Donnie Darko's narrative may not 'make sense', but it clearly suggests a solution in relating to teenagers and alienation. In *Bowling For Columbine* (2002) Michael Moore interviewed rocker Marilyn Manson about the allegation that the Columbine shooters had been moved by Manson's music to commit acts of violence, asking him 'If you were to talk directly to the kids at Columbine and the people in that community, what would you say to them if they were here right now?' Marilyn Manson replied, 'I wouldn't say a single word to them. I would listen to what they have to say. And that's what no one did.' And that's exactly what Donnie is doing. He's listening to the pain of a whole generation of kids. He reflects and absorbs even their most incoherent, melodramatic and misguided rantings. And his response is a profound empathy and, ultimately, self-sacrifice.

'Subordinate terror/kickin' off an era/cold deliverin' pain.' (Public Enemy)

Donnie Darko and *American Psycho* are both narratives that were written by young male authors, about mentally ill young male protagonists, and the films share an instructive set of commonalities and differences. The most critical difference between the two works is that *American Psycho* was originally written just as the 1980s were ending – with an astonishing level of perspective and insight on the part of its young author, whereas Donnie Darko was written as a retrospective comment on the decade, with all the wisdom and sadness of hindsight.

Patrick Bateman and Donnie Darko each take sides in a battle between good and evil, being played out against a landscape of apathy. No one else notices how wrong things are going, but all around them an apocalyptic, 'end of days' scenario is unfolding. Of course, these two characters take up arms on different sides of the final battle – Darko martyrs himself in the interest of salvation, whereas Bateman is pure evil, the beast unleashed.

Both films use the metaphor of mental illness to illuminate the larger pathology of American culture at a particular moment in history, in relation to which the protagonists must define and position themselves. And, as stated earlier, this use of cultural metaphor marks a point of adaptation in the genre of horror. Bateman and Darko are both unreliable narrators who suffer from delusions and hallucinations, yet each is put forth as the only character who 'really sees' the horror unfolding around them. This was, after all, Harold Pinter's point about American war crimes in the 1980s, as cited earlier: While it was all happening it was overwhelmingly surreal – and yet nobody noticed; and now nobody bothers to remember. Except, of course, for the movies which, however flawed and unreliable they may be, act as our cultural memory. Monstrous 80s films, with their crazy prophetic protagonists, serve as a reminder of the madness and monstrosity of the Reagan years, and illuminate the ways in which insanity and apocalyptic vision have become working metaphors in our cinematic lexicon; interpretive tools that we use to understand our present and our past.

'Everyone will suffer': national identity and the spirit of subaltern vengeance in Nakata Hideo's *Ringu* and Gore Verbinski's *The Ring*

Linnie Blake

In 2003, with his eyes firmly set on an Academy Award for Best Actor, Tom Cruise took the eponymous lead in Edward Zwick's *The Last Samurai*. A Union Army captain in the US Civil War, driven to alcoholism by the atrocities of the subsequent Indian Wars, this morally bifurcated man is invited to Japan to advise on the modernisation of the Emperor's army, all part of the Meiji Restoration's quest for *fukoku kyohei*: a rich country with a strong army. In the *bushido* code of the Emperor's enemies, the horse-riding, sword-fighting and ostensibly anachronistic *samurai*, however, our hero finds a model of loyalty, integrity and honour lacking in his previous experience of US social life. Following a frankly absurd slow motion battle sequence (in which the massed ranks of native-born *samurai* are mowed down by the Emperor's US-armed and US-trained machine-gun squadron) our surviving hero becomes the last *samurai* of the film's title. For all his traditional clothing, hairstyle and romantic inclinations though, Captain Algren retains all the US iconicity of Tom Cruise's star image: being less a hybrid of Japanese and American models of masculinity than an embodiment and enactment of a form of US cultural imperialism that is, in part, the subject of this paper. The *bushido* code and indeed all aspects of Japanese culture, is here of interest only in so far as it informs, influences or illuminates US self image: in this instance by transforming a US citizen crisis into an ideal specimen of his race. As I will argue throughout this chapter, this is entirely typical of the attitudes of the US cinematic mainstream towards Japan – whereby Japanese culture is consistently deployed as a means of reaffirming, in highly conservative ways, the cultural superiority of US-style democratic individualism and the bourgeois capitalism it serves.

Such a mode of representation is, of course, traceable to the immediate post-war period, with Cold War films such as *Sands of Iwo Jima* (1949) or *Halls of Montezuma* (1951) revisiting the Pacific War for explicitly nationalitistic purposes, asserting the superiority of US modes of social and political organisation in the face of the deindividuated alterity of the ruthless Japanese threat. It is similarly visible in more socially liberal and ostensibly anti-racist offerings of the Cold War, such as Joshua Logan's *Sayonara* (1957) – a Marlon Brando vehicle that criticised the post-war US policy of preventing GIs from marrying Japanese women by deploying the Japanese *shinju* sub-plot, whereby Red Buttons and his Japanese bride commit lovers' suicide in the face of their social exclusion. Giving up a promising military career and marriage to a General's daughter for his own forbidden love, Brando thus embodies all the rebellious individualism of his earlier characters, whilst Japan provides little more than an exotic backdrop against which he can explore what it means to be a US citizen and a man. The process would, of course, be echoed in Hollywood's wholesale appropriation of film plots and characters drawn from Japanese cinema. Kurosawa Akira's *The Seven Samurai* (1951) would become John Sturgis's *The Magnificent Seven* (1960), whilst the perilous transportation of a politically significant princess, the central plot device of Kurosawa's *The Hidden Fortress* (1958), would be profitably transposed onto George Lucas's *Star Wars* (1977). Such adaptations, of course, erased Japanese cultural specificity, whilst more liberal offerings such as John Boorman's *Hell in the Pacific* (1968) mounted a doomed plea for common humanity in the face of national self interest.

Most commonly, then, Japanese culture and society have been depicted by Hollywood as part of a shoddily schematic binarism, whereby the civilised, democratic and individualistic nature of US society is counterpoised to the savage, despotic and de-individualising tendencies of the Japanese. It is a trend unfortunately visible in recent films like *Empire of the Sun* (1987) and *Pearl Harbor* (2001); whilst even ostensibly anti-racist products such as *Windtalkers* (2002) can be seen to evoke Japanese selfhood predominantly as a means of exploring US social attitudes – specifically US xenophobia and the vexed question of Native American rights. Thus, although it must be acknowledged that the increased popularity in the US of distinctively Japanese genres (such as *anime* or *yakuza eiga*) have put images of Japanese selfhood centre-screen, there remains a tendency to re-cast those images in ways that speak directly to US audiences about themselves.[1] Hence, for all the thermo-nuclear resonance of its title, Ridley Scott's *Black Rain* (1989) is less a Hollywood take on the social and psychological fallout of the US bombing of Hiroshima and Nagasaki (which is the subject matter of Imamura Shohei's film of the same name and date) than a formulaic gangster thriller set against an exotic Japanese backdrop. Even Quentin Tarantino's stylistically hybrid *Kill Bill* can be seen as participating in the trend. 'The Origin of O Ren' narrative of *Kill Bill Part One* (2004), much vaunted as an excellent example of the director's stylistic inventiveness, is little more than an English-narrated *anime* with a score drawn from the quintessentially Hollywood genre of the Western, all brass, maracas and harmonica harmonies. All this, of course, leads up to the truly significant point in O Ren's narrative when, despite being surrounded by her *yakuza* henchmen and practising the Japanese martial arts she has excelled at all her life, the hitherto indestructible assassin is despatched by our all-American heroine The Bride.

Such monstrous adaptation of Japanese history, culture and self-image undertaken by mainstream US cinema is only the starting point of this paper though. What is of real interest here are the ways in which such a project is effectively undercut by the generic conventions of horror cinema, specifically those Japanese horror films most recently subject to adaptation in the United States. Over the past fifteen years, as the United States has sought to increase its international influence over the strategically significant nations of Afghanistan, Iraq, Iran and North Korea, it is notable that there has been an exponential increase in the availability, and hence consumption, of Japanese films in America, whether they are *anime*, *yakuza* or horror.[2] Most popular at the US box office, and the core subject of this chapter, has been Gore Verbinski's 2002 film *The Ring*, a remake of Nakata Hideo's *Ringu* (1998) which was itself an adaptation of Suzuki Koji's 1991 novel *The Ring*. Verbinski's *The Ring* has earned gross international revenues of over $229 million and become the seventh highest grossing horror film in history.[3] Drawing on the Japanese *onryou* or vengeful ghost narrative, whereby unjustly slaughtered women return as semiologically distinctive ghosts to exact their retribution on the living world, both *Ringu* and *The Ring* are ideally positioned to explore the ideological function of models of national identity promulgated by the media in Japanese and US society and internalised by members of each, often in direct contradiction of the realities of national history or contemporary social and cultural practices.[4] Predominantly of course, the capacity of *onryou*-style narratives to undertake such cultural work is a product of the history of the genre in Japan, specifically its implicit opposition to the right-wing militarism that led to the Pacific War. Here the animated female corpse, returning from the dead to demand the resolution of cultural conflicts and retribution for unresolved historical crimes, grants compelling-yet-repulsive access to the political unconscious that lies beneath the psychological unconscious of individual characters or the narrative as a whole. And as I will argue, in both Japanese and US narratives, the vengeful ghost's target is not merely 'the living' but the repressive and totalising ideologies that they have internalised. As this paper will illustrate, then, the generic conventions of the *onryou* may be seen to undermine the imperialistic agendas of both twentieth-century Japan and twenty-first-century America; and in the process the *onryou* calls into question both the value of the *bushido* code in Japan's past and the contemporary fetishisation of family stability, media responsibility and judicial legitimacy in the neo-conservative US. In each case however, the film text is stalked by the spectre of the vengeful female ghost that haunts its bourgeois capitalistic hegemonies and the imperialistic ambitions these narratives uphold.

The *onryou* motif came into its own in the years following America's 1945–1952 cccupation of the defeated Japan when, taking control of all aspects of Japanese social, cultural, economic and political life, America exercised its 'desire to see the Japanese behave like USs (which by definition was good)' (Lu, 1997: 459). Such an unabashedly colonialist agenda encouraged the Japanese people to embrace US models of civil liberties and human rights, particularly those pertaining to freedom of religion, speech, the press and assembly. Abolishing Shinto as the state religion and forcing the Emperor to disavow his divinity, the US occupation thus set out to 'to destroy the wartime militaristic and xenophobic mentality' (Hirano, 1992: 119) that had started with the massacre of hundreds of thousands of Chinese in Nanking in 1937 and ended with America's atom bombing of Nagasaki in 1945. To do so the US introduced the Showa Constitution which entailed the renunciation of war, promoted universal adult suffrage and advocated the equality of the sexes and rights to property, work and trade union membership. Education became a universal right regardless of race, creed, sex, social position or family origin. The Constitution thus set out to enact the US *Declaration of Independence*'s foundational assertion that the supreme aim of government was the promotion of 'life, liberty and the pursuit of happiness' in all its citizens. And to culturally reinforce such values, intrinsically or traditionally Japanese cultural products were heavily censored. Out went all traces of militarism, with sword fight dramas and samurai films being initially banned, as well as some 98 *kabuki* plays. Poetry anthologies were scrutinised, and even Mount Fuji, the object of Shintoist nature worship, became a forbidden subject for visual representation.[5]

Unsurprisingly, such a radical project of re-fashioning Japan in the image of America called into question what it now meant to call oneself Japanese in the modern world and how, indeed, one's cultural identity might be expressed artistically. In one camp, aligned with the nationalistic right, were those proponents of the *bushido* style militarism of the pre-war years; individuals who defended or denied the events of Nanking and justified the human rights atrocities perpetrated during the war years as a necessary part of military strategy. In the other camp, aligned with the peacenik left, were those who decried the militaristic past as a crime against the Japanese people who had been doubly victimised by the punitive dropping of US atom bombs on Hiroshima and Nagasaki. As Shindo Kaneto, director of *The Bell of Nagasaki* (1950) and *Children of Hiroshima* (1952) and, later, of two notable *onryou* films put it, in a rather clumsy translation:

> We might say the atomic bomb had been given to [the] Japanese as a revelation of science who preferred savageness, fanaticism and intolerant Japanese spirit to freedom, culture and science. The atomic bomb was an alarm to civilisation and an awakening towards peace for [the] Japanese. (Hirano, 1992: 64)

What had brought Japan to ruin, the intellectual left argued, was the *bushido* code – not as fetishised by the neo-conservative agenda underpinning *The Last Samurai* or *Kill Bill* but as a form of savage and intolerant fanaticism that exploited the weak, destroyed all that stood in the way of military supremacy and promoted an anti-intellectual and fundamentally irrational form of xenophobic patriarchy. It is no coincidence, then, that in his exploration of *nihonjinron* (or post-war Japanese identity) Shindo should counter the overweening militarism of the recent past with a revival of the figure of the abject woman familiar from a number of ancient storytelling forms. Drawn from the *kaidan* or ghost story but melded with both the demonic woman of *Noh* theatrical tradition (such as the *kyojo-mono* or *shuven-mono*) and the evil woman (*akuba* or *akujo*) of *kabuki* theatre, this abject woman is herself a hybrid. Part-woman-part-cat in the *bakeneko-monu*, part living and part dead elsewhere, she invariably possessed the long dark hair, staring eyes and twitchy unnatural movements that signify supernatural otherness. Thus in Shindo's own *Onibaba* (1964) and *Kuruneko* (1968) and in Kobayashi Masaki's *Kwaidan* (1968) we can see the vengeful feminine principle at work, targeting explicitly the macho militarism of the *bushido* code whilst demanding from beyond the grave a form of justice that restores balance (*wa*) to Japanese social life. In this respect, such figures can be seen as encapsulating Bakhtin's sense of 'pregnant death, a death that gives birth', her 'decaying and deformed flesh' combining 'with the flesh of a new life, conceived but as yet unformed' (Russo, 1990: 325). Such figures are, then, an historically and culturally specific abject. They are 'the jettisoned object [...] radically excluded' that draws the observer 'toward the place where meaning collapses [...] on the edge of non-existence and hallucination' (Russo, 1990: 326).

Clearly it is no coincidence that both *Onibaba* and *Kuroneko* are set in seventeenth-century Japan; also a period of great social disruption, when competing warlords tore the country apart, throwing the peasantry into abject poverty. Hence, in the former film, a mother- and daughter-in-law who live together in an area of towering reeds tire of their diet of mice, worms and snakes and, in the absence of their forcibly conscripted kinsman, murder passing *samurai* – selling their armaments and armour for food. The corpses they throw into the hole of the film's title. This is, as the opening credits indicate, a 'deep and dark' space whose 'silence has endured since ancient times', a space wherein all aspects of Japanese culture and consciousness that cannot be assimilated into a balanced and harmonious world view must be ejected. It is a space iconographically very similar to the subterranean prison of Teshigahara Hiroshi's *The Woman in the Dunes* (1964) and, as we will see, the deep dark well of *Ringu*. Thus dwarfed by their surroundings and buffeted by winds of ill fortune that blow evil for the nation as a whole, they do their best to survive whilst terrible portents that directly evoke the horrors of Hiroshima and Nagasaki abound: 'a black sun rose, the day was night. It's as if the earth was turned upside down.' Clearly, it is *bushido* that has brought them to such a pass and it is unsurprising that when a mask-wearing *samurai* appears, the mother-in-law openly asserts 'men like you killed my son'. He must, in turn, be 'punished [...] for starting a war'. The mask, which hides the masculine principle's dark desires to control and conquer, is thus ripped away. But in placing it on her face, the mother-in-law makes a fatal error. Like the victims of Hiroshima and Nagasaki she becomes horribly mutilated by donning the mask of militarism and for all her shouted protests 'I'm not a demon, I'm a human being', she is swallowed up by the hole. Thus Shindo's realistically realised women, who eat like men and kill like men, and refuse to be sexually exploited whilst being comfortable with their own sexuality, are corrupted by the *bushido* code. For this reason, the mother-in-law will be cast out, being swallowed by the hole as convincingly as is Yamamura Sadako, abject corpse woman of *Ringu*, three centuries later.

Such concerns were echoed in Shindo's follow-up project *Kuruneko*, the tale of a mother- and daughter-in-law whose son and husband has, once more, been carried away to fight in the service of an anonymous lord. In his absence they are raped and murdered by a group of wandering *samurai*. Swearing vengeance on the warrior class 'for warring' and on a world that proclaims 'the weak will always starve', the women enter into a demonic pact. Brought back to life in the guise of rich gentlewomen, they lead *samurai* through the forests to their ghostly home where, having given them the chance to redeem themselves, they transform into black cats and rip out the throats of their unrepentant victims. A generic relative of the *onryou*, this *bakeneko-monu* thus aligns the feminine abject with the verminous and untrustworthy figure of the cat, illustrating the hidden power and resilience of both. Once again, the target is macho militarism. Unfortunately the lost son Haichi, his loyalties divided between his family and his lord, makes a choice that damns him forever. He opts for loyalty to his master's destructive ideal and ends up with nothing; at the close of the film he lies in the burned ruins of his family house as the snow falls upon him and the plaintive cry of a cat howls round him. Having turned his back on his family, having rejected the ideals of balance, continuity and stability embodied in the feminine principle, he is left with nothing; as indeed was Japan following its wartime defeat. It is a dynamic echoed almost exactly, moreover, in the 'Black Hair' episode of *Kwaidan*, whose *samurai* protagonist is haunted by the eponymous tresses of the loyal, humble and self-effacing first wife he abandoned. His death, when it comes, is caused by a vision of his own horribly aged face; and it is precisely this which kills the protagonists in the original Suzuki Koji novel *Ringu* from which Nakata Hideo and Gore Verbinski's films would be adapted.[6]

Suzuki Koji's novel, which began the *Ringu/Ring* series is the story of magazine reporter Asakawa Kazuyuki (the married father of a daughter) who enlists the help of old college associate Takayama Ryuji (a philosopher and self-proclaimed rapist) to trace the origins of a killer videotape. It is a narrative which consistently deploys the metaphor of the virus to explore the politics of individual, gendered and national identity in an age of multi-media representation. Here Sadako is a genetically-male though feminine-seeming hermaphrodite killed by the last survivor of smallpox in Japan, a doctor who raped her and then killed her when he post-coitally glimpsed her abnormal genitalia; the physician's recognition of and patriarchal horror at Sadako's balanced embodiment of masculine and feminine principles leads to her destruction. The video, and its lethal potentiality, is thus a product of Sadako's own telekinetic abilities mixed with the smallpox virus's will to survive by whatever means necessary. Sadako, as spirit of vengeance, therefore asserts her own right to survive, and to reproduce, by becoming both mother and father to a new breed of infected individuals, her meta-hybridity echoed in the book's inference that her father was not in fact human but a water spirit summoned by the real-life ascetic En no Ozunu.

Most notably, though, Sadako's victims do not die because she emerges from the television screen but, as is the case in *Kwaidan*, when their virally damaged hearts stop beating at the sight of a terrifying vision of themselves prematurely aged. Cast off and excluded by the social world of the symbolic order, its representations of itself to itself, its formulation and recognition of the ideologically interpellated subject, Sadako thus occupies a space of thirty-year silence before erupting into the eclectic incomprehensibility of the images captured on the cursed video: perspectivally distorted maternal hair-brushing, the bubbling eruption of Japanese characters, crawling damaged people, a pointing man, the character '*sada*' reflected in a human eye, the corona of light peeping around the partially closed cover of the well. Illustrating the ways in which dominant ideologies assign a state of psychotic meaninglessness to the unheard and unrecognised who deemed thus are excluded from the material world, Sadako's video also proposes a new way of reconceiving and reconfiguring both the subject and his or her society. She is, as Slavoj Zizek following Marx would have it, the spectral apparition who returns to haunt the real that has excluded her; she is the trauma around which contemporary Japanese social reality is structured. Her more direct mode of address is, in the novel, the vision of the self granted to the doomed immediately before their death. She neither appears from the television nor (as in the idiot-proof US version) rasps 'seven days' down the telephone to her victims. When it comes, the message itself is the length of her silence and the ostensible incomprehensibility of her message.

Nakata Hideo's *Ringu*, the first cinematic treatment of Suzuki's novel, was made in 1998 as a recession-hit Japan's technology markets crashed, unemployment soared and the nation seemed plagued both by a rash of insurance-money killings and by a number of apocalyptic quasi-religious groups, such as the Aum Cult who mounted a poison gas attack on the Tokyo subway system. Significantly, Nakata's primary adaptation of the novel erases Sadako's hermaphroditism entirely and replaces the male Asakawa Kazuyuki with the female Asakawa Reiko, also an investigative reporter, but here the separated career-driven mother of a young son, Yoishi. By highlighting an ongoing Japanese adherence to a doctrine of separate spheres of activity for the sexes, whereby women's biological destiny is to nurture the next generation and not compete with men on the job market, Reiko embodies the plight of the ambitious Japanese woman who is also a mother, whilst Sadako becomes the thwarted potentiality of all victims of masculine aggression. Like Kazuyuki, Reiko is investigating the recent urban myth of a lethal videotape when her niece Tomoko and three of her friends mysteriously die. As in the novel, the group have recently holidayed in a cabin on the Izu peninsula where they watched a mysterious videotape. Travelling to the log cabin in question, Reiko watches and subsequently copies the tape for Takayama Ryuji, who retains the name of the novel's protagonist but is now a mathematician and her ex-husband. Discovering that their son Yoishi has watched the tape, the two set out to save their child. There is no implication, however, that such a quest may restore their relationship as there is in the US version. The preservation of the next generation is all important, and heterosexual romance, obligatory in America, is deemed an irrelevance. As in the novel, they travel first to Oshima, the birthplace of the dead psychic Yamamura Shizuko whom they have identified from images on the tape. Here they discover the story of Yamamura Sadako, Shizuko's illegitimate daughter who disappeared some thirty years before having, it turns out, been murdered by her father. Sadako, it seems, has psychically created the video in an attempt to appease her will to avenge father's crimes. Thus, although Reiko and Ryuji locate Sadako's bones in a well beneath the Izu cabin and, as in the novel, arrange for their burial, this does not prevent Ryuji's death as the spectral Sadako emerges, terrifyingly, from his television screen seven days after his initial viewing of the tape. Realising that she saved herself by replicating the tape and passing it on, Reiko helps her son Yoishi to copy the tape and pass it to his grandfather who, it seems, willingly submits to his own fate.

Located in a highly 'Americanised' Japan, Nakata's *Ringu* is nonetheless a major stylistic and political contributor to the *onryou* tradition. Japan is here a world of baseball games on television, western-style homes, career-driven single mothers, advanced news media and the sophisticated technological mediation of everyday life. But it is also a Japan of far-flung islands, isolated villages, traditional rural dwellings complete with *tatami* mats, futons and paper screens, grand-parental devotion to the family, incomprehensible regional dialects and ancient folk superstitions. As is the case with the hermaphrodite Sadako of the novel or the abject Sadako here, to be Japanese is to incorporate a range of seemingly irreconcilable binarisms. On the one hand is the modern, rational, scientific, individualistic, liberal and democratic Japan of the Showa Constitution. On the other is an older, irrational, superstitious Japan of the past, where the wronged woman returns for vengeance on a world that has not only destroyed her but built leisure facilities upon her unmarked grave. It is not, I would argue, that the technological mediation of life propounded by *Ringu* – its video and stills cameras, VCRs, telephones and televisions – is a product of 'the intrusion of "post-human" otherness into everyday life' (White, 2005: 41). It is more that the 'simulacral proliferation of information in a media saturated social sphere' (41) in evidence here evokes what Baudrillard, in *The Transparency of Evil*, would deem the hell of the same, whereby certain pre-Showa forms and models of individual, gendered and familial relations (the problematic Others to dominant social formations and modes of remembering the past) are effectively erased. This is, of course, a theme familiar from the Japanese New Wave, specifically films such as Shohei Imamura's *Kuragejima: Tales from a Southern Island* (1968), where the primitive way of life of remote islanders is counterpoised to that of an urbane engineer visiting from Tokyo and the culture of factories, air travel and Coca-Cola that follows in his wake. The islanders, the film argues, may be savages, but they have the cultural homogeneity and social harmony that is entirely lacking in the modern world. America may have attempted to abnegate the alterity of the Japanese people by first infecting them with its ideology of individualistic democratic progress and then absorbing them into the international marketplace of nations. But in the form of Sadako's video, the hitherto silenced voice of all that has been lost to this process erupts into speech. Modern Japanese life, in Baudrillard's formulation, is thus exposed as life 'after the orgy' whereby ostensible 'political liberation, sexual liberation, liberation of the forces of production [...] women's liberation, children's liberation, liberation of unconscious drives, liberation of art' (Baudrillard, 1993: 3) ushered in by the US occupation presents a simulacral ideal that champions a colonialist agenda by silencing the past. It is, of course, entirely illusory and Sadako exists to expose it as such.

Suzuki Koji has himself asserted that the vengeful female of the *Ringu* cycle was named for one Takahashi Sadako, a real-life psychic of the early 1900s, the protégé of Professor Fukurai on whom Ikuma Heihachiro, Sadako's father in the book, is based.[7] This real-world Sadako was said to possess the gift of *nensha* – the ability to project an image onto film or some other medium. But given the *onryou* tradition of which the film is a part, it must also be recognised that the name 'Sadako', an old-fashioned and little used name meaning 'chaste child', has a great deal of cultural resonance in Japan. Specifically, her naming evokes one Sasaki Sadako (or 'Sadako of the Thousand Paper Cranes'), a child of Hiroshima who died of leukaemia in 1955. In her attempt to escape her inevitable fate, this Sadako fashioned some 644 origami cranes, believing that if she folded 1,000 the gods would make her well again. The 356 outstanding were made by her classmates and buried with her. Sadako's story would in time come to signify the destruction of innocence by war, her name becoming a kind of shorthand for all that was destroyed by Japan's territorial ambitions and America's concomitant decision to unleash the nuclear menace upon the civilians of Japan. In 1958 a memorial to her and other child victims of the bombs was erected in Hiroshima Peace Park with the inscription:

> This is our cry
> This is our prayer
> Peace in the world.[8]

In her terrible vengeance on the living, in her will to replicate herself through the endless and exponential proliferation of cursed videos, in her will to find a voice Sadako can thus be seen to embody, in Spivak's words, 'the kind of Power and Desire that would inhabit the unnamed subject of the Other' (Spivak, 1995 [1983]: 25). Occupying the subaltern position of one whose history has been skilfully concealed and who thus 'cannot speak' for herself she nonetheless tires of 'lying in shadow' (28) and moves, in Nakata's vision, through the television screen into the real world of the present. Moving quite literally through the televisual medium, using it for the transmission of her own long-silenced voice, Sadako becomes that which will not be erased by American colonialism in Japan or by the Japanese refusal to acknowledge the sins of its own past. In keeping with her abject status her text is multiplicitous. She is the living corpse who collapses the boundaries between life and death, good and evil, the human and the inhuman, the natural and the supernatural. She throws old certainties into doubt. She calls into question normative conceptions of what it is to be human and what it now means to be Japanese. In all its elusive and allusive qualities, hers is a form of post-colonial text in which the hitherto silenced story of her people is told. And its message, though altered and adapted for a US audience, offers a warning of great relevance to the neo-conservative America of the neo-imperialist present.

Although made by different directors, the Hollywood adaptations *The Ring* and *The Ring 2* share a common screenwriter in Ehren Kruger. He is perhaps better known for *Arlington Road* (1998) the Mark Pellington-directed exploration of the competing claims to US selfhood proffered respectively by the US government (and its military, legislative and societal agencies) and the right-wing militias that form the nation's political underground. Locating ideals of national identity (loyalty, freedom, independence, self-reliance, hard work, etc.) within the family unit, Kruger's is a tense pre-9/11 evocation both of the horrors and the political efficacy of terrorism, this time home-grown. The form and function of technologically mediated representations of terrorist atrocity (including video footage and stills photography) also comes in for detailed consideration here, as does the role and responsibility of the televisual and print media – both of which are mercilessly indicted for acting in service of dominant ideologies of national identity. An underrated classic, *Arlington Road* is thus intimately concerned with what it means to be an 'American' at the very end of the twentieth century (notably before 9/11) and, specifically, how a deeply divided nation nonetheless asserts and imposes an entirely de-problematised model of its own exeptionalism on the world. Surprisingly perhaps, these are the very interests that Kruger brings to the screenplays of the remakes of Nakata's *Ringu* films. Certainly, Kruger participates in the tendency to evoke Japanese alterity as a means of exploring US selfhood, but he also operates in keeping with the *onryou*'s history, warning against acceptance of totalising formulations of national identity, particularly those promulgated by the neo-conservative ascendancy.

In narrative terms *The Ring* contains some significant alterations to its Japanese source material. The action is relocated to America's Pacific Northwest, specifically the city of Seattle where, interestingly, a peace park named for Seiko Sadako is located. Here the female reporter is Rachel Keller, single parent to the psychically inclined Aidan whose photographer father Noah has no contact with his son prior to the beginning of the narrative. This failed family unit is complemented by the Morgans, whose adopted pre-pubescent daughter Samara, herself possessed of malign supernatural powers, spends much of her short life in a psychiatric institution before being murdered by her adoptive mother and thrown down a well. Here she remains, increasingly decayed and decreasingly child-like, until her rage is projected upwards onto a videotape and the cycle of vengeance and retribution drawn from the Japanese originals begins again. Clearly, then, the US remake of *Ringu* makes reference to its Japanese origins in terms of plot and the iconography of the vengeful *onryou*, but these are very much in keeping with the history of US cinematic attitudes to Japan, a discussion of which opened this paper. Having excluded the original's screenwriter, Takashi Hiroshi, and director, Nakata Hideo, from the credits of *The Ring*, moreover, the filmmakers even opt, in true colonialist style, to evoke a certain 'Japaneseness' for atmospheric purposes. They include, for example, shots of the non-indigenous Japanese maple tree (the fruits of which are called the *samara*). But like the Japanese wall hanging at the Morgan ranch, the Japanese *anime* character in Aidan's room or the ways in which Noah's loft windows resemble Japanese paper screens, these references are merely decorative; being playful touches akin to *The Ring 2* providing Aidan with a physician called Dr Koji. Evidently, and quite typically, what is of interest here is not Japan but the US. Most significant, however, is Kruger's decision to replace the adult Sadako with the pre-pubescent girl child Samara.

Samara's *post mortem* appearance may be drawn from the Japanese *onryou* tradition, all long hair and staring eye, spastic movements and decomposing flesh, but the fact that she is also depicted as a living child is self-evidently a means of exploring the myths and deceptions that underpin the self-image of the United States. From the coruscating indictment of the hypocrisy of the slave-owning Christian South proffered by Mark Twain's eponymous *Huckleberry Finn* (1883) to Holden Caulfield's teenage disgust at the 'phoney' 1950s in Salinger's *The Catcher in the Rye* (1951), US literature has repeatedly evoked the perspective of the child/adolescent as a means of commenting on the failure of the United States to live up to its exeptionalist promise. Most recently, films as diverse as *Kids* (1995), *Gummo* (1997) and *AI* (2001) have continued this practice, depicting the uses and abuses of children and the families that raise them as a means of testing the nation's claims to moral as well as political and economic leadership of the world. If *Ringu* had called into question the whitewashing of the Japanese past by depicting the media-saturated hell of the same that is the present, then *The Ring* undertakes a similarly sceptical treatment of dominant ideologies of identity in its critique of the nuclear family as sustaining institution of advanced US capitalism. Championed as the key means of transmitting social and ethical values by the neo-conservative right, the family is clearly a means of inculcating the child with a sense of self that is firmly embedded in the political necessity of the present whilst allowing for the transmission of property along dynastic lines. But as an excised scene from the film reveals, this cornerstone of neo-conservative rhetoric is seen to be in a perilous condition; a page in the Shelter Mountain Inn's guest book reads: 'I had a lovely vacation with my fat wife who I'm cheating on and who I'll divorce in a year before I get blood cancer and die.' This is, of course, the precise spot upon which the child Samara was murdered by her mother. Rachel Keller, even more preoccupied with her career than was Yamamura Reiko and even more dissatisfied, appears to have little contact with her own family. There are no self-sacrificing grandparents upon whom she can rely to save her son and her relationship with Ruth, her Republican elder sister who aggressively totes 'family values' whilst resenting Rachel's career, is understandably tense. She has, moreover, chosen to have a child with a photographer who participates in the simulacral proliferation of identities that haunts both films whilst describing his own father as 'a disappointment' and taking no interest in the life of his own child. But it is Samara, the child psychiatrically institutionalised by her adoptive parents, who best reveals the mediation of US family life by the machinations of the state; becoming the locus of a series of debates concerning the nature and culture of US society that challenge the Republican right's totalising assertions.

Unlike Sadako, Samara is confined at the behest of her adoptive parents to a psychiatric institution where she is heavily sedated for the protection of the staff, confined under video surveillance to her room and subject to videotaped interviews whilst strapped to heart and brain monitoring electrodes. The subject of rigorous observation that would not be out of place in Foucault's *Madness and Civilization*, she is perfectly positioned, in all her ostensible irrationality, to expose the machinations of the supposedly rational society that so confines her. Hers is not what Marcuse would term the happy consciousness that blindly accepts the status quo, but one that can be neither enticed nor compelled to conform. She feels no pain, needs no sleep, experiences no visible distress at her own isolation and calmly explains her own compulsion to harm. 'You don't want to hurt anyone,' says her doctor. 'But I do,' Samara retorts, adding politely, 'I'm sorry. It won't stop.' As CCTV footage and X-Ray film indicate though, for all her doctors' attempts to mould her thoughts and behaviour, Samara resists her enforced silence in life and overcomes it in death. She can imprint images on X-Ray film, on videotape and on the human psyche: 'Oh Christ!' declares her father immediately before his suicide. 'The things she'd show you.'

In life, then, Samara is viewed as a monster – one who not only mounts an attack on the supposedly sacred bond between a mother and her child by driving her mother mad, but one who destroys her father's livelihood by driving his horses to their deaths. The psychosurgery her father imposes upon her is clearly not enough to make her conform to the lineaments of the bourgeois family, though, and patriarchal revenge is swift. In an extraordinarily pastoral vision sequence her fate is depicted in vibrant colour. Standing in a verdant forest clearing, as horses run on the horizon and choral voices soothe the senses, Samara and her mother stand by the well. 'Isn't it beautiful here Samara,' says her mother, evoking an ideal vision of land and family that is far removed from what is to come. Immediately and violently she covers the child's face with a black plastic bag, smothering her and throwing her ostensibly lifeless body down the well. Anna's act of retributive violence against one unable and unwilling to conform to the pastoral pretensions of this ideal America encapsulates the political significance of the film's deployment of the *onryou* motif. Certainly, Anna's assertion, 'I know things will get better', as the still-living child topples into a watery tomb, rings very hollow indeed. What is most extraordinary, though, is the way in which infanticide is justified by the narrative logic of the film and internalised by its characters.

Resident on Moesko Island between 1970 and 1977 – years which overlap with America's doomed attempt to extend democratic individualism amongst the reluctant peoples of North Vietnam – Samara shares her name with that of a city of tactical importance in both George Bush's Gulf War and his son George W. Bush's sequel. As it also references 'The Appointment in Samarra' [*sic*], a folk tale famously retold by W. Somerset Maugham in Act III of *Sheppey*, a sense of America's appointment with its own destiny abounds.[9] It was clearly wrong to bring the feminised death that is Samara to the island that is an idealised America. She was self-evidently destined to corrupt the retrospectively imagined pastoral perfection of this self-sustaining community just as the original white settlers defiled the fresh green breast of the new world in the sixteenth century. 'Some things aren't meant to be,' the island's doctor remarks of Samara. 'My wife was not supposed to have a child,' Richard Morgan echoes shortly before his rococo though fiercely-edited suicide. But if it was designed to conceal and excuse the Morgans' grotesque murder of Samara, such evocations of Puritan predestination theology fail utterly to convince. They serve, moreover, to remind us that alone amongst the nations of the developed world, certain US states, most notably the Presidential home state of Texas, continue to deploy such arguments in their justification of the execution of those who fail to conform to social and cultural norms. If nothing else, Samara's repeatedly justified murder illustrates how, for all its pretensions to rationality, America is clearly motivated by an irrational will to vengeance on all who challenge its hegemonies. It is a form of vengeance that is shored up where necessary by a highly selective deployment of Judeo-Christian thought. It is the kind of 'eye for an eye' thinking that saw the invasion of Afghanistan and Iraq as vengeance for 9/11 or even saw 9/11 itself as divine punishment for the secularisation of US society.[10] And as the tagline from the trailer excised from the film affirms, it is a way of thinking that ensures that 'everyone will suffer' and suffer justly if they step out of line.

With the family no longer offering refuge from the horrors of advanced industrial capitalism, what is offered as means of alternative comfort is a world of things and representations of things. The protagonists live in expansive rural ranches, trendy urban lofts and affluent suburban houses. They drive expensive cars. They are well dressed and enjoy engaging careers in the media. Their children are educated in well-funded and well-equipped schools. And everyone, apart from the staff and the convenience store proprietor, is both bourgeois and white. This is clearly the sanitised and safe world of 'Fortress America', the artificiality of which is evoked by the blue filter that characterises the Seattle street scenes. It is moreover a world endlessly refracted through an utter superfluity of electronic devices. At every turn, and even more intensely than in *Ringu*, *The Ring* illustrates the ubiquity of media-generated reproductions of identities and ideals. Anna Morgan's story is pieced together from print media archives; Noah's face appears distorted in the local store's CCTV even as he provides Rachel with access to his employer's sophisticated video editing facilities. Television sets and VCRs abound. They dominate family living rooms and invariably appear in hotels and hospitals. As a scene that directly references Hitchcock's *Rear Window* (1954) indicates, the rich diversity of lives and lifestyles of which America boasts has been replaced by a televisually mediated cultural homogeneity that at no point challenges the social and economic status quo. Quite extraordinarily, Richard Morgan's highly fetishistic suicide combines the water that is associated with his murdered daughter, a bridle from his own dead horses and, of course, a television set. Such is the state of US fatherhood! Rachel Keller, the modern US mother, is even knocked into the well that is Samara's final resting place by a television. In a post-9/11 culture in which the horrors of the World Trade Center's destruction is endlessly recycled as justification for curtailments of civil liberties at home and the invasion of Afghanistan and Iraq abroad, Richard Morgan's view of the media seems particularly apposite.[11] In a moment that would make Adorno and Horkheimer proud, he asserts that the media exists not to inform and empower but to 'take one person's tragedy and force the world to experience it; spread it like a sickness'; this, of course, functions as distraction from weightier matters on which the people's opinion is neither called for nor desired. Thus permeated by the state-sponsored and media-disseminated capitalism that shapes the desires and identifications of individuals and social groups, the ostensible homogeneity of America is neatly exposed as a fiction predicated on the exclusion of those *déclassé* subjects who are denied or demonised by a media in thrall to dominant ideologies of nationhood.

Dispossessed of the nation's fictive promises of equality, the medically abused and mother-murdered Samara becomes a peculiarly US form of *onryou*, 'an abstraction used in order to identify the intractability that surfaces *inside* the dominant system' being 'that which the dominant discourse cannot appropriate completely, an otherness that resists containment' (Prakash, 2000: 288). Like Sadako before her, she is ideally positioned to expose the plight of those excluded and silenced by the forces, structures and formations of contemporary society and specifically by those subjects who, by virtue of their internalisation of dominant ideologies of nationhood, are more socially integrated than she. As in *Ringu* what horrifies most is the moment at which the silenced abject erupts into the social world: as thermographic X-Ray, as the visions experienced by Anna Morgan and later Rachel Keller, as material emergence from the television screen and as the spectral video itself. Shown in full and in interpolated montages at significant moments of the narrative, Samara's video as conceived of by Verbinski is far more legible than that of Nakata's Sadako. Its expertly lit monochrome images, ranging from guts being ripped from a human mouth to scenes of Anna Morgan's suicide, are either allegorical of Samara's abuse or directly drawn from her life. And unlike Nakata's images, they display a unifying visual logic of assemblage that links them to the film as a whole – a series of images relating to circles and spirals, for example, creating a continuum between the ostensibly irrational world of the video and the purportedly rational world of the contemporary US. Both, by implication, are grotesquely violent: included images of maggots and crawling people, severed digits, bubbling blood, cancerous cellular division and child murder evoking a world of pain historically omitted from US news coverage of events such as 9/11 or the aftermath of the war in Iraq. In this, Samara's eruption into speech differs radically from the official version of United States history. When she emerges from the television to take Noah's life, Samara is decayed, vengeful and considerably less childlike than she appeared on the hospital video. She will not be silenced, she will not be infantilised. She will have her revenge.

The Verbinski/Kruger adaptation of the *onryou* therefore encapsulates the attempted project of cultural assimilation that has informed US attitudes towards Japanese cinema since the termination of the Pacific War. But equally visible are the ways in which the *onryou* motif is admirably suited to exploring the invidious effects of *all* unified or totalising models of national identity, whether these are Japanese or US. The conventions of the *onryou* can thus be seen to undermine the imperialistic agendas of both twentieth-century Japan and the twenty-first-century US – throwing into question both the value of the *bushido* code in Japan's past and the validity of the exeptionalist model of national identity so beloved of the Republican right; ideals of family stability, communal responsibility and democratic opportunity on which currently neo-conservative models of US cultural superiority rest. Films like *The Last Samurai* might, in other words, participate in the neo-colonialist agenda that has typified cinematic representations of Japan since the 1940s. They do so, moreover, by glorifying the selfsame *bushido* mindset that led to the catastrophic militarisation of Japan in the 1930s. But films like *The Ring* operate rather differently, for to adapt a Japanese *onryou* is to invite subversion of all dominant ideologies. In the light of 9/11 – particularly the paranoia it has inspired at home and the scramble for international influence it has engendered abroad – the US's re-engagement with its onetime colonial subject Japan through the medium of cinematic horror may be profitable, but it is also an ideologically dangerous project. Thus, for all its ostensible political conservativism, Verbinski and Kruger's re-visioning of *Ringu* insistently calls into question the mass-culturally mediated self-image of a nation that against all the evidence, daily asserts itself to be 'one nation, indivisible under God'.

Notes

The unfilmable? H. P. Lovecraft and the cinema by Julian Petley

1 Of this passage, Houllebecq grimly but appositely remarks: 'O humans at the end of the twentieth century, this desolate cosmos is absolutely our own ... Today, more so than ever before, we can utter the *declaration of principles* that begins *Arthur Jermyn* as our own' (2005: 33).

2 This is a reference to another mythos, that of Nigel Kneale's Professor Quatermass, since Hobb's End is the site of the discovery of the Martian spaceship in *Quatermass and the Pit* (Roy Ward Baker: 1967).

Imperfect geometry: identity and culture in Clive Barker's 'The Forbidden' and Bernard Rose's Candyman by Brigid Cherry

1 Analysis here could focus on a number of different psychographic or demographic profiles, but for reasons of space gender has been chosen as the main focus of this account. Certainly gendered and queer identities are especially relevant to the study of Clive Barker as a queer author. The responses of these identity groups, as well as those of ethnic audiences, demand further study.

2 See, for example, Berenstein, 1996; Cherry, 1999; Pinedo, 1997; and Williamson, 2001.

3 See Cherry, 1999 for a summary of this research.

4 In total, 336 films were named by 107 of the participants. See Cherry, 2005, for the full top 40.

5 In fact, for some of the fans the fascination with Clive Barker and his work overrides other considerations; for these fans *Candyman* is a Barker film and they do not overtly acknowledge Rose as either director or scriptwriter.

6 A discussion of the appeal of *Hellraiser* can be found in Cherry, 2005.

7 Even where not scriptwriting or directing, Barker had approval of or input into each of these films or the projects were assigned to individ-

uals he trusted creatively. See Winter, 2001.

8 Specifically by Stephen King, Bram Stoker, Angela Carter, Shirley Jackson, Edgar Allen Poe, Anne Rice, Whitley Striber, Mary Shelley, Dennis Wheatley and Thomas Harris.

9 See Schneider, 2004 for a discussion of aesthetics. Schneider's focus on horror which stands the test of time might profitably be widened to include examples of horror which hold strong appeals for specific identity groups.

10 See Benshoff, 1997 for a fuller account of the straight queer in Barker's work.

11 See Jancovich, 1992.

12 Whilst there are clear links between horror cinema and the Gothic in its various forms, it may not seem entirely intuitive to refer to the fairy tale in this context. However, many of the female fans taking part in the study pinpointed the origins of their taste for horror to fairy tales and other forms of children's literature and entertainment. Furthermore Clive Barker has stated that he draws on the fairy tale as one source of inspiration in his writing. See interviews with Barker in Jones, 1991 10, or 394, for example.

13 See Briefel and Ngai, 2000; Hill, 1997; and Pinedo, 1997.

14 This is not intended to suggest any invalidity in Kuhn's work. Rather it is hoped that it would add additional insight into such theoretical analysis.

15 Splatterpunk fiction arose in the late 1980s and generally consists of explicit gore, violence and mutilation. It is typified by the work of David J. Schow, John Skipp and Craig Spector. Splat lit is closely allied to splatter cinema, originating in the work of low-budget film makers such as Herschell Gorden Lewis and continuing through body horror, the slasher film and various strains of the 'video nasty'.

16 Kern also discusses *Hellraiser* in terms of splatter, describing it as a 'hard-core, gore film classic' (Kern, 1996: 56).

17 The repetition of the monster's name while looking in the mirror to call it up is taken from the 'Bloody Mary' urban myth.

18 Children would tout their guy around local streets asking for a 'penny for the guy' and the money so collected used to buy fireworks to be set off as they burnt their guy on the bonfire. This traditional event is now more often referred to as Firework Night and the making and burning of the guy has largely fallen away.

19 When discussing these elements of the text, one American fan made the assumption that the Candyman was a clown.

20 Script available online at www.clivebarker.info/candyman.html.

21 With the focus on the connotations of anti-Catholicism, race seems to have become a structuring absence in the short story. Anne-Marie's face is described at one point as 'the colour and texture of stale

dough' (21) and the Candyman has 'skin the colour of buttermilk' (6). Other characters, the middle-aged women and the boy, lack any signifiers of ethnic origin and only the shopkeeper is given a specific identity, stereotypically Pakistani. Published in 1985, this is only four years after the Toxteth riots – incited in part by police harassment of black youth – had taken place.

22 'A Little Bit of Hamlet: A Conversation between Clive Barker and Dennis Etchison', 25 February 1987, UCLA Extension Writers Program. Transcript in Jones, 1991, 47–65.

Out from the realist underground; or, the Baron of Blood visits Cannes: recursive and self-reflexive patterns in David Cronenberg's Videodrome *and* eXistenZ *by Steffen Hantke*

1 These intermediate films are *The Dead Zone* (1983), based on the novel by Stephen King; *The Fly* (1986), based on a story by George Langelaan, as well as on Kurt Neumann's 1958 film with Vincent Price and Patricia Owens; *Dead Ringers* (1988), based on the novel *Twins* by Bari Wood; *Naked Lunch* (1991), based on William Burrough's novel; *M. Butterfly* (1993), based on the play by David Hwang; and *Crash* (1996), based on J. G. Ballard's novel.

2 For detailed information on the Genie Awards and on Cronenberg's record, see www.academy.ca/hist/history.cfm?rtype=1&curstep=4&nname=David+Cronenberg.

3 Similarly, *Spider* (2002), the film following *eXistenZ*, is based on Patrick McGrath's novel of the same title.

4 The other film Thomson mentions in this context is *The Dead Zone*.

5 'At this time, tax-shelter incentives were introduced in Canada to encourage private investment in an indigenous film industry. This system, later perceived as a hideous loophole and consequently stopped, allowed anyone with money to burn to promise investment in a specific production. At that point, the investor could write off tax owed on a much larger sum, actually contributing a much smaller amount to the making of a movie. Promissory notes to provide the remaining finance further down the line – should it be needed – were security enough. Given Canada's fiscal year, this meant that in October potential investors panicked and looked around for film productions in which to invest their profits. The film industry consequently began to starve for eight months of the year, prior to new, feverish activity which began to occur in November/December' (Rodley, 1992: 68–9).

6 See, for example, the David Cronenberg fan site *The Plasma Pool* (http://plasmapool.esmartweb.com/), or a website called *Cronendrome* www.blue-bottle.co.uk/cronenframe.htm).

7 'Cronenberg has said the film's point of departure was an interview he once did with Salman Rushdie, but as Kim Newman has pointed out elsewhere in these pages, its more compelling literary source is the haunted fiction of Philip K. Dick. Compared to Dick's writing at its ontologically insecure best, though, *eXistenZ* looks as trifling as it is diverting: a little too perky, a little too pat' (Kevin Jackson). The interview itself can be found at: 'Cronenberg Meets Rushdie.' *Shift Magazine*, June/July 1995: www.davidcronenberg.de/cr_rushd. htm.

8 Contrary to expectation, Cronenberg does not project himself into Geller because of the negative publicity over such films as *Crash*, but rather in the context of technology. 'I torture myself about the inevitability of being dated on film,' he states. 'The technology will make you obsolete even if the story doesn't [. . .] Because there are kids who can't watch black and white, they won't watch a black and white film.' Out of the question whether 'a game designer could never be an artist' arises the figure of Allegra Geller ('Cronenberg Meets Rushdie.' *Shift Magazine*, June/July 1995. www.davidcronenberg.de/cr_rushd .htm).

9 See, for example, this assessment by Stephen Hunter in the *Washington Post*: 'As it turns out, the last few seconds of the movie justify the jejune stupidity and grossness that have come before, the 89 minutes of stilted dialogue, disgusting spectacle and frying-pan-flat performances' (np). James Berardinelli launches the same complaint: 'By the time the film limps to the ending, we're expecting at least one of the climactic twists, and its obviousness leaves a bad taste. It probably would have been more interesting for Cronenberg *not* to employ such an transparent "surprise"' (np).

'These children that you spit on': horror and generic hybridity by Andy W. Smith

1 Source: Internet Movie Data Base, 6 January 2006.

2 Taken from Newman, 2002.

3 The slasher film 'Final Girl' is the sexually untainted heroine, usually with a boy's name, who faces up to the monster/killer at the end of the movie and prevails. See the character of Laurie, played by Jamie Lee Curtis, as an exemplar of the 'Final Girl' in Carpenter's *Halloween* (1978).

4 *Rosemary's Baby* (Roman Polanski, 1968); *The Exorcist* (William Friedkin, 1973); *The Omen* (Richard Donner, 1976).

5 See Williams, 1996 for a more in-depth analysis of political metaphors in horror cinema.

6 This conclusion is intercut with the film's theme song: 'Don't You Forget About Me' by the Scottish rock group Simple Minds, a suit-

ably rousing 1980s guitar anthem with appropriate lyrics of teenage angst and desire for recognition.

7 Other 'Brat Pack 'movies from this period included Hughes' *Sixteen Candles* (1984) and *Weird Science* (1985), as well as *Pretty in Pink* (1986, written by Hughes and directed by Howard Deutch) and *St Elmo's Fire* (Joel Schumacher: 1985). The 'Brat Pack' consisted of a loose affiliation of actors all playing similar types of roles in the aforementioned movies. These actors included (in no particular order) Andrew McCarthy, Ally Sheedy, Judd Nelson, Demi Moore, Molly Ringwald, Rob Lowe, Emilio Estevez, James Spader, Anthony Michael Hall and Matthew Broderick.

8 The game is prefaced by Pink Floyd's song 'Another Brick in the Wall', whose refrain runs 'We don't need no education' in another witty combination of cultural references.

'Our reaction was only human': monstrous becomings in Abel Ferrara's Body Snatchers *by Jay McRoy*

1 For compelling historical and cultural analyses of this lengthy ideological conflict, see, among other texts, Thompson, 1982a, 1982b; Heller and Barson 2001; Kuznick and Gilbert, 2001; Gerstle, 2001; Miller, 1999 and Kramer, 1999.

2 Several of these texts are mentioned throughout my paper, however some of the better recent scholarship discussing the metaphoric depiction of US Cold War panic in science fiction films includes: Hendershot 1999, 2001 and Seed, 1999.

3 In *Terminal Identity*, Scott Bukatman posits *Invasion of the Body Snatchers* as paradigmatic of the alien invasion trope. In such films, he argues, '[t]he human is threatened by outside forces that are antithetical to "the human": That is, they are not mammalian; they are "clusters" rather than "individuals"; and they have no emotions (clearly the defining human quality in traditional SF: *never* do humans encounter *more* emotional creatures than themselves)' (Bukatman, 1993: 270).

4 See also *I Married a Monster from Outer Space* (USA, Gene Fowler, Jr.: 1958).

5 While Twitchell's book does not contain an elaborate exploration of *Invasion of the Body Snatchers* as a distinctly Cold War-era film, he does offer an intriguing reading of the 'pod people' as a form of zombified body.

6 See King, 1981, 18–20.

7 A similar form of narrative instability functions as a prominent trope in Abel Ferrara's vastly underrated *New Rose Hotel* (1998).

8 See, in particular, Clive Barker's *Hellraiser* (USA, 1987) and

Nightbreed (USA, 1990), and David Cronenberg's *Videodrome* (USA, 1983), *Naked Lunch* (USA, 1991), and *eXistenZ* (USA, 1999).

9 Perhaps the finest and most memorable example of sexist posturing in Siegel's film occurs when Dr Miles Binnell (Kevin McCarthy), after kissing his recently transformed love interest and failing to receive the 'gender appropriate' response, declares: 'I had been afraid many times in my life, but I never knew what true fear was until I kissed Becky.' For an engaging analysis of this scene, see Byers, 1989.

The Gorgon: *adapting classical myth as Gothic romance by I. Q. Hunter*

1 Phil Hardy (ed.), *The Aurum Film Encyclopedia: Horror*, revised edition (London: Aurum, 1993): 154. The entry's inaccurate plot description, in which Carla becomes Paul's *father's* companion, conveniently rewrites the film as an Oedipal family romance. See also Creed, 1993: 151–66.

2 For an especially rich interpretation of the Medusa, see Warner, 1996

3 Creed, 1993: 66; Shuttle and Redgrove, 1986: 248. *The Wise Wound* includes a sensitive and enlightening discussion of *The Gorgon* in relation to cultural fantasies about menstruation (247–9).

4 On gerontophobia in the British horror film, see I. Q. Hunter, 1996: 45–55; Steve Chibnall, 2002, esp. pp. 158–61.

5 There's a sympathetic reading of the Medusa along these lines in Cixous, 1976: 875–99.

6 See Hunter, 2000b: 86.

7 Compare with Tony Harrison's poem, 'The Gaze of the Gorgon' (Harrison, 1992: 57–75), in which the Gorgon has precisely this symbolic function.

8 On *Moon Zero Two*, see Hunter, 2000a: 16–25.

9 Hutchings argues that resistance to the feminising anti-heroism of the nannying, castrating Welfare State may have played some part in this. Hutchings, 1993a: 54–7.

Marion Crane dies twice by Murray Pomerance

1 A version of this chapter first appeared in Pomerance, 2001. The editors thank SUNY Press for permission to reproduce the essay.

Adapting legends: urban legends and their adaptation in horror cinema by Mikel J. Koven

1 Parts of this paper were originally presented at the 2000 annual Perspectives on Contemporary Legends conference, Edinburgh, UK.

2 And interestingly, these films almost completely drop those points of folkloristic interest in their sequels: *Urban Legends: The Final Cut*

(US/Canada, 2000, John Ottman), *Candyman: Farewell to the Flesh* (US, 1995, Bill Condon), and *Candyman: Day of the Dead* (US, 1999, Turi Meyer).

3 See www.snopes.com/horrors/parental/shannon.htm.

Gothic horrors, family secrets, and the patriarchal imperative: the early horror films of Mario Bava by Reynold Humphries

1 For information concerning titles, along with detailed synopses and analyses, see Howarth, 2002. For the sake of coherency, I shall use the Italian titles as I have been able to view the original, uncut Italian prints with sub-titles.

2 In which case Melissa is also a victim and her bouncing ball can be seen as a reference to *M* and the killer's first victim.

3 Freud remarked that expressions such as this and 'beside oneself' showed language representing split subject positions.

4 A different version of the analysis of *Sei donne per l'assassino* originally appeared in the online journal *Kinoeye*. My thanks to Steven Schneider for allowing me to use it here.

'Everyone will suffer' – national identity and the spirit of subaltern vengeance in Nakata Hideo's Ringu and Gore Verbinski's The Ring by Linnie Blake

1 Popular *yakuza* dramas would include Kitano Takeshi's *Violent Cop* (1989), *Boiling Point* (1990), *Sonatine* (1993) and his LA-set crossover success *Brother* (1997), and Miike Takeshi's *Shinzuku Triad Society* (1995), *Dead or Alive* (1999, 2000, 2002) and *Ichi the Killer* (2001). Most popular *anime* would include Otomoto Katsuhiio's Akira (1988), Oshii Mamoru's *Ghost in the Shell* (1995) and Miyazaki Hayao's *Spirited Away* (2001) – the last the highest grossing Japanese film ever made.

2 The cult status of Japanese horror was established as early as the 1990s, with Tsuukamoto Shinya's *Tetsuo: The Iron Man* (1991) and *Tetsuo 2: Bodyhammer* (1991). More recently Miike Takeshi's *Audition* (2001), Ishii Takeshi's *Freeze Me* (2002) and Kitamura Ryuhei's *Versus* (2000) have continued the trend whilst Fukasaku Kinji's *Battle Royale* (2001) and *Battle Royale II* (2003), Nakata Hideo's *Ringu* (1998), *Ringu 2* (1999) and *Dark Water* (2003), and Shimuzu Takashi's *Ju-On: The Grudge* (2002) have met with such large-scale US interest that the Nakata and Shimuzu films have been profitably re-made in the US for an international English-speaking audience.

3 In the period between its release and the time of writing (November 2005) *The Ring* has taken $229,100,000 at the box office and

$20,670,000 in domestic rentals alone. See *The Numbers:* www.the-numbers.com/movies/2002/TRING/html.

4 '*Onryou* is the Japanese term for a vengeful ghost. *Onryou* are usually girls or young women and have slow and spastic movements. Male *Onryou*, though much more rarer [*sic*] are much more violent and have hands that are always clenching into fists and unclenching. It is believed that these spirits are created when a person is very cruely murdered. They kill all they see, and the people they kill become one of them. These *yokai* are commonly associated with vengeance and violent justice.' From *Wikpedia, the Free Encyclopedia*: http://en.wikipedia.org/wiki/Onryou, accessed 9 September 2005.

5 See, for example, 'Chapter Two: Prohibited Subjects', Kyoko, 1992.

6 Even before Gore Verbinski undertook his remake of *The Ring* for US audiences or long before Nakata was himself invited to direct the US *The Ring* 2 (2005) there have been numerous other filmic, television and manga versions of the *Ringu* story in Asia, and several sequels. In terms of novels, Suzuki's *The Spiral* or *Rasen* (1995) sees the pathologist Andou Mitsuo undertaking an autopsy on Ryuji, his former classmate, finding a viral code within his DNA and undertaking his own hunt for Sadako having read the now-dead Asakawa's narrative of events. In January 1998 and February 1999 Suzuki also published *Loop* and *The Birthday*, short stories on the same subject. He penned the manga version in 1996, with art by Nagai Kourjirou. This was, however, overtaken by manga versions of the *Ringu* and *Ringu 2*, written by Takahashi Hiroshi, art by Inagaki Miscio and published in 1999. An English translation of *Ringu* by Naomi Kokubo appeared in 2003 and of *Ringu 2* by Steve Hoffman in 2004. There have been television specials: *Kanzenban*, *Saishuushou* and *Rasen: The Series* and a prequel *Ringu 0* (2000) directed not by Nakata but by Tsuruta Norio. In 1999, a South Korean version *The Ring Virus* was released, directed by Kim Dong-bin. More faithful to the Suzuki novel, and containing the original rape/virus thesis it is, nonetheless, cinematographically derivative of the Japanese original.

7 *The Ring World*: www.theringworld. com, accessed 9 September 2005.

8 Such echoes are doubly resonant, moreover, if we consider Imamura Shohei's film *Intentions of Murder* (1964), the heroine of which is also called Sadako – a country girl who refuses to commit suicide when raped, and in time grows strong enough to dominate the upper-class household that once entirely controlled her. This Sadako thus encapsulates a pronounced feminine strength that overcomes all patriarchal attacks upon her, becoming eventually 'a matriarchal

ruler [...] the priestess archetype [...] ruling over the tribe [...] the ancient Shamaness of Japanese mythology' (Desser, 1988: 126).

9 'The speaker is Death. There was a merchant in Baghdad who sent his servant to market to buy provisions and in a little while the servant came back, white and trembling, and said, Master, just now when I was in the marketplace I was jostled by a woman in the crowd and when I turned I saw it was Death that jostled me. She looked at me and made a threatening gesture, now lend me your horse, and I will ride away from the city and avoid my fate. I will go to Samarra and there Death will not find me. The merchant lent him his horse, and the servant mounted it, and he dug his spurs in its flanks and as fast as the horse could gallop he went. Then the merchant went down to the marketplace and he saw me standing in the crowd and he came to me and said, Why did you make a threatening gesture to my servant when you saw him this morning? That was not a threatening gesture, I said, it was only a start of surprise. I was astonished to see him in Baghdad, for I had an appointment with him in Samarra.' Maugham, 1933, quoted in Salmon, 1998: 27.

10 As the evangelical minister Jerry Falwell remarked on the religious chat show *The 700 Club* in the week of the bombing of the World Trade Center, 'What we saw on Tuesday, as terrible as it is, could be miniscule if, in fact, God continues to lift the curtain and allow the enemies of America to give us probably what we deserve [...] the pagans and the abortionists and the feminists and the gays and the lesbians [...] the ACLU, People for the US Way, all of them who try and secularise America.' (Wheen, 2004: 183–4).

11 Establishing an Office of Homeland Security beyond the scrutiny of Congress and introducing legislation that had major implications for US citizens' legal rights in terms of freedom of association, information and speech, the right to legal representation and to trial by jury, the so-called P.A.T.R.I.O.T. Act has brought about a radical transformation to the relationship between the US people, their police forces and the US military; one that is highly reminiscent of President Nixon's wholesale surveillance of potentially damaging oppositional groups in the name of freedom, specifically freedom from the evils of communism. And as in the Nixon period, such developments have been reflected in film culture in general and in the genre of cinematic horror in particular.

Bibliography

Abel, R. (1984), *French Cinema: The First Wave, 1915–1929*, Princeton, NJ: Princeton University Press.

Adorno, T. and Horkheimer, T. (1986) [1944], 'The Culture Industry: Enlightenment as Mass Deception', trans. J. Cumming, *Dialectic of Englightenment*, London: Verso, 120–68.

Artaud, A. (1988), *Antonin Artaud Selected Writings* (ed.) Susan Sontag, Berkeley: Los Angeles University of California Press.

Baldick, C. (1987), *In Frankenstein's Shadow: Myth, Monstrosity, and Nineteenth-Century Writing*, Oxford: Oxford University Press.

Bankhead, T. (1952), *Tallulah: My Autobiography*, London, Victor Gollancz.

Barker, C. (1985), *Clive Barker's Books of Blood Vol. V*, London: Sphere.

Barrymore, J. (1926), *Confessions of an Actor*, London, Holden.

Baudrillard, J. (1993) [1976], *Symbolic Exchange and Death*, trans. I. H. Grant, London: Sage.

—— (2002) [1990], *The Transparency of Evil: Essays on Extreme Phenomena*, trans. J. Benedict, London and New York: Verso.

Beasley-Murray, J. and Moreiras, A. (eds) (2001), *Subaltern Affect*, Special Issue of *Angelaki:* Journal of the Theoretical Humanities, 6.1, London and New York: Routledge Journals, Taylor & Francis Ltd.

Benjamin, W. (1968), 'The Work of Art in the Age of Mechanical Reproduction', *Illuminations*, trans. H. Zohn, New York: Harcourt Brace Jovanovich, 217–52.

—— (1986), 'Surrealism, The Last Snapshot of the European Intelligentsia', in *Reflections: Essays, Aphorisms, Autobio-*

graphical Writings, trans. E. Jephcott, New York: Schocken, 177–92.

Benshoff, H. (1997), *Monsters in the Closet: Homosexuality and the Horror Film*, Manchester: Manchester University Press.

Berardinalli, J. (1999), 'Review of *eXistenZ*', *ReelViews:* www.moviereviews.colossus.net/movies/e/existenz.html, accessed 20 March 2004.

Berenstein, R. J. (1996), *Attack of the Leading Ladies: Gender, Sexuality, and Spectatorship* in Classic Horror Cinema, New York: Columbia University Press.

Bloch, R. (1989) [1959], *Psycho*, New York: Tor.

Bordwell, D. (1980) [1974], *French Impressionist Cinema: Film Culture, Film Theory, and Film* Style, North Stratford, NH: Ayer Company Publishers.

—— and Thompson, K. (1986), *Film Art: An Introduction, Second Edition*, New York: Alfred A. Knopf.

Bowser, E. (1980), *The Transformation of Cinema: 1907–15*, New York: Scribner.

Boyer, P. (2001), *Religion Explained: The Evolutionary Origins of Religious Thought*, New York: Basic Books.

Brakhage, S. (1976), *Metaphors on Vision*, New York: Anthology Film Archives.

Braudy, L. (1972), 'Hitchcock, Truffaut, and the Irresponsible Audience,' in A. J. LaValley (ed.), *Focus on Hitchcock*, Englewood Cliffs, NJ: Prentice-Hall, 116–72.

Briefel, A. and Ngai, S. (2000), '*Candyman*: Urban Space, Fear, and Entitlement', in A. Silver and J. Ursini (eds), *Horror Film Reader*, New York: Limelight Editions, 281–304.

Brilliant, R. (1997) [1991], *Portraiture*, London: Reaktion Books Limited.

Bronfen, E. (1998), 'A Womb of One's Own, or the Strange Case of David Cronenberg', in *The Knotted Subject: Hysteria and its Dicontents*, Princeton, NJ: Princeton University Press, 381–409.

Brophy, P. (2000), 'Horrality: The Textuality of Contemporary Horror Films', in K. Gelder (ed.), *The Horror Reader*, London and New York: Routledge, 276–84.

Brunvand, J. H. (1981), *The Vanishing Hitchhiker: American Urban Legends & Their Meanings*, New York: W. W. Norton.

—— (1986), *The Mexican Pet: More 'New' Urban Legends and*

Some Old Favorites. New York: W. W. Norton.
—— (1993), 'A Blast Heard Round the World', *Contemporary Legend* 3: 103–20.
Bukatman, S. (1993), *Terminal Identity: The Virtual Subject in Postmodern Science Fiction*, Durham NC: Duke University Press.
Burke, K. (1969), *A Grammar of Motives*, Berkeley: University of California Press.
Buruma, I. (1995), *The Wages of Guilt: Memories of War in Germany and Japan*, London: Vintage.
Byers, T. B. (1989), 'Kissing Becky: Masculine Fears and Misogynist Moments in Science Fiction Films', Arizona Quarterly, vol. 45 no. 3, Autumn, 77–95.
Caesar, E. (2005), 'The Cult of Donnie Darko', *The Independent* on-line: http://enjoyment.independent.co.uk/film/features/article303185.ece, accessed 2 August 2005.
Campbell, R. (1986), '*Dr Jekyll and Mr Hyde*', in J. Sullivan (ed.) *The Penguin Encyclopedia of Horror and the Supernatural*, Harmondsworth: Penguin, 129–30.
Carey, J. (1974), 'Spatial and Temporal Transitions in American Fiction Films', *Studies in the Anthropology of Visual Communication* 1:1 (Fall), 45–50.
Carroll, N. (1990), *The Philosophy of Horror*, London and New York: Routledge.
Carter, L. (1975), *Lovecraft: A Look Behind the Cthulhu Mythos*, St Albans: Granada Publishing.
Castle, T. (1995), *The Female Thermometer: Eighteenth-Century Culture and the Invention of the Uncanny*, New York: Oxford University Press.
Cavell, S. (1979), *The World Viewed, Enlarged Edition*, Cambridge, MA: Harvard University Press.
Chauhuri, S. (1977), 'Visit of the Body Snatchers: Alien Invasion Themes in Vampire Narratives', *Camera Obscura*, 40–1, 180–98.
Chaw, W. (2004), 'Cronenberg Re-examines Cronenberg', *The Film Freak Central Interview*, on-line, www.filmfreakcentral.net/notes/dcronenbergretrointerview.htm, accessed 4 March 2004.
Cherry, B. (1999),'Refusing to Refuse to Look: Female Viewers of the Horror Film', in R. Maltby and M. Stokes (eds), *Identifying*

Hollywood Audiences, London: BFI.

—— (2005), 'Broken Homes, Tortured Flesh: *Hellraiser* and the Feminine Aesthetic of Horror Cinema', *Film International*, 5:17, 10–21.

Chibnall, S. (2002), 'A Heritage of Evil: Pete Walker and The Politics of Gothic Revisionism', in S. Chibnall and J. Petley (eds), *British Horror Cinema*, London: Routledge.

Cixous, H. (1976), 'The Laugh of the Medusa', trans. K. Cohen and P. Cohen, *Signs* 1 (Summer): 875–99.

Clark, T. J. (1984), *The Painting of Modern Life*, Princeton, NJ: Princeton University Press.

Clover, C. J. (1989) *Her Body, Himself: Gender in the Slasher Film*, in J. Donald (ed.) *Fantasy and the Cinema*, London: British Film Institute.

Cohan, S. and Hark, I. R. (1993), *Screening the Male: Exploring Masculinities in Hollywood Cinema*, London and New York: Routledge.

Combs, J. (1993), 'From the Great War to the Gulf War: Popular Entertainment and the Legitimation of Warfare', in R. E. Denton Jr (ed.), *The Media and the Persian Gulf War*, Westport, CT: Greenwood Press.

Conrich, I. (2000), 'An Aesthetic Sense: Cronenberg and Neo-horror Film Culture', in M. Grant (ed.), *The Modern Fantastic: The Films of David Cronenberg*, London: Flicks, 35–49.

—— (2004), 'Before Sound: Universal, Silent Cinema, and the Last of the Horror-Spectaculars', in S. Prince (ed.), *The Horror Film*, New Brunswick: Rutgers University Press, 40–57.

Corber, R. J. (1993), *In the Name of National Security: Hitchcock, Homophobia, and the Political Construction of Gender in Postwar America*, Raleigh and Durham: Duke University Press.

Crane, J. (2000), 'A Body Apart: Cronenberg and Genre', in M Grant (ed.), *The Modern Fantastic: The Films of David Cronenberg*, Trowbridge: Flicks Books, 50–69.

Creed, B. (1993), *The Monstrous Feminine: Film, Feminism, Psychoanalysis*, London and New York: Routledge.

Cristobal, R. (1994), 'A Latin Mini-Renaissance', *World Press Review*, January, 50.

de Camp, L. S. (1975), *Lovecraft: A Biography*, London: New English Library.

Dégh, L. (1995) 'Does the Word "Dog" Bite? Ostensive Action: A Means of Legend-Telling', *Narratives in Society: A Performer-Centered Study of Narration*, FF Communications No. 255, Helsinki: Suomalainen Tiedeakotemia Academia Scientiarum Fennica, 236–62.

Deren, M. (2005), *Essential Deren: Collected Writings on Film by Maya Deren* (ed.) B. R. McPherson, Kingston, New York: Documentext, McPherson & Company.

Desser, D. (1988), *Eros Plus Massacre: An Introduction to the Japanese New Wave Cinema*, Bloomington and Indianapolis: Indiana University Press.

Dissanayake, W. (ed.) (1988), *Cinema and Cultural Identity: Reflections on Films from Japan, India and China*, Lanham, New York and London: University of America Press.

Dixon, W. W. (1991), *The Charm of Evil: The Life and Films of Terence Fisher*, Metuchen, NJ: Scarecrow Press.

—— (2000), 'Transferring the Novel's Gothic Sensibilities to the Screen', in D. Nardo (ed.), *Readings on Frankenstein*, San Diego CA: Greenhaven, 115–28.

Douchet, J. (1960), 'Hitch et son public', *Cahiers du cinema*, no. 113.

—— (1999), *Hitchcock,* Paris: Cahiers du Cinéma, 7–15.

Edmundson, M. (1997), *Nightmare on Main Street: Angels, Sadomasochism, and the Culture of Gothic*, Cambridge, MA: Harvard University Press.

Flitterman-Lewis, S. (1987), 'The Image and the Spark: Dulac and Artaud Reviewed', in R. E. Kuenzili (ed.), *Dada and Surrealist Film*, New York: Willis, Locker and Owens, 110–27.

Foresti, G. (2002), *Corman Lovecraft: Le Rencontre Fantastique*, Paris: Dreamland Editeur.

Foucault, M. (1979) [1961], *Madness and Civilisation: A History of Insanity in the Age of Reason*, trans. R. Howard, London: Tavistock.

Freeland, C. (2000), *The Naked and the Undead: Evil and the Appeal of Horror*, Boulder: Westview Press.

Friedan, B. (1959), *The Feminine Mystique*, New York: W. W. Norton.

Fulcanelli (1999), *The Dwellings of the Philosophers*, trans. B. Donvez and L. Perrin, Boulder: Archive Press and Communications.

Garton, J. W. (1980), *The Film Acting of John Barrymore*, New York: Arno.

Gelder, K. (ed.) (2000), *The Horror Reader*, London and New York: Routledge.

Georges, R. A. (1971), 'The General Concept of Legend: Some Assumptions to be Reexamined and Reassessed', in W. D. Hand (ed.), *American Folk Legend: A Symposium*, Berkley: University of California Press, 1–19.

Gerstle, G. (2001), *American Crucible: Race and Nation in the 20th Century*, Princeton, NJ: Princeton University Press.

Gibson, W. (1984), *Neuromancer*, New York: Ace.

Glazer, M. (2002), 'The Vanishing Hitchhiker in South Texas: Tellers, Circumstances and Gender', Conference Paper Delivered at the 2002 Annual Perspectives on Contemporary Legend Conference, Sheffield, UK.

Goffman, E. (1974), *Frame Analysis: An Essay on the Organization of Experience*, Cambridge, MA: Harvard University Press.

—— (1976), 'Gender Advertisements', *Studies in the Anthropology of Visual Communication* 3:2, (Fall), 69–154.

Goldberg, J. (1967), *The Demon in the Mirror*, unpublished manuscript.

Gombrich, E. (1960), *Art and Illusion*, Princeton: Princeton University Press.

Grant, B. K. (1998), 'Rich and Strange: The Yuppie Horror Film,' in S. Neale and M. Smith (eds), *Contemporary Hollywood Cinema*, London: Routledge, 207–28.

Grant, M. (2000), 'Introduction', in M. Grant (ed.), *The Modern Fantastic: The Films of David Cronenberg*, Trowbridge: Flicks Books, 1–35.

Greenberg, H. R. (1993), *Screen Memories: Hollywood Cinema on the Psychoanalytic Couch*, New York: Columbia University Press.

Grider, S. (1981), 'The Media Narraform: Symbiosis of Mass Media and Oral Tradition', *Arv* 37: 125–31.

Gunning, T. (1989), 'Films that Tell Time: The Paradoxes of the Cinema of Ken Jacobs', in *Ken Jacobs: A Retrospective*, New York: The American Museum of the Moving Image.

Hardy, P. (ed.), (1993), *The Aurum Film Encyclopedia: Horror* (revised edition), London: Aurum.

Harrison, T. (1992), *The Gaze of the Gorgon*, London: Bloodaxe.

Harvey, D. (1989), *The Condition of Postmodernity: An Enquiry into the Origins of Social Change*, Oxford: Blackwell.

Hawkins, J. (2000) *Cutting Edge: Art-Horror and the Horrific Avant-Garde*, Minneapolis and London: University of Minnesota Press.

Heller, S. and Barson, M. (2001), *Red Scared!: The Commie Menace in Propaganda and Popular Culture*, San Francisco: Chronicle Books.

Hendershot, C. (1999), *Paranoia, the Bomb, and 1950s Science Fiction Films,* Ohio: Bowling Green Press.

—— (2001), 'Anti-Communism and Ambivalence in *Red Planet Mars, Invasion USA*, and *The Beast of Yucca Flats*', *Science Fiction Studies* 84, vol. 28, part 2 (July), 246–60.

Hendry, J. (1996), *Understanding Japanese Society*, Nissan Institute/Routledge Japanese Studies Series, London: Routledge.

Hill, M. (1997), 'Can Whiteness Speak?: Institutional Anomalies, Ontological Disasters, and Three Hollywood Films', in M. Wray and A. Newitz (eds), *White Trash: Race and Class in America,* London: Routledge, 155–73.

Hirano, K. (1992), *Mr Smith Goes to Tokyo: Japanese Cinema Under the US Occupation*, Washington and London: Smithsonian Institution Press.

Hoberman, J. (1994), 'Paranoia and the Pods', *Sight and Sound* 4, no. 5 (May), 28–31.

Holden, S. (2000), 'Murderer! Fiend! (But Well Dressed)', *New York Times* on-line: http://query.nytimes.com/gst/fullpage.html?res=9B05E6DC113EF937A25757C0A9669C8B63, accessed 14 April 2000.

Houellebecq, M. (2005), *H. P. Lovecraft: Against the World, Against Life*, San Francisco: Believer Books.

Howarth, T. (2002), *The Haunted World of Mario Bava*, London: Fab Press.

Hunter, I. Q. (1996), 'Deadly Manors: the Country House in British Exploitation Films', in P. Cooke, David Sadler and Nicholas Zurbrugg (eds), *Locating Identity: Essays on Nation, Community and the Self*, Leicester: De Montfort University.

—— (2000a), 'Brits in space', *Filmhäftet* 112 (4): 16–25.

—— (2000b), '*The Legend of the 7 Golden Vampires*',

Postcolonial Studies 3.1 (April): 86.
Hunter, J. (ed.) (2002), *The Bad Mirror*, New York and London: Creation Books.
Hunter, S. (1999), 'Innards Sanctum', *Washington Post* online, 23 April: www.washingtonpost.com/wpsrv/style/longterm /movies/videos/existenzhunter.htm.
Hutchings, P. (1993a) *Hammer and Beyond: The British Horror Film*, Manchester: Manchester University Press.
—— (1993b), 'Masculinity and the Horror Film', in P. Kirkham and J. Thumim (eds), *You Tarzan: Masculinity, Movies and Men*, London: Lawrence and Wishart, 84–94.
—— (2002), *Terence Fisher*, Manchester: Manchester University Press.
Jackson, K. (1999) 'Review of *eXistenZ*', *Sight and Sound* on line: www.bfi.org.uk/sightandsound/review/101, accessed 13 December 2006.
Jackson, R. (1995) [1981], *Fantasy: The Literature of Subversion*, London and New York: Routledge.
Jacobs, K. (1997a) *Catalogue Notes*, New York: The Film-Maker's Cooperative.
—— (1997b), 'Program Notes', for D. Schwartz (Editor and Chief Curator), *Nervous System Film Performance I: From Muybrige to Brooklyn Bridge*, Berlin: 27th International Forum of New Cinema, International Berlin Film Festival.
—— (1999), 'Interview', with H. Kreisler, *Conversations with History*, Institute of International Studies, Berkeley: University of California.
—— (2002), 'Notes for *Tom Tom the Piper's Son (1969–71)*', Paris: Re: Voir, Gartenberg Media Enterprises, Inc.
—— (2004), 'Program Notes', *Time after Time – In and Around The Nervous Magic Lantern and Nervous System of Ken Jacobs*, Brussels: Filmmuseum/Musee du Cinema.
James, J. (1988), 'Introduction: Apocalyptic Visions Past and Present', in W. J. Cloonan and J. James (eds), *Apocalyptic Visions Past and Present: Selected Papers from the Eighth and Ninth Annual Florida State University Conferences on Literature and Film*, Tallahassee: Florida State University Press.
Jancovich, M. (1992), *Horror: The Film Reader*, London and New York: Routledge.
Jay, M. (1993), *Downcast Eyes: The Denigration of Vision in*

Twentieth-Century French Thought, Berkeley: University of California Press.

Johnstone, N. (1999), *Abel Ferrara: The King of New York*, London and New York: Omnibus Press.

Jones, S. (ed.) (1991), *Clive Barker's Shadows in Eden: The Books, Films and Art of Clive* Barker, Lancaster, PA: Underwood-Miller.

Joshi, S. T. (1996), *H. P. Lovecraft: A Life*, Rhode Island: Necronomicon Press.

Jung, C. G. (1964), *Man and his Symbols*, London: Aldus.

Kavanaugh, J. H. (1980), '"*Son of a Bitch*": Feminism, Humanism and Science in *Alien*', *October* 13 (Summer), 90–100.

Kendrick, W. (1991), *The Thrill of Fear*, New York: Grove Press, 1991.

Kent, T. (1986), *Interpretation and Genre*, New Jersey: Associated University Press.

Kern, L. J. (1996), 'American "Grand Guignol": Splatterpunk Gore, Sadean Morality and Socially Redemptive Violence', *Journal of American Culture*, 19:2, 47–59.

King, S. (1981), *Danse Macabre*, New York: Everest.

—— (1993), *Danse Macabre*, London: Warner Books.

Koven, M. J. (1999), '*Candyman* Can: Film and Ostension', *Contemporary Legend*, N. S. 2: 137–54.

—— (2000), '"Have I Got a Monster for You!": Some Thoughts on the Golem, *The X-Files* and the Jewish Horror Movie', *Folklore* 111.2, 217–30.

—— (2003), 'The Terror Tale: Urban Legends and The Slasher Film', *Scope: An* on-line *journal of film studies* on-line, April: www.nottingham.ac.uk/film/journal.

Kramer, H. (199), *The Twilight of the Intellectuals. Culture and Politics in the Era of the Cold War*, Chicago: Ivan R. Dee, Inc.

Kraniauskas, J. (1998), '*Cronos* and the Political Economy of Vampirism: Notes on a Historical Constellation', in F. Barker et al. (eds), *Cannibalism and the Colonial World*, Cambridge: Cambridge University Press, 142–57.

Kristeva, J. (1993), *Nations Without Nationalism*, trans. L. S. Roudiez, New York: Columbia.

Kuhn, A. (2001), '"What's the matter, Trevor? Scared of something?": Representing the Monstrous-feminine in *Candyman*', Paper given at Postmodern Practices Conference, 23–25

November on-line: webdoc.sub.gwdg.de/edoc/ia/eese/artic20/kuhn/1_2000.html.

Kuznick, P. J. and Gilbert, J. (2001), *Rethinking Cold War Culture*, Washington: Smithsonian Institute Press.

Kyoko, H. (1992), *Mr Smith Goes to Tokyo: Japanese Cinema Under US Occupation 1945–1952,* Washington and London: Smithsonian Institution Press.

Latham, R. (2002), *Consuming Youth: Vampires, Cyborgs, and the Culture of Consumption*, Chicago and London: University of Chicago Press.

Lavalley, A. J. (1979), 'The Stage and Film Children of Frankenstein: A Survey', in G. Levine and U. C. Knoepflmacher (eds), *The Endurance of Frankenstein*, Berkeley: University of California Press, 243–89.

Lévy, M. (1988), *Lovecraft: A Study in the Fantastic*, Detroit: Wayne State University Press.

Leibman, N. (1995), *Living Room Lectures: The Fifties Family in Film and Television*, Austin: University of Texas Press.

Lovecraft, H. P. (1973), *Supernatural Horror in Literature*, New York: Dover Publications.

—— (1999), *The Call of Cthulhu and Other Weird Stories*, London: Penguin.

—— (2001), *The Thing on the Doorstep and Other Weird* Stories, London: Penguin.

—— (2005),*The Dreams in the Witch House and Other Weird Stories*, London: Penguin.

Lu, D. J. (1997), *Japan: A Documentary History. Volume II. The Late Tokugawa Period to the Present*, Armonk and London: East Gate.

Lucas, N. (producer) (1999), *Dial H for Hitchcock: The Genius Behind the Showman*, Universal TV Entertainment.

Mank, G. W. (1994), *Hollywood Cauldron: Thirteen Horror Films from the Genre's Golden* Age, Jefferson: McFarland.

Marcuse, H. (1972) [1964], *One Dimensional Man*, London: Abacus.

Marling, K. A. (1994), *As Seen on TV: The Visual Culture of Everyday Life in the 1950s*, Cambridge, MA: Harvard University Press.

Maslin, J. (1994), 'Undead Again: A Suave Vampire' review, *New York Times*, 24 March, C16.

Massumi, B. (1993), 'Everywhere You Want to Be: Introduction to Fear', in B. Massumi (ed.), *The Politics of Everyday Fear*, Minnesota: The University of Minnesota Press, 3–38.

Maugham, W. S. (1933) *Sheppey*, London: William Heinemann.

McGilligan, P. (2003), *Alfred Hitchcock: A Life in Darkness and Light*, New York: Regan.

McLarty, L. (1996), '"Beyond the Veil of the Flesh": Cronenberg and the Disembodiment of Horror', in B. K. Grany (ed.), *The Dread of Difference: Gender and the Horror Film*, Austin: University of Texas Press, 231–53.

Meikle, D. (1996), *A History of Horrors: The Rise and Fall of the House of Hammer*, Lanham, MD: Scarecrow Press.

Mendik, X. (2000), 'Logic, Creativity, and (critical) misinterpretations: An Interview with David Cronenberg', in M. Grant (ed.), *The Modern Fantastic: The Films of David Cronenberg*, Trowbridge: Flicks Books, 168–86.

Migliore, A. and Strysik, J. (2000), *The Lurker in the Lobby: A Guide to the Cinema of H. P.* Lovecraft, Seattle: Armitage House.

Mikkelson, B. (2002), 'Shannon's Friend'. *The Urban Legends Reference Page* on-line: www.snopes.com/horrors/parental /shannon.htm, accessed 23 October 2002.

Miller, D. (1999), *The Cold War: A Military History*, New York: St Martin's Press.

Miller, J. (1983), *States of Mind*, New York: Pantheon.

Miller, N. Z. (1996), *Immunization Theory vs. Reality: Exposé on Vaccinations*, Santa Fe, New Mexico: New Atlantean Press.

Mitchell, C. P. (2001), *The Complete H. P. Lovecraft Filmography*, Westport: Greenwood Press.

Modleski, T. (1988), *The Women Who Knew Too Much: Hitchcock and Feminist Theory*, New York: Methuen.

Moore, R. O. (1999), *Savage Theory*, Durham, NC: Duke University Press.

Morton, T. (ed.) (2002), *A Routledge Literary Sourcebook on Mary Shelley's Frankenstein*, London and New York: Routledge.

Mossman, M. (2001) 'Acts of Becoming: Autobiography, *Frankenstein*, and the Postmodern Body', *Postmodern Culture*, vol. 11, no. 3 (May). on-line: jefferson.village.virginia .edu/pmc/current.issue/11.3 mossman.html, accessed 9 March 2006.

Mulvey, L. (1975), 'Visual Pleasure and Narrative Cinema', *Screen* 16(3), 6–18.

Murphy, M. (1995), '*The Gorgon*', *Dark Terrors* 11 (December), 9.

Naremore, J. (1973), *Filmguide to 'Psycho'*, Bloomington: Indiana University Press.

Neale, S. (1989), *Issues of Difference: Alien and Blade Runner* in J. Donald (ed.), *Fantasy and the Cinema*, London: British Film Institute, 213–23.

Newman, K. (1999), *Cat People*, London: British Film Institute.

—— (2002) *Science Fiction/Horror: A Sight and Sound Reader*, London: British Film Institute.

Nollen, S. A. (1994), *Robert Louis Stevenson: Life, Literature and the Silver Screen,* Jefferson: McFarland.

The Numbers (2005), on-line: www.the-numbers.com/movies /2002/TRING/html, accessed 4 November 2005.

O'Donnell, P. (2000), *Latent Destinies: Cultural Paranoia and Contemporary U. S. Narrative*, Durham and London: Duke University Press.

Oakley, A. (1972), *Sex, Gender, and Society,* New York: Harper and Row.

Oring, E. (1986), 'Folk Narratives', in Elliott Oring (ed.), *Folk Groups and Folklore Genres: An Introduction*, Logan: Utah State University Press, 121–45.

Penley, C. (1989), *Time Travel, Prime Scene and the Critical Dystopia* in J. Donald (ed.), *Fantasy and the Cinema*, London: British Film Institute.

Pinedo, I. C. (1997), *Recreational Terror: Women and the Pleasures of Horror Film Viewing,* Albany, NY: State University of New York Press.

Pinter, H. (2005), 'Nobel Prize Acceptance Speech', 7 December, 2005, on-line: http://nobelprize.org/literature/laureates/2005 /pinter-lecture-e.html.

Poe, E. A. (1975), *The Complete Tales and Poems of Edgar Allan Poe*, New York: Vintage Books, Random House.

Pomerance, M. (ed.) (2001), *Ladies and Gentleman, Boys and Girls: Gender in Film at the End of the Twentieth Century,* Albany: State University of New York Press.

Prakash, G. (2000), 'The Impossibility of Subaltern History', *Nepantla: Views from South* 1(2), 287–94.

Praz, M. (1951), *The Romantic Agony* (second edition), trans. A. Davidson, London: Oxford University Press.

Rambaldi, M. (2004), 'Biography for David Cronenberg', *The Internet Movie Database*. on-line: www.imdb.com/name/nm0000343/bio, accessed 19 March 2004.

Rank, O. (1958), 'The Double as Immortal Self', *Beyond Psychology*, New York: Dover Publications, Inc.

Rigby, J. (2000), *English Gothic: A Century of Horror Cinema*, London: Reynolds & Hearn.

The Ring World (2005), on-line: www.theringworld.com/japan.php, accessed 9 September 2005.

Ringel, H. (1975a) 'Terence Fisher Underlining, interview by Harry Ringel', *Cinefantastique*, 4.3.

—— (1975b), 'Terence Fisher: The Human Side', *Cinefantastique* 4.3.

Roberts, A. (2000), *Science Fiction (The New Critical Idiom)*, London and New York: Routledge.

Rodley, C. (ed.), (1902) *Cronenberg on Cronenberg*, London and Boston: Faber & Faber.

Romney, J. (1994), 'Beatific Blood Suckers', review, *New Statesmen and Society*, 2 December, 34.

—— (2002), 'Morbid, Eighties Surrealism, Lovely', *The Independent on Sunday* on-line, 27 October: http://enjoyment.independent.co.uk/film/reviews/article141314.ece

Roth, M. (2000), 'Twice Two: *The Fly* and *Invasion of the Body Snatchers*', *Discourse* 22, no. 1. (Winter), 103–16.

Rothman, W. (1982), *Hitchcock: The Murderous Gaze*, Cambridge MA: Harvard University Press.

Rowe, C. (1974), 'Illuminating Lucifer', *Film Quarterly 27*, Summer, California: University of California Press.

Russo, M. (1997), 'Female Grotesques: Carnival and Theory', in K. Conboy, N. Mdiena and S. Stanbury (eds), *Writing on the Body: Female Embodiment and Feminist Theory*, New York: Columbia University Press, 318–36.

Salinger, J. D. (1994) [1951] *The Catcher in the Rye*, London: Penguin.

Salmon, W. C. (1998), *Causality and Explanation*, New York: Oxford University Press.

Sarris, A. (1978), 'Peas in a Pod', *Village Voice* 23 (25 December).

Schneider, S. J. (2004), 'Toward an Aesthetics of Cinematic

Horror', in Stephen Prince (ed.), *The Horror Film*, Piscataway, NJ: Rutgers University Press.

Schwartz, D. (ed. and Chief Curator) (1997), *Nervous System Film Performance I: From Muybrige to Brooklyn Bridge*, Berlin: 27th International Forum of New Cinema, International Berlin Film Festival.

Shary, T. (2002), *Generation Multiplex: The Image of Youth in Contemporary American Cinema*, Austin: University of Texas Press.

Shelley, M. (1998) [1818], *Frankenstein,* 1818 edition, (ed.) M. Butler, Oxford: Oxford University Press.

Shift Magazine (1995), 'Cronenberg Meets Rushdie', June/July, on-line: www.davidcronenberg.de/cr_rushd.htm.

Shuttle, P. and Redgrove, P. (1986), *The Wise Wound: Menstruation and Everywoman* (revised edition), London: Paladin.

Sitney, P. A. (1978), *Visionary Film: The American Avant-Garde 1943–1978,* second edition, Oxford: Oxford University Press.

Skal, D. J. (1973), *The Horror Show: A Cultural History of Horror*, London: Plexus.

—— (2001), *The Monster Show: A Cultural History of Horror*, New York: Faber and Faber.

Smith, A. (2004), *Victorian Demons: Medicine, Masculinity and the Gothic at the fin de siècle*, Manchester: Manchester University Press.

Smith, B. G. (2002), *Global Feminisms Since 1945*, London and New York: Routledge.

Smith, D. G. (2006), *H. P. Lovecraft in Popular Culture*, Jefferson: MacFarland.

Smith, P. (1992), '"Read All about It! Elvis Eaten by Drug-Crazed Alligators": Contemporary Legend and the Popular Press', *Contemporary Legend* 2, 41–70.

—— (1999), 'Contemporary Legend on Film and Television: Some Observations', *Contemporary Legend* n. s. 2, 137–54.

—— and Hobbs, S. (1990), 'Films Using Contemporary Legend Themes/ Motifs' in G. Bennett and P. Smith (eds), *Contemporary Legend: the First Five Years: Abstracts and Bibliographies from the Sheffield Conferences on Contemporary Legend 1982–1986*, Sheffield: Sheffield Academic Press, 138–48.

Sobchack, V. (1995), '"Surge and Splendor": A Phenomenology of the Hollywood Historical Epic', in B. K. Grant (ed.), *Film Genre Reader II*, Austin: University of Texas Press.

Solomon, P. (2003), 'The Frame', *Millennium Film Journal* 35/36, Fall, 120–35.

Spivak, G. C. (1995) [1983], 'Can the Subaltern Speak? Speculations on Widow Sacrifice', in B. Ashcroft, G. Griffiths and H. Tiffin (eds), *The Post Colonial Studies Reader*, London and New York: Routledge, 24–9.

Sterritt, D. (1993), *The Films of Alfred Hitchcock,* New York: Cambridge University Press.

Stoker, B. (1997) *Dracula,* (eds) N. Auerbach and D. J. Skal, New York: W. W. Norton.

Taubin, A. (2001), 'Amazed and Confused at Sundance: Troubled Buyers and True Believers', *Village Voice*, on-line: www.villagevoice.com/film/0106,taubin,22024,20.html, accessed 13 December 2006.

Thompson, E. P. (1982a), *Beyond the Cold War: A New Approach to the Arms Race and Nuclear Annihilation*, New York: Pantheon.

—— (1982b), *Extremism and Cold War*, London: Verso.

Thomson, D. (2002), 'David Cronenberg', *The New Biographical Dictionary of Film*, New York: Knopf, 189–90.

Truffaut, F. (1985), *Hitchcock,* New York: Simon and Schuster.

Twain, M. (1967) [1883], *The Adventures of Huckleberry Finn*, London: Minster.

Twitchell, J. (1985), *Dreadful Pleasures: An Anatomy of Modern Horror*, Oxford and New York: Oxford University Press.

Vidler, A. (1992), *The Architectural Uncanny: Essays in the Modern Unhomely*, Cambridge, MA: MIT Press.

Warner, M. (1996), *Monuments and Maidens: The Allegory of the Female Form*, London: Vintage.

White, E. (1995), '"Once They Were Men, Now They're Land Crabs": Monstrous Becomings in Evolutionist Cinema', in Halberstam, and I. Livingston (eds), *Posthuman Bodies*, Bloomington and Indianapolis: Indiana University Press.

—— (2005), 'Case Study: Nakata Hideo's *Ringu* and *Ringu 2*', in J. McRoy (ed.), *Japanese Horror Cinema*, Edinburgh: Edinburgh University Press.

Wheen, F. (2004), *How Mumbo-Jumbo Conquered the World,*

London: Harper Perennial.

Wiebel Jr, F. (2003), 'Edison's *Frankenstein*', in C. Yambar and R. Bihun (eds), *Edison's Frankenstein: A Graphic Adaptation of a Lost American Horror Classic*, Pittsburgh: Comic Library International, 47–58.

Wikpedia, the Free Encyclopedia, on-line: en.wikipedia.org/wiki /Onryou, accessed 9 September 2005.

Williams, L. R. (1999), 'The Inside-Out of Masculinity: David Cronenberg's Visceral Pleasures', in M. Aaron (ed.), *The Body's Perilous Pleasures: Dangerous Desires and Contemporary Culture*, Edinburgh: Edinburgh University Press, 30–48.

Williams, T. (1996), *Hearths of Darkness*, London: Associated University Presses.

Williamson, M. (2001), 'Vampires and Goths: Fandom, Gender and Cult Dress', in J. William and J. F. Keenan (eds), *Dressed to Impress: Looking the Part*, Oxford: Berg.

Willingham, R. (1994), *Science Fiction and the Theatre*, Westport, Connecticut: Greenwood.

Wilson, C. (1976), *The Strength to Dream: Literature and the Imagination*, London: Abacus.

Winter, D. E. (2001), *Clive Barker: The Dark Fantastic*, London: Harper Collins.

Wischhusen S. (ed.) (1975), *The Hour of One: Six Gothic Melodramas*, London: Gordon Fraser.

Wood, R. (1986), *Hollywood from Vietnam to Reagan*, New York: Columbia University Press.

—— (2002), *Hitchcock's Films Revisited, Revised Edition*, New York: Columbia University Press.

Yetiv, S. A. (1997), *The Persian Gulf Crises*, Westport, CT: Greenwood Press.

Zizek, S. (1994), 'Introduction: The Spectre of Ideology', in S. Zizek (ed), *Mapping Ideology*, London and New York: Verso, 1–33.

Index

CPSIA information can be obtained
at www.ICGtesting.com
Printed in the USA
BVHW042325120319
542489BV00011B/246/P

9 781784 992484